MURDER IN MIAMI

ALSO BY NOEL HYND

The Russian Trilogy

Conspiracy in Kiev
Midnight in Madrid
Countdown in Cairo

The Cuban Trilogy

Hostage in Havana
Murder in Miami
Payback in Panama (forthcoming)

Available in ebook format, including Kindle

Flowers from Berlin
Revenge
The Sandler Inquiry
The Enemy Within
False Flags: Betrayal in London

THE CUBAN ★ TRILOGY

NOEL HYND

MURDER IN MIAMI

BOOK TWO

ZONDERVAN®

ZONDERVAN.com/
AUTHORTRACKER
follow your favorite authors

ZONDERVAN

Murder in Miami
Copyright © 2012 by Noel Hynd

This title is also available as a Zondervan ebook.
Visit www.zondervan.com/ebooks.

This title is also available in a Zondervan audio edition.
Visit www.zondervan.fm.

Requests for information should be addressed to:
Zondervan, *Grand Rapids, Michigan* 49530

Library of Congress Cataloging-in-Publication Data

Hynd, Noel.
      Murder in Miami / Noel Hynd.
          p. cm. — (The Cuban trilogy ; 2)
      ISBN 978-0-310-32456-0 (softcover)
      1. Miami (Fla.) — Fiction. I. Title.
PS3558.Y54M87 2012
813'.54 — dc23   2010050742

Cover design: James Hall / JWH Graphic Arts
Cover photography or illustration: 123RF.com
Interior illustration: istockphoto®
Interior design: Michelle Espinoza
Editorial team: Andy Meisenheimer, Sue Brower, Bob Hudson, Alicia Sheppard

Printed in the United States of America

12 13 14 15 16 /DCI/ 22 21 20 19 18 17 16 15 14 13 12 11 10 9 8 7 6 5 4 3 2 1

In memory of Manny Myers, M.D.,
friend and mentor on many
humanitarian missions to Honduras.
Your friendship, guidance, and
wisdom will be missed by all.

ONE

Shortly after 2:00 a.m., erupting in a flurry of noise and flashing lights on an otherwise quiet autumn night in Rome, six armored SUVs from the Italian National Police skidded to a stop in front of the Excelsior Hotel, a magnificent white palace on the Via Veneto. The hotel glimmered in the September moonlight and the soft glow of the streetlights. The majestic old hotel hardly looked like a target, but a target it was this early morning.

From the lead SUV, an austere, lantern-jawed plainclothes commander named Benito Cabrini, a captain in an elite unit of the *carabinieri*, bolted onto the sidewalk, his feet hitting the ground even before his vehicle had come to a complete stop. Cabrini quickly wrapped a bulletproof vest around his midsection, jammed a riot helmet on his head, visor up, and drew a nine-millimeter Beretta automatic from under his suit jacket. He turned and gave sharp hand signals to the two dozen men leaping out of the vehicles behind him, sprinkling his paramilitary command style with his own creative profanities.

The hotel's concierge staff, in gold-braided uniforms and dark suits, fell away quickly. They recognized one of Italy's crack anti-terror teams.

Cabrini barked into a mobile phone and shouted urgent orders at four teams of men, all brandishing either automatic weapons or battering rams. They fell into their assigned positions. *"Andiamo!"* Cabrini yelled, motioning the men under his command to move into the hotel.

They made their way through a gaggle of leggy English models and their escorts, who nursed champagne directly from the bottles. They gave way quickly from the entrance area. An American couple—he in a suit and tie, she in a green silk dress—

11

recoiled sharply as the police brigade surged toward the hotel's grand entrance. A group of German lawyers and American film producers disbanded quickly and moved down the sidewalk.

Twenty heavily armored squad members poured out of a second armada of cars. Behind them, local police set a perimeter on the Via Veneto, complete with red and blue flashing lights and aggressively brandished weapons. On all sides of the hotel, exits were secured by paramilitary cops in riot gear. Tourists and frisky late-night revelers froze in their tracks, at gunpoint if necessary, keeping their hands visible, of course.

Two months of intelligence gathering — by satellite, internet, and old-fashioned shoe leather — and another three weeks of observation had led to this night.

Lights flashed; walkie-talkies crackled. A squad of ten armed men in black protective gear rushed through the front entrance, securing that passageway and pushing late-arriving guests out of the way.

The Excelsior was a monument to turn-of-the-twentieth-century style and anchored Rome's most celebrated avenue, famous for its boutiques and named after Italy's sole victory in World War I. Long a magnet for wealthy tourists, statesmen, retired generals, artists, and actors, the Excelsior was as distinctive as the Coliseum and the Pantheon down the slope of the Via Veneto.

But tonight, to Captain Cabrini, it was just another big building that needed some doors bashed in.

Cabrini led a dozen of his men past the plush sofas and small statues to the main elevator. The other two elevators had been secured on the ground floor, and a detachment of local police were already positioned in the three staircases, a grand one and two emergency ones in the back. The elevator, as plush, gilded, and comfortable as the lobby, rose to the sixth floor, where Captain Cabrini led his men into the hallway. Local police had taken up positions on the floor. The commander of the local *carabinieri* gave Cabrini a pair of hand signals, first to indicate the correct suite — *numero 612* — and a second to indicate no one had come or gone from the floor since their arrival fifteen minutes earlier.

"Benissimo!" Cabrini snorted softly. "Let's take them!"

Cabrini arrived at door 612. He was not a man given to gentle entrances; nor, when so much diligent effort had gone into locating these suspects, was he given to giving his prey any warning.

With a gentle hand, he tried the doorknob, stepped back, drew his pistol, and signaled to two men who carried a five-foot steel battering ram.

Cabrini gave another sharp nod. "Go!" The two men smashed their ram into the door. The first hit set off a loud crack that could be heard for several floors in all directions. It lifted the door from its frame but it stayed connected to its lock. The second thrust ram followed in less than three seconds and was harder than the first, smashing the door loose and sending it flying into the dark living area of the suite.

Darkness quickly turned to brightness. Cabrini, weapon in hand, was the first in the room. He turned the lights on — a luxury suite with deep carpets, a splendid sofa, a wall television, several sitting areas, and antique oak writing desk. There was no movement.

To the side was a double doorway, leading to the bedroom.

Cabrini didn't have to tell his men. Two with Uzis rushed through the doors into the bedroom, weapons aloft, where they found two beds turned down for the evening, complete with complimentary chocolates, a rose, and a breakfast menu.

The closet doors were open. Bathrooms, window ledges, under the beds. They patted down the walls for hidden exits or places of concealment.

They found no one. Nothing.

For two full minutes, no one spoke.

Finally, *"Nessuno,"* said Luigi Ridelletti, Cabrini's second-in-command. *No one.*

Grudgingly, Cabrini put away his weapon. He stalked slowly

around the bedroom, examining everything, working his eyes over the details, large and small, seething. No clothes in the drawers, no toiletries in the bathroom, no papers sitting around. A few dresser drawers were ajar, and some hangers were on the floor of the closet.

"Our friends left early," Cabrini finally said. "Quickly and efficiently," he added. "But early nonetheless." He paused. "Must have had another engagement." None of his troops saw fit to interrupt him.

"Coincidence?" Ridelletti asked.

"They were probably warned," Cabrini said. "Someone was obviously here. Who else other than fugitives behaves like this? Got a tip and ran fast. Have the airports notified. Check all flights, though I doubt it will do any good."

Ridelletti reached for a cell phone and followed the command.

Cabrini sauntered back to the living room. He eyed the surroundings. Original paintings hung on the wall. The sofa was deep and new. The windows were open slightly and looked over the Via Veneto, the sleeping city, and seven hills of Rome.

Then, turning, the captain spotted something, one small thing that was out of place. Something silver and cylindrical lay on the writing table. He walked over, bent down, and examined it without touching it. A silver fountain pen, engraved with a name. He recognized the logo of Tiffany & Company.

He eyed it with sharp suspicion. He had seen little objects like this rigged to trigger explosives so powerful that they could bring down buildings. But he was also an impetuous man as well as one who understood his suspects.

They wouldn't bomb him, the couple who had been in this fine suite. They had nothing against him. His job was to apprehend them; theirs was to evade him.

Nothing personal.

Ridelletti appeared at Cabrini's side.

"Should we call the bomb squad?" Ridelletti asked.

"I don't think so," Cabrini said. "Stay where you are."

Cabrini reached into his pocket for a pair of latex gloves. He pulled them on and picked up the pen. He read the name engraved on it and raised an eyebrow. "Nice instrument," he said. He flipped off the cap. As it clicked, he turned to his associate. "Boom!" he said in a low whisper.

Ridelletti flinched. Cabrini snorted a low laugh.

He wrapped the pen in a handkerchief and dropped it in his pocket.

"*Va bene.* They're gone. They beat us," he said. "Should we ask about the cost of the door?" Ridelletti asked.

"Dust for fingerprints, do the photographs, and then we go," Cabrini said. "The door fell off its hinges by itself. Italy is broke. We have nothing to do with the door."

"Yes, sir," said Ridelletti.

"All this for nothing," Cabrini said with an inventive burst of obscenities. "Let's wrap up and go home."

TWO

In New York City, on West 21st Street in the Chelsea district, the third-floor resident, known to her neighbors as Susanna Ferrara, a smart, nicely attired quiet brunette in her early thirties, had an important morning ritual, which was not known to her neighbors. The last thing she did before stepping out into the hallway in front of her small apartment was to check the Glock 12 she wore on the right side beneath her suit jacket. The weapon was loaded, locked, and ready. If the Glock was ready to start the day, so was she. She had just returned from a week's vacation in California, where she had attended the wedding of two friends, Paul and Teresa. She felt refreshed and, as she phrased it, ready to return to the financial battlefields.

These were no ordinary battlefields, however.

Alex LaDuca, employee of Fin Cen, the financial frauds division of the United States Treasury Department, found the hallway gloriously quiet and empty, just the way she liked it. She bypassed the elevator and walked down two flights of stairs. The building was a pleasant one, a solid five-story prewar brick structure. It had been renovated in the 1980s into smart co-ops, two bedrooms in most cases, four units per floor, except for the penthouse, which occupied the entire fifth floor and led to a private roof garden.

Alex, living under the name of Susanna Ferrara, had moved out of her high-rise on the West Side where a series of bullets had come through the plateglass window one evening, thanks to an assassin sent by Señora Yardena Dosi. Alex had sold that co-op and purchased this one, a smaller and more modest self-contained third-floor unit. Alex had a master bedroom, a comfortable living room, kitchen and dining area, plus a smaller extra bedroom, which Alex used as a study, an entertainment room, and a library. It also had a big convertible sofa in case any old friends wished to crash.

The building was within walking distance of the quirky smart shops of Greenwich Village and Chelsea on Seventh and Eighth Avenues, and it was located on a quiet tree-lined street. No coincidence there. The large maples provided a perfect shield for her front windows, obliterating any possibility of more potshots. Just for good measure, however, special panes of bulletproof glass were placed in all her windows, and the apartment was equipped with a sophisticated security system. The blinds were permanently pulled.

No one in the seventeen-unit building knew her real name or what she actually did for a living. Her cover story was that she was in the financial industry — true, sort of — as a bond trader — false, sort of. Since many of her adversaries were in the habit of posting bond following their indictments, this part of the cover had a certain linguistic irony.

The previous few years had taken their toll, as everyone had said they would. There had been the catastrophe in Kiev, which left her fiancé dead; then the long endgame with a Ukrainian-Russian mobster named Yuri Federov — which still maintained a ripple effect to this day; followed by a dicey episode in Spain and an even dicier one in Cuba. All this was piled on top of the fact that "Mata Hari Dosi," as Alex had nicknamed Yardena Dosi at the office, was still lurking somewhere in North Africa, presumably plotting her next move and a return to business.

Alex had her people out on the Dosi watch, looking for and interpreting shreds of information. But Alex had a few tricks up her sleeve too. She had been in the business long enough to establish her own alliances in Europe and the Americas. She could pull a few strings and make life hot for the Dosi lady too. And she saw no reason not to.

This morning, as Alex left for work, she wore a navy skirt just above the knee and a blue blazer and good walking shoes.

At 7:50 a.m., she stepped out onto New York's West 21st Street, between Ninth and Tenth Avenues, and into a bright new September day in Manhattan. Alex found the hint of autumn in the air invigorating. It was her favorite season, especially now, living in Manhattan.

As was her habit, she did a quick scan of the street, the passersby, the parked cars. She quickly processed which were familiar and which were not. Even in a city with such built-in anonymity, she had to decide which tinted window, odd antenna, or suspicious license plate might pose a threat.

She saw nothing that suggested a problem.

So, this being an ordinary morning, a ten-minute walk would take her to the downtown IRT for a ten-minute subway ride, which would take her on a final ten-minute walk to her office building on West Street and eventually to her desk on the fifty-seventh floor. From there, she would oversee various ongoing assaults against the financially corrupt, dishonest, or plain old-fashioned crooked.

Sometimes it was loathsome work, often tedious, normally thankless, continually frustrating, and sometimes dangerous. It was the type of work that caused a sane normal woman to burn out within a matter of years, destroyed one's nerves, precluded romance or family life, and made cynicism a daily participatory sport. When it took her out into the field, it made blouses stick to her ribs and intensified the usual paranoia.

She wondered how long she could do this.

She had money in the bank — nearly two million dollars — from a recent, highly unlikely inheritance. So she didn't have to live this way. But she was drawn to her work and continued — for now, anyway. It wasn't that she loved it so much as she was bitten by it. There was something about the danger and the excitement, past, present, and future. There was, as Winston Churchill once said, nothing more exhilarating than to be shot at and missed. This had happened more than once.

She emerged from the subway in lower Manhattan — a sudden rain cloud had come out of nowhere, darkening the skies and shrouding the tops of the tall buildings along Duane and Wall Streets. Alex moved quickly among the other workers seeking the lobbies of office buildings as the morning shower fell in thick drops.

Sometimes, timing was everything. Later she remembered thinking that thought quite a bit: Timing was everything. This was one of those days when the past and the future would start to mesh together.

THREE

Arriving on her floor at 8:33 a.m., Alex walked through the metal detector and into Fin Cen's suite.

"Good morning," she said to Stacey, her assistant.

"Morning," Stacey answered. She handed Alex a batch of message slips, passing them over an array of framed photos of her current *amazing* boyfriend, who was *even more amazing* than the one she had just dumped. Alex could tell that there were at least a dozen slips. Normal. The world didn't stop spinning while she slept, so why would the incoming messages?

Yet she was anxious to read her email this morning. Things had been heating up in Europe. A solid trail had apparently been established for the heads of the Dosis' international money-laundering operation.

During the spring, before going to Cuba, Alex and those under her command in New York and around Central and South America had delivered a punishing blow to the international money-laundering operation headed by Yardena Dosi and her husband, Misha. Alex's operation, known at Fin Cen as Operation Párajo, had left the Dosis' Panama-based operation in disarray, but the principals had escaped, traveling a zigzag path around Central and South America as well as Europe, evading arrest at every juncture, before settling down in an estate in Morocco.

There, it was said, Señora Dosi sat on her porch, stared at the ocean, hurled epithets at the sky, swore revenge, and even worse, plotted it.

One attempt to assassinate Alex had failed. It failed by a few inches, but it failed nonetheless. The attempt had driven Alex first to a Cuban operation so she could lay low and then to the Susanna Ferrara identity in New York — just in case.

"Protective cover" was the euphemism. Prosecutions were continuing, but the scurrilous Dosis were still out there, ready to bounce off the ropes and come back into the ring swinging with everything they had. So Alex would continue to live under her nom de guerre. The Dosis were a big battle in a major war.

It was also known that Señora Dosi and her husband slipped away to Europe from time to time, making generous use of their collection of fraudulent passports.

Alex was awaiting word: had the Italians made the capture?

"You need to go to De Salvo's office," Stacey said as Alex tried to blow past her. Andrew De Salvo was Alex's boss at the Financial Crimes Enforcement Network.

"Why?" Alex asked. "What's up?"

Stacey shrugged. "He wants to see you. Right now."

"Does it have to be right now, or can it be 'right now' in five minutes?" Alex asked.

"Five minutes might work, but I didn't say so," Stacey said.

"Okay," Alex said, still moving. "You haven't seen me yet."

Alex moved behind her desk and dropped her attaché case. She turned on her secured computer and waited for it to boot up.

On another computer screen, she did a quick scan of her emails to see if anything was blowing up in any of her lesser operations worldwide. The internet seas seemed calm. So did the personal ones when she checked her personal email. Maybe too calm, she thought with her normal touch of paranoia. She flicked through the message slips. No problems. Then the secure network kicked in. She leaned forward and saw a message that she recognized as her contact in Rome. Her pulse quickened.

There was nothing in the subject slot, and the sender's name was a jumble of encrypted letters. But she knew it was Captain Cabrini, her contact.

She waited. The message opened. It was in Italian and short and sweet — like a slap in the face.

Cabrini wrote: "Your birds have flown. Regrets. Your next move?"

Normally, Alex didn't curse, but this morning, at this moment, as she watched weeks of work explode in her face, she made an exception.

She plopped back in her chair and folded her arms. She was sure the Italians had had the Dosis in their grip. How had they gotten away? Had they sensed something? Had someone tipped them off? It made no sense. She didn't know whether to be angry or demoralized, so she tried to move to a mental place between the two.

Stacey appeared at the door and made a subtle gesture toward De Salvo's office. The boss was waiting.

Alex nodded. She glanced at her watch. Quarter of nine. Time to get back in gear. She would pick up the pieces later. She wouldn't be able to fully assess the damage until she talked to some of her surrogates on the ground in Italy. She was learning. The job was like that. And of course, the boss probably had a heads-up on what had happened. No doubt, that was what he wanted to discuss.

Okay. She bounced to her feet and strode down the corridor to Andrew De Salvo's corner suite.

Elsa Nussman, the boss's assistant, sat guard outside. "Go on in," Elsa said. "He's waiting."

Alex knocked, opened the door, and stepped in. De Salvo looked up in his distinguished, if slightly stooped way. De Salvo was a midwesterner from Indiana, just past sixty. He had been in New York and Washington for thirty years, not all of them happy. He smiled, which was a good start. His blue eyes showed indictment fatigue, a hazard of the profession. Alex guessed that hers would probably look that way too in the not-too-distant future.

"Good morning, Alex," he said.

"Morning, Andy," she said. First name familiarity had finally set in after a few months on the job. "What's up?" she asked.

Alex slid into a chair before her boss's desk. She waited.

"A couple of things," De Salvo said.

"The disaster in Rome?" she asked.

"What disaster in Rome?"

She recovered. "Sorry. You talk first."

"I can hardly wait to hear about a disaster in a foreign capital."

"You go ahead, then I'll fill you in."

"Well, first," he said, "I got a call from a gentleman in Washington. Works for a congressman in Virginia. There's some congressional committee looking into Fin Cen, how we work, what we do, how we justify our budget, assuming that we do justify our budget. Since you're now second-in-command in this office, he's going to want to talk to you."

Alex shrugged. "Is that a problem?"

"I don't see it as one," De Salvo said. "Not yet, anyway, but you know how Washington works. You never know where something's going to lead. Politics!"

"Politics?" she asked.

"Just be prepared to feed the beast. Give them what they need, not a scrap more."

"Are we talking about a telephone interview, or do I have to go to Washington?" Alex asked. "Or does he come here?"

"He comes here, thank heaven. Next week sometime, or maybe the following week. Or not at all if they get swept away by something else. Who knows? It's all by appointment and coordinating schedules. I have to service the little twit also. Meals, entertainment, and intrusive updates on what we do here. It's a pain. Anyway, just answer everything honestly and with a positive spin. That might be enough to keep him happy, at least on your part. Half the time they're just looking for a reason to visit New York."

"All right. Seems harmless."

"Not always," De Salvo answered. "So now, here's number two. I'll just give you the headline in case I go under a truck in the next few minutes," he continued.

"Not a bad idea," she said.

"You're wanted in Florida," he said.

"Wanted?" Alex asked.

"Strongly desired," he said. "Is that a better way to put it or worse?"

"'Wanted' as in someone wishes to see me?" Alex asked. "Or 'wanted' as in my picture is on display in the post office?"

"Good question. Maybe both," De Salvo said. "But one thing I know is this: the name Ivar Mejías obviously needs no introduction to you."

She snorted slightly. "Hardly. He hasn't left for Spain yet?"

"Nope. Still in Miami with his lovely wife of all these years," De Salvo said. "Scheduled to leave in another week, as I understand. He wants to talk to you."

"In person, I assume."

"That's the way Mejías framed it," De Salvo said. "He's been talking to some CIA people out of the Miami office, FBI as well. I'm told his wife has a few things to say too. He's wrapped up with them but still seems to have a few goodies remaining for you. A list of names of some sort. For you and you alone. Does that make any sense?"

She thought about it. Mejías was a recent defector from Cuba, the centerpiece of a dodgy operation that Alex had come in on earlier this year. Alex had helped to guide Mejías and his wife off the south shore of the island, with the help of a CIA pilot, on a hot morning that preceding June. It was made even hotter by the gunfire from the militia that accompanied their departure.

"I don't know how much sense it makes until I talk to him," Alex said. "How's that for an answer?"

"It's the one I expected," De Salvo said. "Listen, the sooner you get down to South Beach to talk to him, the sooner he's off to Spain and out of our hair. So," he said, his voice trailing off suggestively, "if it could be done sooner rather than later ..."

"My schedule's impacted for the next three days," she said. "What about the weekend? I could get a Saturday flight, see him late Saturday or Sunday, maybe get a little downtime on the beach, and be back by Monday morning. Would that work?"

"If it works for Mejías and it works for you, it works for me."

De Salvo reached for a pen and wrote down a phone number. "Phone him and set it up," he said. "Keep in mind it's storm season in Florida — hurricanes — and travel safe."

"Thanks."

He handed her the number. "Ever see *Key Largo*?"

Alex laughed. "A long time ago."

"Well, I saw it even longer ago. Lauren Bacall was beautiful. Now," he said, leaning back, "Rome. All roads lead there. There was something you were going to tell me ..."

"The Dosis," she said. "We thought we had them, but they slipped away again."

He digested it quickly. "It happens," he said. "Stay on their tails."

"Maybe we can discuss it," she said. "Tomorrow?"

"That'll work."

"Thanks."

She held Mejías's phone number in her hand and headed for the door. "Alex," her boss called to her. She stopped in the doorway and turned. He said, "Don't let it get you down. And don't let it kill you either. We deal in batting averages here. No one hits a thousand, and very few hit four hundred."

"Got it," she said. She smiled for the first time since arriving at work. "Thanks again."

Twice that afternoon, she tried to phone Mejías in Miami. Twice the calls jumped to voice mail and Alex left messages.

In Alex's line of work, there really was no such thing as an operation that came to a definite conclusion.

How long had it been, she asked herself. Ten weeks? Twelve weeks, since the defector Ivar Mejías and his wife, Juanita, had arrived in Florida after a lifetime undercover in Cuba? They had delivered, following some short, bumpy, and unofficial flights from Santiago to Belize to Key West, sheaves of documents providing information about many previously unresolved issues of

Cuban-American relations. The pro-Castro Cubans had been understandably furious with the defection, and the rancor had gone all the way to the top. The presidents of both nations had been briefed. Neither were happy as neither had been seeking to provoke an incident when a more cooperative era of post-Castroism seemed to lie in the near future.

Señor and Señora Mejías had settled in at an undisclosed location in Miami, waiting for the CIA to get its paperwork together and send them to Spain, where both Mejías and his wife claimed citizenship.

By 6:00 that evening, Alex gave up on expecting her calls to be returned during business hours. She had left her cell phone number and indicated that she would be receptive to a call at any hour. That was the best she could do.

At 6:30, Alex switched off the three computers on her desk and traded her work shoes for a pair of Nike running shoes. She took the elevator down to the lobby and celebrated the close of a relatively tranquil work day after the morning's bad news.

FOUR

Alex slipped her small attaché case into a Thomas Bihn backpack and started the trek uptown. On nights when she couldn't get to the gym, and felt secure enough not to use Fin Cen's secure car service, the two-mile walk did her good. She delighted in inventing a wandering path that led her up Seventh Avenue through the West Village — never exactly the same route for security's sake — where she could stop at any one of a number of small restaurants or takeout places. It was on these walks that she wondered about her future. As much as she enjoyed her work, office or field, she knew that it couldn't last. Everyone burned out eventually. Another two years for her, maybe? Three?

She had already been contemplating something less contentious and less dangerous in the private sector. Plus, as a Christian, she knew she might even accomplish some greater good in the world. She was fluent in five languages — English, Spanish, French, Italian, and Russian — and adept in a sixth — Ukrainian — so surely she could play a role somewhere that could change people's lives for the better. And with a two-million-dollar inheritance of sorts, a gift from a dying acquaintance, sitting largely untouched in the bank, gathering healthy interest, she could afford to spend time helping the poor and oppressed. She remembered the time she had spent in Venezuela the year before, just after Robert's death. She longed to return to the people she had lived with, prayed with, broken bread with.

The money allowed her to think outside the box. She could quit Fin Cen tomorrow if she wanted to. She could spend time as a missionary in Africa or Haiti or South America for a dollar a year, if she saw fit. It would be a much more fulfilling use of her time.

Of course, she could, with all her newly gained wealth, buy herself a beach condo in the south of France and be a party girl, sitting on a beautiful beach, staying rigorously fit, wearing the smallest two-piece bathing attire that the local laws and common sense permitted, sipping sinful iced drinks, flirting shamelessly with any interesting man whose attention she caught, and reading all the books that she had never quite had the time to catch up with. She could spend her nights in the discos and clubs of Rome, Barcelona, and Gibraltar, or maybe Ibiza, Mykonos, or Majorca, dancing with irresistibly handsome men or terminal bad boys, watching dawn approach and flitting from one questionable relationship to the next.

Of course, even on the beach, in her straw beach bag, right there next to the bottled water, raisins, oatmeal crunch bars, and sunscreen, she would have to keep her proactive life insurance policy — her Glock 12. There was always, even for a woman enjoying the sunshine of early retirement, the chance that on some sunny afternoon, an old adversary would step from the shadows into the sunlight and force a moment of reckoning.

"Always keep a weapon handy," her friend Sam Deal had once remarked. "You never know when Christian charity runs out and you just might have to blow some fire-breathing heathen away."

Sure, Sam, she thought with a laugh. *That's how the world works, doesn't it?*

Then she laughed to herself on the subject of such a sybaritic lifestyle. If the shoe didn't fit, she wasn't going to wear it. And this one didn't fit, so why even bother to try it on? Maybe she just didn't have the nerve, she laughed to herself.

In terms of personal relationships, the shadow of the enormous loss she had suffered eighteen months ago in Ukraine — the death of her fiancé — had finally started to recede. She felt she was approaching life and relationships again with a clearer vision and a sense of purpose. Was she, at last, ready to meet someone, a man who might become a life partner, hopefully one who shared the faith and values that she had grown up with? She didn't know. Life was impure and imperfect: she knew this better now than she had a few years earlier. Compromise and readjustment weren't just spectator sports; they were daily acts, usually small but sometimes large. She would let herself remain in God's hands and see where he led her.

She sighed as she walked. A resolute loneliness overshadowed her life right now, sometimes causing her to question her decision to try to stay true to God's leading. She wondered whether she was being too picky, too old-fashioned, too out of touch with the modern world. But being ready for a new romance and spotting an appropriate partner on the horizon were two entirely different things. Well, she allowed to herself, whatever was going to happen was going to happen, God willing. So she would accept each day as a blessing.

She stopped at a small grocery on 18th Street and bought a few takeout items for dinner. She arrived back at her building at 8:00, tired and anxious to do nothing more than have dinner, read a little, listen to music, relax, shower, and hit the pillow early so she could be rested for her next grueling workday.

She knew most of her neighbors by sight, though none of them in any depth, which is how she preferred it. The residents were mostly professional people, a highly affluent armada of lawyers, doctors, bankers, and other corporate types. Alex knew a bit about some of them.

The Levinson family lived across from her, Barbara and Michael, their two-year-old daughter, Sasha, and a housekeeper from Nicaragua. Richard and Judy Seltzer and their family lived on the fourth floor; he was a superstar hand surgeon at Cornell Medical Center. Jim Bandy on three was a men's fashion designer whose work was frequently in the newspapers, and Rebecca Stein, also on four, was a corporate attorney who worked at Fiftieth and Fifth.

Then there was the building celebrity, an actor named Eric Robertson, who was living temporarily in the unit just below

Alex's, subletting from an entertainment lawyer who was currently in London. Robertson, famous for his roles in several films, was now in a solid supporting role on Broadway in a revival of *South Pacific*. He played Lt. Joe Cable, the young American officer who falls in love with an Asian woman. Alex had caught a glimpse of the handsome Robertson twice at odd hours, and he had seemed pleasant enough, unpretentious. They had exchanged a quick hello.

Alex saw her neighbors in the hallways, in the mail room, and occasionally on the street or in neighborhood shops. She always had a good word and a smile. Beyond that, they were only acquaintances, and she hoped it would remain that way. It was a comfortable place to live in and retreat to after work. It was secure and had the sophistication she appreciated in a world-class city. She was, for the first time in many months, starting to be happy. The challenges of her job were still there, as were the challenges of the life of faith that she tried to lead. None of that was going away. But the return of some happiness was a welcome event.

When Alex entered the building this September evening, Mrs. Seltzer, the upstairs neighbor, was in the lobby with her daughter, chatting with Rebecca Stein, their friend from the fourth floor. They nodded to Alex as she went to her mailbox.

"Hello, Susanna," one of them said. They knew her by her cover name. Alex politely answered as she juggled mail from her box.

"Just getting home?" Rebecca asked.

"Long day," said Alex. They looked at her, expecting more. Alex dusted off a little white lie. "Asian bonds," she said. "The whole market is in disarray. Don't know what's crazier these days, Tokyo or Singapore. Paperwork keeps me late."

"Everyone is either overworked or unemployed these days," Judy added.

"Isn't *that* the truth!" the other woman said. "My niece

graduated from NYU in American Civilization and is working at Starbucks."

"Which Starbucks?"

"Does it matter?"

The ladies shook their heads and shifted the discussion from world finance back to people — more notably, gossip. Rebecca had spotted "the big-shot actor," as she called him, that afternoon in the lobby, and Eric had said hello. Now both women were remarking on how good-looking he was, as well as down-to-earth and polite. Alex smiled pleasantly and locked her mailbox.

"Have you seen him?" Judy asked her.

"Who?" Alex answered.

"Our resident celebrity?"

"Only from a distance," Alex answered.

"Isn't he *gorgeous*?" Judy asked. "If I were a single young woman like you, I'd jump him in a heartbeat."

"After you stood in line for a few hours!" Rebecca said with a laugh.

"And not that he'd ask me," Judy laughed.

"Good night, ladies," Alex said, smiling good-naturedly and checking out of the conversation. "I'll leave you to your entertaining daydreams."

Their mischievous laughter followed Alex to the elevator.

Life in the big city.

Alex checked her security systems and found her apartment the way she had left it. She unlocked the door, still in thought, but not so much that she ignored the alarm switch hidden in her closet. She had forty-five seconds to get to it and enter a three-digit code that turned it off.

She thought about the conversation in the lobby. There was nothing unusual about celebrities in New York. Since living there, Alex had spotted quite a few. Robert De Niro lived in SoHo and was often seen at a little Italian restaurant on Bleecker Street, which Alex frequently passed. Just the previous week, Alex had

seen Matthew Broderick and Sarah Jessica Parker at a neighborhood flower shop. Twice she had spotted Bill Murray at her local
dry cleaner's, and another time Jon Bon Jovi had passed her on
the street.

Big deal. Standard Manhattan fare. She had developed the
blasé attitude of a seasoned New Yorker who just wanted to
maintain her own privacy and achieve her own goals — and allow
others to do the same.

Being shot at always kept things in perspective.

FIVE

A thousand miles to the south, in Miami's South Beach, James Kevork stood in the front vestibule of the bar and rock club he managed. He surveyed the crowded dance floor, then peered out the front door at a line of shaggy-haired young men in leather jackets, closely cut young men in black T-shirts, couples in groups and alone, and an armada of beautiful and leggy young girls, accompanied and alone, in breathtaking attire.

James grinned. He had been on a roll for the last few years, an excellent roll.

He had carefully nurtured his music clientele and had developed a sharp sense of what his crowd wanted to see, hear, and drink. His crowd was the twenty-one-to-twenty-five set who lived in the area, kids from the city and the suburbs with the hot wheels and the fake IDs, and all the other trendoids who flocked to South Beach after dark.

He leaned close to his employee, Harout, a sturdy, massive fellow immigrant from the former Soviet republic of Armenia. Harout was his loyal keeper of the front gates. James spoke softly into the larger man's ear.

"Twelve more bodies," James said. "Female. Get more unattached girls in here."

Success in this business was often gained or lost in the management of the line of people waiting to pay for admission, as well as the blend of what was inside the club. Make them stand in line too long and they'll move to another club. But let them in too quickly — or worse, have no line out front — then young people decide there's nothing special about this place and move on. Edge them closer, entice them, then get them in, and it was like a license to empty their pockets on overpriced liquor and smokes. This all factored in with the "unattached female" ratio. Keep it high so the unattached males in the club would stay, dance, and spend.

Obediently, Harout counted out the next dozen people in line. The number stopped in the middle of a gaggle of girls. Suburbanites, James quickly recognized, New Yorkers on vacation, aspiring actresses and models and hairdressers all tarted up for the evening, showbiz wannabes.

Harout turned a glance to his boss for visual instruction. Cut off at the previous group or bring in a few extra girls. It was a no-brainer. The girls looked good. The lead girl gave the manager an imploring gesture, hands folded as if she were begging or in prayer. Her big Lady-Gaga-ish eyes darted back and forth between Harout and James.

James laughed. He gave a quick wink and a smile. "Sure thing," he said.

Harout motioned and allowed the girls to enter. They rushed in with a flurry of excited voices and bare arms and legs. The lead girl gave James, who was three times her age, a quick hug of thanks and continued along.

James, who was left in a small fog of the girl's perfume, smiled. Life was good. The club was hopping. He was worth a pile of money, and everything was coming up roses. Best of all, the night was young.

A few miles to the north, in a gritty commercial neighborhood of Miami, Tommy Vierra stood on a loading platform and watched a yellow rental truck back up to his storage unit. It was after midnight on Northwest 75th Street, on a block of twenty-year-old cinder-block-and-steel warehouses. The only other waking creatures within a hundred yards were the cats and rats that crawled through the parking lot at night stalking each other, and the insects that swarmed around the vapor lights that lit the area.

This was how Tommy Vierra liked it. The cats, the rats, and

the insects were reliable; he had never met one that could talk, much less testify in court.

Vierra was middle-aged and portly, with silver-gray hair pulled back in a ponytail and a rude pug nose that looked as if it had been rearranged a few times. His arms were big and flabby; a shirt, with smiling red, yellow, and blue pelicans, hung on him like a tent. Long hip-hop cargo shorts hung beyond the knees of his thick gray legs. In one of the bulky pockets rested a handgun.

Tommy signaled to the driver to ease closer to the landing port, which was elevated about four feet above the pavement. Then with a slashing downward swing of the arm, he motioned for the truck to stop. He barked a short profane command at the same time.

The truck jerked to a halt, and there was a sound of heavy merchandise shifting within the cargo area.

No matter. The delivery was FOB: In this case, *Floated* Off a Boat. It was from a Panamanian freighter, if truth were known, which was only one step removed from having fallen off a truck.

The driver and passenger leaped out of the cab. Vierra raised the steel door to the storage unit, and at the same time the driver and passenger raised the rear door of the truck. Then everyone pitched in, putting a couple of hand trolleys to use, moving cargo from the truck to the storage unit.

Twelve washing machines and seven dryers, Vierra noted. A dozen microwave ovens and sixteen gas stoves. Not a bad haul. Vierra went through some mental arithmetic. About three dozen swag appliances. He could turn these over for about $100 to $150 profit on each if he moved them quickly and to the right "discount" stores that serviced the slums of Miami's Overtown.

The unloading was swift and efficient. The men from the truck quickly closed their cargo door and turned to Vierra.

As Vierra reached into his pocket, his shirt gave way and for a moment his huge belly was visible. Then his hand emerged from his pocket with a green roll of double-digit bills. He squeezed it so securely that Presidents Jacksons and Grant almost yelped. He peeled off fifty dollars to each delivery guy, then gave each an appreciative smack on the shoulder.

They nodded, climbed back in the truck, and drove off into the night. Vierra pulled down the gate to his storage unit, double padlocked it, and jumped clumsily down to the warm asphalt of the parking lot.

He hulked through the empty lot to his car, a battered blue Chevrolet with a huge trunk, a big grill, and a major-league dent in the driver's side rear door. He lurched into the driver's seat and turned a key in the ignition. The engine turned over obediently, and he was gone within two minutes.

At the same time, a man named Nick Skypios was also concluding his day's business. On a block in Coconut Grove, Nick was tabulating his evening's receipts in the back room of Cypress, the small Greek restaurant that he ran. As always, the Grove remained a trendy upscale neighborhood with shops, cafés, and a carnival-like nightlife atmosphere.

The cleanup crew was in the kitchen, unloading the dishwasher and inventorying the provisions left over. They would be used for specials the next evening. Nick's brother Chris was up front, concocting a list of liquors that needed to be restocked. The front door was locked, and as extra security, Chris Skypios kept a loaded shotgun under the bar. The weapon was a good luck charm. Keep it there and one would never need it.

Nick Skypios was doing nicely during the recession. Lunchhour business was brisk and dinner business was steady. Nick kept his place open an hour later than the eateries in the Italian neighborhoods and often caught a late crowd from the Marlins, the Dolphins, the Heat, or even the Panthers. The professional sports teams drew tens of thousands of extra people into the neighborhood about a hundred and sixty times a year. Nick's place was positioned well to take advantage.

A watchful eye from the local police was helpful for safety

and the shotgun had a perfect record as a talisman. Nick's two sons were in a local parochial school, his wife was pregnant with their third child — they were trying for a girl this time — and Chris at the bar had found a location in Surfside, the small but growing neighborhood between Bal Harbour and Miami Beach, that might be optimal for a Cypress II, which would be a co-venture between the two brothers.

Who knew? They were on a roll.

The brothers closed their restaurant at 1:30 a.m., their workday done. They would return in nine hours. Chris left first. Then Nick. The neighborhood was silent now; most lights along the residential brownstones that lined the block were off.

Chris had the shorter drive, back to Miami Lakes, a mixed middle-income neighborhood where he owned his own home. He rolled through a series of three stop signs, found US 1 and the fast lane.

Like the massive freighters along the Port of Miami, all was comparatively smooth sailing.

SIX

At work the next morning, Alex recommenced her battle with the Dosi organization. She spoke to and exchanged emails with several police commanders and honchos around the world — Spanish with her peers in Central and South America; French with contacts in Morocco who had a purported lead on the Dosis' whereabouts in that North African nation. She used English to run down a rumor that the Dosis had a banking conduit in the Republic of Ireland. Neither the Moroccan nor the Irish lead materialized, but neither could be dismissed either. To the contrary, both still offered tantalizing possibilities.

For her inquiries, she used secured telephone and email lines, scrambled and encrypted. She controlled her codes from her desk. On the wall across the room, given over to charts and graphics following the Dosi network, she had posted large surveillance pictures of the Dosis, pictures taken of the couple in Panama by the CIA eighteen months earlier. The pictures were there so that Alex would not forget who her enemy was. She looked them in the eye several times a day. They had sent bullets into her home and come within inches of killing her. Any criminal who had hired professionals to take a shot at a federal investigator would not hesitate to make another attempt.

Operation Párajo, it was called. It was a chess game of sorts, as Andrew De Salvo had pointed out, a battle of queens in which a stalemate was not possible. It would only end when one queen fell. Alex's nerves hadn't quite been the same since the opening gambit.

With this in mind, Alex's battle with the Dosi organization was now two pronged. First, she was attempting to drive the remnants of their organization into financial ruin. Second, she was unleashing an ever wider cyber dragnet for the key leader in the organization, Yardena Dosi herself.

Señora Dosi, Israeli born and brandishing passports and citizenship papers with the flair that some women display for shoes, was the financial brains of the organization; her husband, the muscle.

"Don't most marriages work that way?" De Salvo grumbled at their working lunch that next day over fruit and half sandwiches sent in from a Wall Street deli.

"Yes," Alex admitted, "but this one is more venal."

De Salvo was using the occasion to look over reports Alex had written, summarizing her progress against the Dosis. Her boss looked anxious and tired these days, more so than usual. He had been commuting to and from Washington the few last weeks, and a recent FBI inquiry into Fin Cen's activities was proving to be an increasing distraction, as were the lists of questions being assembled by irritating congressional interns. Even worse were his own questions about those questions: why, for example, had his agency, which had always been apolitical, suddenly drawn scrutiny from Congress? Where was this coming from? There were no ready answers.

Operation Párajo, which Alex had conceived and commanded, had been a joint strike of American and Panamanian military and law enforcement agencies against the Dosis' criminal money-laundering enterprise. Their international empire may have operated from Panama, but its reach extended well into the United States and Canada. The Dosis and their surrogates financed the bulk of the illegal drugs and weapons on North American streets. Alex had chosen to attack their revenue stream, successfully compromising their supply chains and financial underpinnings.

The house of illegal cards had started to tumble many months earlier when a Venezuelan narcotics trafficker solicited a Panama City customs inspector to ease the smuggling of twenty bales of US currency into Panama. The smuggler gave up the link to two individuals: Misha and Yardena Dosi. The Dosis held both

Israeli and Panamanian passports, as well as several "escape" passports, including South African and Canadian. Fin Cen had become interested in Señor and Señora Dosi after the US Drug Enforcement Administration established that Misha Dosi maintained several islands on both of Panama's coasts, islands that have been used for running narcotics and currency via a fleet of state-of-the-art speedboats. On the Caribbean coast of Panama, Señora Dosi owned two islands in the Islas Marias archipelago. On the Pacific side, Señor Dosi owned Isla Escondida, near the Panamanian coastal town of San Carlos.

The Dosis' central company, Nauticabonita, was the top marine-supplies business in the country but was even more important as an instrument to launder the money that financed drugs, armies of narcotics cartels, and homicides of politicians, police, honest competitors, or anyone else around the world who got in the Dosis' way.

From her office at Fin Cen, Alex had initiated the takedown phase of a major criminal empire and the two major players behind it. Not surprisingly, the Dosis were lashing back with a fury that was almost without precedent, having orchestrated one bold attempt on Alex's life already.

"This is quite impressive," De Salvo said of Alex's reports. "The Dosis might be able to hide for the rest of their lives, but they won't be able to do a fraction of the business they used to."

"I thought I'd apprehended them this week in Rome," Alex said. "We had tracked some passports, some airport IDs. I paid a source in Morocco two thousand dollars out of the Rodent Fund for some information. I still think the information was good."

De Salvo looked up. "It could have been. Not the first time someone's been betrayed from within Europe or North Africa."

"It smarts anyway."

"Tell me about it," he said with irony. He looked back down at her reports. He continued to read and listen at the same time.

Alex said, "My guess is they have millions of dollars stashed away. They'd be fools if they didn't — and they're not fools. We know that. In any case, I'm tracing every financial dealing they've done over the last ten years. They've got money stashed away in the usual places: Cayman Islands, Switzerland, Bahamian and Panamanian offshores. But there's some unusual stuff too: Argentina, Peru, Singapore. My guess is they can live comfortably, but not under their own names and not in any place that maintains a reasonable extradition treaty with the United States. One little slip on a business ledger," she said, "and I can impound millions. One little slip personally, and I can have them arrested. That's if they show up at the wrong place and if I can get the right local people on the case."

"No wonder they want to kill you," De Salvo said.

"These are evil people," she said. "They account for a lot of misery in the world, in our country and others. I'll keep going after them with every tool that I have. It's that simple."

He raised his eye glasses and looked at her. "Promise me you're still being careful," he said.

"I am. Very."

"*Are* you?"

"Yes."

"Sometimes I wonder whether it's all worth it, Alex," he said. "You're young. You have choices. I've been in the harness here for so long that I don't know much else."

"The work is addictive," she said. "So are the challenges."

"Oh, I know that," De Salvo said. "But I also know about addictions, where they often lead you. We used to be such a classy bunch in government and financial security. Now we're so crass. *Vulgar* is the word. We're the investigators, but we spend half our time being investigated. We deplore what our opponents do, then half the time we have to sink to their level to get them. Do you feel the ends justify the means? I've never asked you that."

"Sometimes," she said.

"Good answer," he said. "Everything is a situation, right?"

"Most everything."

He smiled. "Do you still have all that money in the bank?"

"Yes, I do."

"All of it?" he asked.

"Pretty much," she said.

"You're elusive this morning, Alex. What does 'pretty much' mean?"

"It means the money is gathering interest," she said. "It racks up a couple of thousand dollars a month. I take some of it off the top and give it to charities. I've been blessed, so I pass the blessings along."

"Charities?" he repeated.

"Compassion International, Kiva, Water.org. There's also a scholarship program at the boarding school I went to. I chip in." She paused. "I like Kiva in particular. Microloans for people to set up businesses or repair homes around the world. I have about five thousand dollars out on the streets of Central America."

De Salvo raised an eyebrow. "What if you never see it again? No big deal?"

"You know the phrase 'there but for the grace of God'? Everything I have is God's grace in my life," she said. "If I never see it again, no big deal. If it *does* come back, so much the better. I'll probably lend it out again, same way."

"Keep lending it until it *doesn't* come back?" he asked.

"I don't see it that way."

"Well, more power to you," he said. "Call me a jaded old goat, but I'm not sure I'd still be coming into work if I had all that *efectivo* locked away."

"You *are* a jaded old goat," she said.

"I am. I might buy myself a nice chalet in Austria and go on an indefinite skiing vacation. Charity starts at home. Or maybe I'd buy a food truck, you know, one of those roach coaches you see out there at Battery Park at lunch hour. Get out there and spend some time with the proletariat, if you know what I mean." Alex smiled in response. "Or maybe get remarried and start a Von Trapp – style family. Ever heard me yodel?"

She smiled. "No."

"Well, you won't. Not until some hood leaves me a pile of money too. Then I'll yodel to my heart's content. Not before."

"We're all grateful, Andy."

"I'll bet. So I guess that's why the Almighty funneled the dough to you and not to me. Go figure."

Alex laughed. De Salvo rubbed his tired eyes and returned his attention to the documents before him. Alex had never seen him so tired, so peeved, so distant from the job before him. He was sixty-two, she knew, and she wondered if he was planning to take early retirement. He hadn't mentioned it, but he was constantly hinting. There was even a rumor that Alex was being groomed as his successor. But if De Salvo retired at sixty-five, would Washington give the post to a young woman of thirty-three, which was how old Alex would be in two years?

The correlating rumor was that someone from the US Attorney's office would move over and take the post, a man in his forties. But would that be seen as a slap at Alex?

Conversely, *young*, *smart*, and *energetic*, were the adjectives normally tossed about when the future leadership of Fin Cen was discussed. And Alex's qualifications — young, smart, and energetic, multilingual, with several years of experience — trumped even that. Of course, if she could drive a spike into Yardena Dosi's black heart, Alex would look even better.

For a moment, looking back to the documents before him, De Salvo tilted his glasses to magnify. He was, she guessed, looking at some of the footnotes in her report, which were in a smaller font. Turning the pages with his long fingers, his expression morphed into a frown, then a grin.

"Ah, now *this* is interesting," he said. "You managed to freeze the assets of two of their subsidiaries in Morocco. How on earth did you do that?" he asked pleasantly. "The Moroccans don't normally do anything for us. How did you get compliance on *that*?"

"I took a long shot, and it paid off," she said. "Our sources tell us that the Dosis are hiding out in Morocco, as you know. So I've pushed the envelope in the region, spread some money around in exchange for small secrets. Technically, a state of hostilities exists between Morocco and Israel. I had a Swiss solicitor go into a hall of records in Rabat and enter Señora Dosi's passport against the ownership of her companies. It was enough to get assets frozen until there's a hearing."

"I assume you kept American fingerprints off it?" De Salvo asked.

"Of course," Alex said. "And the hearing dockets are back-logged so the assets are frozen for a good eighteen months. Meanwhile, we'll see who responds to the complaint, then we'll start looking into their legal connections." She paused.

"Clever," he said lightly. "You didn't go to law school, did you, Alex?"

"No."

He shook his head. "You'd be even more dangerous if you had," he said, handing her report back. "Excellent work. Out-standing. Keep doing what you're doing."

"Thank you." She held up the report. "We finished with this?"

"I am."

"Good." She walked across the room and dropped it into the shredder, which ate it, then pulverized it.

"Anything else?" he asked.

"I'd like to bring some more of my European surrogates into this," she said. "I have contacts in Spain and an exceptional one in Italy. Completely trustworthy. I'd like to see if I can work a false-flag operation against the Dosis through Europe. Something significant. I don't think they'd be looking for it." She paused. "I also have a contact in China. It would be more difficult to get in touch with him, but I can do it."

"Who are the contacts?" De Salvo asked.

"In China, a man named Peter Chang. I worked with him in Madrid. I have only a vague way to contact him, but I consider him a friend, one who'll do me favors. Also from Madrid, a man named Colonel Pendraza of the Spanish Policia Nacional. He's older, nearing retirement, but still has considerable influence in Spanish security. He's something of a surly old *franquista*. Personally, he's a little too far right for my tastes, but we're friendly. Then there's a man in Rome, Gian Antonio Rizzo, formerly of the Roman city police but also a CIA contact. He confirmed that the Dosis fingerprints were all over the suite in Rome. He also sent me a hotel surveillance film showing them leaving. They were there, and we weren't far behind."

"You've got quite a little black book for a gun totin' single girl, don't you?" De Salvo said wryly.

She took it the way it was intended, as a compliment. "I'm thinking globally with the Dosi operation," she said. "They have fewer legal restraints on them since they will break any law in any nation, but I have more extensive resources. So I want to play the game from my strengths, not theirs."

"Obviously."

"Also, considering what's at stake, and considering that one attempt to arrest the Dosis in Rome may have been compromised by a security breach, I feel more confident using my own people. Make sense?"

"Of course." He shrugged. He glanced at the clock. "What do you need from me?"

"Your permission. Proper documentation to cover myself so no one down the road alleges that I acted alone or overstepped. To contact people on this level, Colonel Pendraza, for example, I need authorization from the top of Fin Cen. That's you."

"Draw up the papers. I'll sign them."

"I've already drawn them up," she said.

She produced two documents and handed them to De Salvo. He read them carefully, then signed.

SEVEN

In cloudy, humid Miami, Nick Skypios, sleeping late after a late night at his Greek restaurant in Coconut Grove, was as concerned as he was tired. There were hints of trouble. His sources of financing were making noises about getting some of their investment money back. This was in conflict with what the off-the-record financing agreement had been. The sources told him that he would have five years to repay the seed money. That was part of their master plan to launder their investment into an American bank. Now they were cutting the time from five years to two.

Outrageous! Nick thought. That could press him into having to go to the banks to make up the difference. And that might inadvertently make him vulnerable due to some other legal and fiduciary shortcuts he had taken. No wonder he had started answering questions off the record to some federal prosecutors who had taken an interest in his financing arrangements.

Right now, though, there was nothing to do except wait ... wait for the Feds to make their next move. Nick wasn't worried, but then again, he was. His business was doing well. If only the powers that be would leave him alone. He turned on the music system in the living room of his condo. Some Victoria Halkiti would help him get started. Secretly, he was in love with the perky-voiced Victoria. She sang splendidly in Greek but was a golden girl, half Swedish, half Greek, born in Scandinavia. Nearing forty, Nick had grown up with her music, even saw her in concert once. He pumped up some volume and felt better about things.

He made coffee and checked the time. He needed to get

moving a little faster. The new people in the restaurant kitchen needed supervision. He needed to drive over to the Grove and be there by 11:30 to oversee the lunch hour.

He ducked into the shower. He felt refreshed when he came out, dried himself off, and walked into his living room. Then he felt a cold, hard fear, worse than anything he had ever felt in his life.

He had a visitor, uninvited and unwelcome. The man sat in the armchair in the far corner to Nick's left. It was the only blind corner in the room, the only place where Nick wouldn't have seen someone immediately and been able to access one of the several guns that he kept around his home.

Nick cursed to himself. The visitor held a massive pistol, pointed right at the center of Nick's chest.

"Hello, Nick. Please don't move. Moving targets make a mess."

Nick trembled. He glared back. "Please don't. I don't have any money here. I'll give you — "

The visitor raised a finger to his lips to indicate silence. "Who's this girl singing?" the visitor asked. "I like her. Sexy. I just wish I could understand what she was saying. I guess it's Greek to both of us."

"She's singing in English," Nick said.

"Is she? I didn't notice."

A gloved hand went to the tuner. The volume turned up. Skypios could read the intruder's intentions. He wondered if he could jump back and be out the door before the trigger was pulled. He bolted toward the hallway. At the same instant the pistol erupted.

The bullet caught Skypios in the center of the chest. It shattered his breastbone as the shot tore upward through the flesh and bone of his body. The second shot, fired a quarter second after the first, crashed into a rib bone on the left side. It ripped into the right ventricle of the heart.

All Nick felt was the overwhelming pain in his chest. He staggered and knew that he was going to fall. He tumbled against the wall and sprawled over a table. Then he slumped to the floor. His visitor came in close as Nick's eyes flickered and put a final shot into Nick's head, right between the eyes.

EIGHT

From the secure phone in her office, Alex called Miami again and, quite by surprise, managed to get Major Mejías, her recent Cuban defector, on the line. They spoke in Spanish.

At first the conversation was halting, awkward to the point of banal: the weather, the Miami traffic, the deplorable daytime content of the Spanish-language television stations. Then Alex moved to the purpose of the call, arranging some face time, and the conversation took a more resilient tone.

The major would be moving to Spain by the end of the following week, he said, echoing what Alex already knew, and there were some things that he wanted to discuss with Alex — and only Alex. For such topics, a face-to-face meeting was essential.

Alex arranged to meet Mejías at an outdoor café called La Veranda, a place she knew to be secure but visible. La Veranda was one of the terraces of the art deco hotels that lined South Beach's Ocean Drive, terraces that had once been filled with metal chairs for snowbird retirees but had now, since the revival of South Beach a couple of decades earlier, been turned into restaurants from which one could look at the palm trees and the human parade that passed incessantly.

They agreed upon the following Sunday at 3:00 in the afternoon. Señora Mejías would be present also, which was fine with Alex.

Mejías said he could cover what he wanted to cover in an hour. It concerned a list of names, he promised, persons who would be of interest to Alex in her ongoing work.

"On the big investigation I'm working on?" she asked.

"That could be the case," he answered. "We shall see in person, yes?"

"Yes," she said.

"I look forward to it," he said.

The major sounded cheerful but anxious to see her. It was a given that he wished to be on his way to Spain as soon as possible. Miami, he said, was a very sunny place for a lot of very shady Cubans.

But once Alex had set the meeting for Sunday afternoon, Mejías's tone became more festive, and the rest of the conversation had a valedictory ring. Could Alex make sure that the proper agencies had all of his banking information, Mejías asked, as apparently he was to draw a "retirement" salary out of some rodent fund that the CIA had established for such warriors on the front lines of freedom.

Alex said she would cover the details if he gave them to her. She picked up a pen and prepared to make handwritten notes as he proceeded. But Mejías laughed and refused to say much more. "We can talk on Sunday," he said. "I will also tell you about my personal relationship with Fidel Castro," he said. "It dated from the same era." He threw Alex only a few tidbits and they seemed designed to tease, as if he wanted to make sure that she showed up.

"My activities started out small and then went larger," Mejías said. "Little tidbits of information about Castro, I will give you. I was scrupulous only to hurt Castro and not Cuba. I care more about promoting Cuban democracy than about advancing the American cause. You understand?"

Alex said she did and that they would talk more on the weekend. She also knew that by scheduling the meeting for Sunday, she would need to use Monday as a fallback day, in case anything went wrong or anything led to something larger that would require her to extend her trip.

The major rang off in an upbeat mood.

NINE

On Friday evening, one of Alex's oldest friends, Laura Chapman, was in town. Laura worked a similar job in Washington and knew Alex's true identity as well as her current protective cover. Laura was between flights, on her way to London, and Alex allowed her to use the extra bedroom that night. As it turned out, they both had to be at Kennedy International Airport the next morning.

They met after Alex's workday and had dinner at an Italian place called Grana on Fourth Street in Greenwich Village. Then they took in a movie at a theater off Waverly Place and went out for a snack and a nightcap afterward — a healthy pop of Jamba Juice on Eighth Street. There they caught up with each other and let the passing scene on the sidewalk amuse them.

They returned to West 21st Street by taxi. When they arrived, Alex had a sudden start, which caused her to run the palm of her hand over her weapon momentarily. Laura, picking up on the vibe and also armed, did the same.

A long black vehicle was parked in front of Alex's building, one that reminded Alex of the limousine belonging to Paul Guarneri, a central figure in the Cuba operation earlier that year. Guarneri still professed romantic intentions toward Alex — of course, she had no interest in seeing him. Alex might have terminated the relationship completely, but she also knew that such men had their purposes. So she kept him at arm's length, no closer, no further, and had recently agreed to have coffee or a drink with him. But that didn't mean he had stopped calling, nor was he above showing up unannounced. So Alex looked carefully at the vehicle.

"Trouble?" Laura Chapman asked.

"You never know," Alex answered.

"Driver," Alex said. "Please circle the block, come back, and drop us a few buildings away, okay?"

From beneath his turban, the driver said he would. He kept the meter running.

Alex checked her watch. It was after midnight. They circled cautiously and returned. The taxi pulled to a halt four doors down, per Alex's instructions.

"What do you think?" Laura asked.

"We're probably okay," Alex said. "Let's just be cautious."

"Okay."

Alex paid. She and Laura stepped out. They kept their hands on their weapons, though the weapons remained concealed.

A burly driver came quickly around the limo, glowered in the direction of the two women, then opened the rear door. A man's legs swung out, followed by the rest of his tall athletic body. He glanced in their direction as he stood on the sidewalk and spoke to his driver.

It was Eric Robertson, the actor and building celebrity.

"Is that who I think it is?" Laura asked.

"Yup. He lives downstairs from me."

"Are you *kidding*?"

"Would I make up something like that?"

"And you haven't punched a hole in your floor yet?"

"I'm afraid not."

"Do you *know* him?" Laura asked.

"We spoke in the mail room once," Alex said.

"And he *lives* here?"

"I'm told he's subletting," Alex whispered. "He's in *South Pacific* for eight weeks. Or twelve. Then he's off to do a movie. I hear the building gossip now and then. It's unavoidable."

After another few seconds, "I'm still a teenybopper at heart," Laura said. "I want him."

"You and a few hundred thousand other women in New York and California. So put your name on the list."

Laura laughed. "Right," she said. "Well, you can see why. He's gorgeous."

Eric Robertson thanked his driver, turned, and wandered toward the building. He was tall and handsome, wearing slim jeans and a smart leather bomber jacket. As fate would have it, he arrived at the street level door at exactly the same moment as Alex and Laura.

They stopped. So did he.

"Hi," he said.

"Hi," Alex answered.

His gaze swept from one to the other. He knew he had been recognized, but neither woman would acknowledge it. He unleashed a million-kilowatt movie-star smile.

"Hello," Laura chipped in, late.

There was an awkward moment, everyone being too polite, when no one moved.

"Well, *someone* must go first," Robertson said with mock formality. "How about I unlock and hold this door and you lovely ladies can precede me through it?"

"That would be wonderful," Alex said.

"Yes," Laura added. "Definitely. It would be great."

"Well, then, let's get on with it," Robertson said cheerfully.

With a strong arm and deft motion, he swept the key from his pocket, opened the door, and held it wide. Alex and Laura passed through.

"Thank you," they both said.

"My pleasure," he said with a slight and excessively polite nod.

When the door closed behind them, Laura turned impetuously back to him. "How did the show go tonight?" she asked.

Alex cringed. But Eric laughed again. "Well, no one threw rotten eggs or overripe tomatoes, the critics have already had their day and didn't hurt us, no one fell off the stage during the dance numbers, and the performance sold out. So by those standards, I guess it was a success."

"Well, that's good," Laura said.

"You bet it is," he said with a wink. "Good night, ladies."

"Good night."

"Good night."

Robertson bounded up the steps to the second floor. Laura and Alex took the elevator to the third.

"'Ladies,'" Laura repeated in the elevator. "'*Ladies*'! What a stud muffin," Laura said. "I should have asked for an autograph. My arm. That's it. I should have had him autograph my arm."

"I'm glad you didn't."

Alex found herself wondering why a man that good looking would be alone on a Friday night. Alex expressed the thought to Laura.

"Silly," Laura said. "His girl is probably waiting for him downstairs, or he's just turning around to change and he'll be on his way out again. Actors!" she said, as if that explained everything. "They get around. You know what they're like."

"Actors," Alex agreed. "But if he was going out again, why did he dismiss his driver?"

"Who knows?" Laura said.

Alex unlocked her door, and they entered her apartment.

The two women began packing for the airport. At one point, to her abiding shame, Laura put an ear to the floor to listen but reported nothing.

"I know, I know. I have a wonderful boyfriend, and I've behaved like a flirty schoolgirl this evening. Shame on me."

"You said it," Alex answered. "I didn't."

TEN

Slightly before 1:00 p.m. on Saturday afternoon, Alex pulled her rental car to a halt in front of the Park Central Hotel in Miami Beach. She parked behind a black 1937 Plymouth coupe, similar to the one in which Humphrey Bogart and Ida Lupino fled in *High Sierra*. The car was parked there to lend some "deco glamour" to the hotel. Alex stepped out of her car and into the Miami afternoon. The day was balmy, partially cloudy with the usual sneaky humidity.

Alex checked into the funky old hotel and was pleased to find that her room had the standard louvered windows of South Beach and modest but decent furniture. The room was decorated with photos of South Beach in the 1920s, including one of young women in early two-piece bathing suits, posing in front of a sign forbidding such bathing attire.

Of course, these fresh young women were now old crones or dead, Alex thought. In the elevator was an old ad that advertised rooms "from five dollars."

She showered quickly and put on fresh clothes: a casual khaki skirt and a navy blouse. She kept her firearm in her shoulder bag and wore her cell phone on the left side, turned off.

She glanced at herself in the mirror. She was pleased with what she saw, the right balance between sexy-attractive and confident-no-nonsense. For better or worse, this was the image she usually tried to project. She had a quiet dinner at the hotel restaurant and worked on her laptop, reviewing the files on Mejías and the more extensive ones on the Dosi empire. Nothing new fell into place.

The next morning she rose early. She found a small Episcopal church near the Park Central and went to the 8:30 service, though her assignment in Miami was more on her mind than the liturgy. In the late morning, she went for a three-mile run along the beach. It reinvigorated her, even with her Glock in a specially designed holster on her back beneath a baggy T-shirt. She kept her ID and permit in a runner's wallet on her arm.

A quick swim after the run and a light lunch took her through the noon hour. Then she checked email, text messages, and phone messages. She found nothing important, so she dressed for her meeting with the Mejíases. She wore the same outfit as the previous evening, the Glock again in a shoulder bag.

She left the hotel a few minutes before 2:00 p.m. and drove to her proposed rendezvous point with Señor and Señora Mejías: La Veranda, an outdoor café on Ocean Drive, open, bustling, and adjacent to the beach. It was across a busy street from a grand hotel, with a view of the sand and the Atlantic Ocean, beyond a stand of spiky philodendrons that established the perimeter of the café.

She found a seat at an empty table and positioned herself with her back to the wall, a standard precaution on any assignment. Nearby, a pair of twitchy, noisy parrots held court in a white enamel cage, glaring disapprovingly at the diners. One of the parrots, Alex noticed with a smirk, had the vocabulary of a sailor who had been at sea too long, thanks presumably to some of the mischief makers among the clientele.

She kept a nervous eye on all the accesses and exits.

One of the parrots sounded off again in a voice that was staccato and metallic, as scratchy as an old phonograph record.

A waiter came to Alex's table. She ordered an iced coffee. The waiter vanished.

A few minutes passed. Alex kept watching the street for any signs of surveillance. She saw none. Her gaze worked the open café. As she looked again for Mejías and his wife, a distant feeling of paranoia was upon her again, a healthy enough situation.

Not far from her, a fat man with salt-and-pepper hair had a pair of boilermakers lined up. He gazed out across the water as if trying to forget something. Across from her a fiftyish woman, with a blouse the color of a goldfish and an emerald-and-diamond ring the size of a quarter, ate with a wiry man half her age. The latter seemed to be courting the former — or was it the other way around? Amazing in what directions a bulging bank account can propel one's life, Alex thought. She also noted a single woman dining on something that looked healthy, at least from a distance. The woman was clad in a Tahitian-style head wrap, a pink blouse, purple harem pants and sneakers. After every few bites, her eyes worked the room.

Alex's coffee arrived. She made small talk with the waiter, whose name was Alfredo. Though she had heard him conversing in Spanish, Alex talked to him in English; it made it easier to eavesdrop if no one knew she spoke Spanish.

Time passed. No Mejías. No Señora Mejías. She began to smell complications.

A pelican landed clumsily on one of the railings that partitioned the café from the beach. It had barely stopped flapping when it took off again, sailing on a hot breeze toward a piling fifty yards away where it found a more enjoyable class of people and birds.

At 2:30 Alex phoned Mejías's cell number. Nothing. She had a home number for him also. She tried it. It answered but jumped to voice mail. Increasingly anxious, Alex waited as the ensuing minutes morphed into an hour. A blandly handsome man in a navy polo shirt and white slacks came in, holding hands with a luscious six-foot blonde in a denim mini. They had South Beach modeling agency tattooed all over them — a perfect cover. But the waiter knew them. He provided menus quickly and a pair of frozen margaritas almost as fast. There were also a couple of klatches of young tourists. Alex spotted a green Michigan State T-shirt on a young man and a pretty girl in University of North Carolina gym shorts.

She left the tourists and continued to work the café with her eyes.

She glanced at her watch. Where were they?

Nearby, a pair of loud voices speaking rapid-fire Spanish jarred her. She turned fast. Her senses bolted, then eased as she tuned into the conversation. Two young men were talking baseball, arguing about some game. What was it about Cubans? she wondered. They spoke the fastest-cadenced Spanish on the planet, always seeming in a rush to finish their sentences and start the next one. Fidel had lasted half a century, but no sentence in Cubanglish lasted more than three seconds. Go figure.

The young men stopped talking and glanced at her, thinking she was flirting. She turned away. The last thing she needed was unwelcome suitors. She glanced at her watch. More than an hour blown now.

This was bad. She tried the phone numbers again.

Again, nothing.

At 3:45, disgusted, she tossed a ten-dollar bill onto the table for her coffee and a generous tip and walked back to the car.

The humidity had kicked in more heavily. Beneath her blouse, she was sweating. But it wasn't just the heat; it was a bad feeling. She knew the day was going off the rails. When she reached her car she examined it carefully for any sign of tampering. No bomb, no bug, or so she hoped. In a further paranoid moment, she crouched down and glanced underneath. No surprises that would blow her into oblivion.

She unlocked the car, fed Mejías's home address into the rental's GPS, and drove, starting off with a brisk and flagrant illegal U-turn when she spotted a window in the traffic.

She crossed the causeway, left Miami Beach, and approached Little Havana. Keeping one eye on the rearview mirror, she made sure she had no trackers and guided the rental vehicle down a couple of side streets.

As she rounded the last corner, she saw a small armada of police cars in front of an address halfway down the block, with a crowd of anxious onlookers huddled across the street.

Several cars from the Miami Police Department had set a

perimeter. There was yellow tape all over and blue strobe lights flashing in every direction. Police radios crackled into the scorching air.

In the air-conditioned quiet of her car, Alex muttered a low profanity. After pulling into an empty parking place, she stepped out into the suffocating Florida heat. Three Miami cops turned and assessed her. They were strong young guys in tan shirt sleeves. Powerful bronzed arms and the sturdy T-square shoulders of gymnasts. Shields glimmering. Sunglasses, all of them. Big black weapons at their hips. Spanish names, hard eyes, lantern jaws.

She steadied herself and went to work.

The house they surrounded was a three-story deco-streamlined building with a pastel paint job. Blue and pink on white stucco. The street seemed quiet, or at least until today. As Alex took three steps forward, one of the uniformed men intercepted her, raising a powerful hand.

"Sorry, ma'am. Can't go any further."

She read his name plate. Ramirez. She resisted the temptation to slip into Spanish.

"I'm with the United States Department of Treasury," Alex said. "I was scheduled to meet with Ivar Mejías. I'm going to reach under my jacket and show you my ID. I've also got a weapon in my bag. You okay with this?"

"Let's see what you have," Ramirez said.

Alex reached with her left hand and flashed her Fin Cen shield. With a movement of her other wrist, she pulled open her shoulder bag and showed him her Glock.

"Okay," the cop said.

"Who's your commander?" Alex asked.

"Lieutenant Woodbine."

"Where's he? Or she?"

"Inside," Ramirez said, nodding toward the house.

"Where's Mejías?" she asked.

"Inside too."

"Dead?"

"I'll walk you in," Ramirez said. "Put your ID where people can see it so no one shoots you, okay?"

Alex fixed it to her breast pocket. "Was that a bad joke?" she asked.

"Not meant to be one."

"Okay," she said. "ID in place."

Ramirez led Alex to the ranking officer on the scene. He was Lt. Clarence Woodbine, a lanky African-American with closely cropped grayish hair. He had a misshapen nose, probably from collision with a few fists over the years, and a zigzag scar across the left temple. He reminded Alex of someone, but she couldn't place it.

Woodbine had an attitude to match the temperature. He was on a cell phone in the living room when Ramirez guided her to him. He ended the call. Ramirez introduced them, then quickly disappeared.

The lieutenant glowered at her, then at her Department of the Treasury shield, and didn't react well to either.

"So, what are you doing here?" he asked before she could say anything.

"I'm on a case," she said.

"Hell of a coincidence — I am too."

"I'm also armed," she said.

"Show me."

Alex opened the bag and gave Woodbine a glimpse of her weapon.

"You got a permit for that Glock?" he asked.

"Would I show it to you if I didn't?"

"Maybe."

"I have a permit," she continued. "Federal."

"Got a Florida permit?"

"Washington trumps pink plastic flamingos. I'm on an assignment."

"Pretty women shouldn't get mixed up in murders."

"Chauvinists shouldn't be lieutenants."

"That's your opinion."

"You're right. It is. Where's Mejías?" she asked.

"Upstairs ... reclining. What do you want him for?"

"A friendly conversation."

"About what?"

"A federal matter."

"What sort?"

"The sort I can't discuss with you without proper clearance," she said. "Where's his wife?"

"Don't know. Somewhere," said Woodbine.

"'Somewhere' as in, you know where but won't tell me, or 'somewhere' as in you don't know?"

Woodbine shrugged. "Maybe if you told me something, I'd tell you something."

Alex came back at him, sotto voce. "Mejías was in the Cuban government until a few weeks ago. Mid-level intelligence stuff," Alex said. "I was the agent who went down to Havana to smuggle him out. We've been nursing him along, debriefing — not me, but others ... CIA, Treasury — getting him ready to travel. Mejías and his wife." She paused.

"Interesting," Woodbine said. "Is there more?"

"I spoke to him on Friday by secure phone. He wanted to talk about something important. In person. We had a meeting set up for today, so I flew down."

"From DC?"

"New York," Alex said.

Woodbine nodded. "Okay. That's good. Now we're being friendlier," he said.

"Speak for yourself," Alex said.

"I am." He gave a grudging smile. "That explains a lot," he said.

"Good. Now you owe me a little."

"Yeah," he said. "You want to talk to him?"

"Yes."

"Follow me," he said. "You'll get your chance."

He motioned to the stairs.

Alex moved through the living room. Lamps were overturned and shattered, so were plates. Walls had been broken. Someone had come in and gone ballistic. Alex and Woodbine climbed the steps.

On the second floor there was another cluster of Miami police, male and female, harness and plainclothes, dusting everything, taking pictures. Alex noticed a trail of blood on the floor, which led to what looked like a bedroom. There was extensive breakage of furniture, and blood a few feet up on the wall.

She followed Woodbine across the upstairs landing and into the bedroom. The door was partly open, and beyond it, voices. Detectives. A dozen crime-scene techies trying to do their thing while not obliterating evidence. Alex knew how it went.

The room was hot and oppressive. Someone had killed the air-conditioning in this part of the house — almost as if they'd cranked the heat, but second stories in Miami were like this. A closet door was open, and she knew that's where the real horror was. The door — what remained of it — was ajar. It had been smashed apart by bullet holes. Blood flowed from the closet onto the floor.

She looked.

"There he is," said Woodbine. "Talk to him if you want."

Alex saw the bullet-riddled body of Ivar Mejías. Someone had won the brawl, beaten him, thrown him in the closet, locked him in, then stepped back and hammered the closet with bullets. From the size of the holes in the door — and in the body — it looked like the work of an automatic pistol, .9mm maybe.

Sick, unspeakable, and vengeful.

"Who found him?" Alex asked in a low voice.

"His wife," Woodbine said. "She went out about ten this morning, came back about ten thirty. He was alive when she left ... dead when she returned. She said she went to the bodega for groceries. She sounds credible. Badly shaken up. Hysterical. We're checking her story."

"Obviously. Where is she now?" Alex asked. "You have her?"

"We *had* her," Woodbine said. He followed that with a torrent of obscenities, one of the most colorful Alex had ever suffered through.

"Translation?"

"Our people barely had their feet in the place when your friends arrived."

"What friends? I didn't know I had any friends here."

"The first batch of Feds," Woodbine said.

"Who?"

"Guys in white shirts and dark suits. Obnoxious bunch."

"FBI?" Alex asked. "Miami office?"

"Try some other initials," he said, "and it's not IRS or EPA."

"Langley, Virginia. CIA, local annex."

"That would be it," he said. Another round of profanity followed.

They stepped away from the closet. Woodbine fished in his pocket and produced a business card. CIA shield, Miami address, an agent named Lionel Dickey, whom Woodbine loathed in particular.

"Little sawed-off runt," Woodbine said. "I know the type. So do you."

Alex took the card. She went to write down the information, but Woodbine said she could keep it. He had an extra.

"You can line a latrine in the ladies' room with it for all I care," Woodbine said. "I'm not calling him. He's blocking my case, and he knows he's doing it. They're sitting on her till we give up. I know how it works. I get a high-profile homicide, and they make sure I can't close it. Thanks so much. If you want to talk to the new widow, call Dickey — and get ready to wait in line for a taste of noncooperation."

"Got it," Alex said. "Thanks. I'll see what I can do."

"Sure you will. All you lousy Feds are the same. And now you come in here giving me a girlie-girl smile and sashaying around in a skirt, but you all chow down from the same trough. Get me? I got no use for any of you. You don't help me, I don't help you. So do what you want and get out of here, Alex Whoever, because I don't want to see you again. So get lost."

"I can grant you some favors," Alex said, "but that's not one of them."

She pulled one of her business cards from a pocket and handed it to him.

"Thanks," he said. He tore it in half and dropped the pieces on the floor. "Consider that a hint."

"May I see your hand?" she said.

"My *what*?"

"Your hand," she repeated. She took out a ballpoint pen. "Your palm."

He held out his left hand. She grabbed his wrist firmly, and then in bold strokes wrote her cell number on the light part of his flesh. He was so stunned that he didn't pull his hand away until she had written all seven numbers.

"That's a two-one-two number," she said. "I look forward to hearing from you."

Woodbine looked at his hand and cursed.

ELEVEN

What if you stay in Miami for a few days?" De Salvo asked Alex on the phone later that evening. "Can you talk to the CIA people. I'll pull the strings from here to get you the audience. Do you know anyone in the Miami office?"

"No. But I have the card of a case officer," she said. "I don't want to give the name over the phone. I'm not sure we're secure."

"We're not," De Salvo said. It was Sunday evening, and he was at a pro football game, The Giants — his team — playing Dallas in New Jersey. In the background, she could hear the noise of the crowd.

"I also have a contact," she said. "Friend of a friend."

The contact at the CIA was Laura Chapman's boyfriend, Rick McCarron. Laura and Rick had one of those long-distance relationships dictated by modern employment. Laura worked in DC, Rick in Miami. One weekend a month, Laura would fly to Miami; one weekend a month, Rick would fly to Washington. For them it worked, or at least currently it did.

Alex had never met Rick, though once or twice he had answered the phone on weekends when Alex had phoned Laura. Still, a contact was a contact.

"The main thing is to find out what Mejías wanted to discuss," De Salvo said. "Agreed?"

"Agreed," Alex said.

"Must have been something significant," said De Salvo.

Alex answered, "A list of names, that's what he alluded to. Important, I'd guess."

"So you're willing to stay there and follow it up?"

"Absolutely," Alex answered.

"Go for it," De Salvo said.

For most of Monday morning and the early afternoon, Alex worked on her laptop near the hotel pool. She made phone calls all over Miami but felt stonewalled by the results. Woodbine, McCarron, local FBI office. She left messages, but no one called her back. The only thing she learned — from a reporter at a local Spanish-language newspaper when she cold called — was the time and place of Mejías's funeral. It would be the next day at a Roman Catholic church in little Havana.

Later in the afternoon she went for a long walk and in the evening went to the beach, which she found joyless. She missed New York, she missed her friends, she still hurt over the tragedy that had cost her fiancé his life those many months ago in snowy Kiev. She thought of all the money she had in the bank and wondered what God's plan was for her, if indeed there was one. She wondered if she was straying from it. She wondered if she thought too much.

She later phoned Lieutenant Woodbine again to see if there was anything new on the case. This time her call connected. But when she finally got him, he hung up on her.

Alex thought about the irony of it all. Mejías had kept his own council in Cuba, laid low for decades, had finally made his escape with his wife, and then murderers had found him in the United States. That was the broad overview. How much lurked beneath the surface was another question. Beyond the irony, what was going on?

It seemed too coincidental that he was killed just minutes before he was to meet with Alex. Miami crawled with Cubans and Caribbean ex-pats of all persuasions, but surely Mejías would have known to be careful. And surely his wife, Juanita, would have been watching his back. How could all this have happened and why? Alex asked herself. There were so many possible explanations that she cringed.

Both pro-Castro and anti-Castro people had a world of grievances. Gangsters? Someone with an old personal vendetta? Something to do with the CIA — or something *not* to do with the CIA?

Then there was the crime scene. There was something hyperintense about it, something that raised it to an odd level. Alex had not been able to pinpoint it at the time — smashed lamps, punched walls, a barrage of bullets far beyond what was necessary for a "simple" execution — but now she had it. There had been a frenzied *passion* to the killing, as if it had been in retribution for something, a score that had been a long time in the settling.

Then there was Señora Mejías. She claims to have been away when the intruder entered. Coincidence or by design? Then a violent confrontation had followed. Mejías had fought his assailant but had gone upstairs instead of out? Why? To get a weapon? Maybe. But Mejías, as Alex remembered, was fit and a bit of a bull himself. Yet he'd been no match for whoever had killed him. Or had he been outnumbered? Had there been more than one assailant?

And why? Recent payback? Or payback from long ago? Mejías's past was nothing if not complicated. Where had the moment of reckoning been born? The deceased probably didn't even know all the enemies he had made. So how was Alex supposed to figure it out?

The dark angel on one of Alex's shoulders asked this question: Had there been collusion with the widow? Had Juanita really been absent? Had she been a witness? Perhaps even a collaborator?

Alex shook her head. The more she examined it, the more the questions multiplied.

For Señora Mejías, Alex's empathy was immeasurable.

TWELVE

James Kevork, the club owner in South Beach, was having a midnight dinner in his office behind the club when the first two men in Miami Police uniforms came to see him. It was hardly a quiet moment as the music from the bar and dance floor boomed heavily around him, even on a Monday night. Then again, the music and activity from the entertainment area was a beautiful sound. Business was jumping.

He reacted politely and asked the policemen what he could do for them, speaking louder than normal to be heard above the very profitable din.

The first cop began a rambling inquiry about security at the club. He focused on that and then made an allusion to whether or not kids were partying with drugs. Then there was something about underage drinking.

"I keep an eye on everything," Kevork said, keeping a current eye on the security monitor in his office as he spoke to them. He got the idea that the cops were edging toward an extra shakedown of some sort. The lead guy sure wasn't getting to the point of the visit; of that much Kevork was certain. "You can go out and card people yourselves if you want, but you won't find much."

It was a bluff, of course. The last thing Kevork needed was uniformed Miami cops wading into his sea of partygoers, mingling with the precocious nineteen-year-olds, and wrecking the party atmosphere. Crockett and Stubbs this wasn't.

Kevork drew a breath and held on to what remained of his patience. The local city police were a nuisance that had to be indulged to get business done. One never knew when one might need them. Who knew? Some idiot might try to hold up the joint some night, and who was he going to call? What did one pay protection money for, after all?

But he also pondered how stupid these uniformed grunts could be, coming by to ask for an extra payoff, if that's what they were there for. Wasn't it obvious that his office had a surveillance camera rolling? The camera was right up there in an overhead corner, a little red light flashing every three seconds to show that it was connected and working. There was nothing that transpired in that office that Kevork couldn't revisit, review, or screen for someone else, from some guy's mistress to a precinct commander. Well, if these guys were dumb enough to make their pitch on camera, he was going to capture it. Later on, he could decide what use it might be.

The club owner leaned back in his chair. "Gentlemen, really," he said indulgently, "I'm sure you have other more interesting things to do than talk to me. And I have a club to manage tonight. What can I do for you? What would be your pleasure? Let's get to the point."

The door to the office opened again and a third man in uniform entered. He nodded to the other two. The first officer turned back to Kevork. For a moment everyone stood there as if no one knew what to do next.

Kevork had a bad feeling about all this. He looked quickly at all three faces and searched them, trying to figure out what was wrong. Then, too late, he had it — the little light on the security camera was solid. The system was off. It had been disconnected in the last few seconds, most likely by the last man to enter. And in the same moment, Kevork realized that he had only a few moments to live.

Even so, in a lucid reflex for life, he lunged for the pistol that he kept in his top drawer. But he wasn't fast enough. Two of the fake uniformed cops drew their own weapons and opened fire. They were good at what they were there to do, hammering point blank blasts at Kevork's head, neck, and upper chest. They fired four shots each.

The bullets were powerful, propelling him backward. For a moment, Kevork's body remained upright, propped up by his chair, despite the blood and bullet damage to the wall behind him. Then it gave a final huge spasm and slid down heavily. It hit the floor, lying on its side. The third assailant deftly leaned over and fired a single shot into the side of Kevork's head, just above the ear.

For a moment, the assassins stared at what they had done, not in disbelief but with a sense of accomplishment. Then one of them, using gloves, fixed the lock on the door so that it would latch after they left. They hurried out the back exit and went quickly down the alley where they removed their uniforms into a garbage bag and disappeared in separate directions into the buoyant nighttime atmosphere of South Beach. The neighborhood would have to rock on without James Kevork.

THIRTEEN

On the bright humid Tuesday morning that followed, Alex followed on foot as the funeral procession for Ivar Mejías moved slowly through four city blocks in Little Havana. The day had already started with a glitch. She had dropped her sunglasses in the lobby of the hotel, and they had smashed. A hundred dollars later in the hotel gift store, she was equipped with a new pair of Ray Bans. *Sic transit fortuna.*

Now, equipped with her new shades, she followed the slow, moody procession through the streets, through an atmospheric neighborhood that was home not just to residents from Cuba, but also from Honduras and Nicaragua. At its heart was Calle Ocho, lined with authentic Cuban restaurants, cigar factories, fruit stands, cafeterias, art galleries, and theaters. She could smell the freshly baked *chicharrones* and *merenguitos* as she walked.

The heat was already murder, and the humidity made it first-degree. The procession wound from Caballero Rivero Woodlawn funeral home and stopped at a pair of restaurants, La Carreta and Versailles on Calle Ocho, places Alex knew were landmarks for the Cuban exile community and their half century of descendants. The procession then continued to St. Michael's Catholic Church on West Flagler Street. The tropical sun gave no one a break.

St. Michael's was relatively modern, dating from the 1940s, Alex guessed. She followed the others into the church, and she slid into a pew toward the rear. She quickly scanned the mourners and counted about a hundred, maybe a hundred twenty-five, which was interesting because Mejías had only been in this neighborhood for a few months. Yes, the community here was strong, but how had so many people gotten to know him so quickly?

At the entrance, in the vestibule, candles had been lit for the deceased. In the pews, some mourners held candles, the symbol of keeping a spirit — the Spirit — present in this world. A huge crucifix dominated the front of the church.

As she spent a moment in silent prayer, she fingered the miniature cross at her neck. Then her left earring irritated her. She readjusted it. Today she had chosen a pair of recently purchased small gold hoop earrings with clasps. The left clasp pinched. Or was it maybe the oppressive heat and humidity, changing the texture of her skin and the touch of the metal?

Alex loosened the clasp slightly and readjusted the earring. It all added to her sense of anxiety, of being unnerved.

Then there was movement to her right.

Alex turned her head. Señora Mejías came slowly down the center aisle, escorted by a young man of about forty. He looked like a younger version of the major, which stunned Alex. Was he their son? If so, where had he come from? How was he in the United States? How could they have had a son already in the United States? More questions arose in her mind.

Alex's eyes shifted back to the widow. She wore black, no surprise there. Her sleeves were long, and large, dark round glasses, presumably to hide tears and red eyes, obscured most of her face.

Near the altar, mourners steadily filed past the open silver casket that fronted a wall emblazoned with white roses. At the appropriate moment, Alex fell in line and passed by the open coffin. She took an extra moment to nod and say a final prayer for the man's soul. Whatever else the man may have done during his time on earth, he had saved her life. Alex was grateful and for a moment fought back tears. Death was so hard and finite when contained in a coffin. It seemed as if it were only yesterday that she and Mejías's wife were running for the CIA aircraft taking off from Communist Cuba's south shore.

With gratitude that bordered on affection, Alex touched the casket as she slowly passed it. She let her fingers linger,

In his coffin, Mejías clasped a white rosary. Around his neck a kerchief bore the colors of Cuba: red, white, and blue, same as the American flag, and Alex reflected that this was not a complete coincidence. A Cuban flag had also been carefully folded and placed beneath his head.

Involuntarily, Alex's eyes scanned with professional intensity. Mejías had suffered head wounds from the fusillade of shots that had killed him. The undertakers had done a commendable job of covering them, but because she knew where to look, Alex could see where they had been.

She turned away, preferring not to look too carefully.

From somewhere, a voice in Spanish intoned a prayer to Saint Michael, or San Miguel, as he was called here. The accent was Cuban, the voice that of an older man. Alex guessed it was the priest. "Saint Michael, Archangel, defend us in battle. Be our protection against the wickedness and snares of the devil. May God rebuke him, we humbly pray; and do Thou, O Prince of the Heavenly Host, by the Divine Power of God, cast into hell, Satan and all the evil spirits, who roam throughout the world seeking the ruin of souls. Amen."

Alex respectfully crossed herself and left the viewing area. She turned and followed the aisle back to her seat. Involuntarily, images came back to her from Ukraine, the impressive service that had been held in an Eastern Orthodox church before all hell had broken loose and an attack had rained down on the American president, her fiancé had been killed, and everyone had fled to the airport.

Back in her pew, Alex was joined by a middle-aged woman, with skin the color of light coffee, who sat a few feet away. The woman was dressed entirely *de luto*, in the black of mourning. She wore a flat hat — almost gaucho style — and a veil. She was in her early twenties, Alex guessed, though she couldn't see her face clearly. On the other side of her was a young man with a Cuban face, a T-shirt, and a Marlins cap. All around, other mourners glanced to each other, whispered privately, nodded, shook heads, and shifted their weight from side-to-side.

The woman in the veil nodded to Alex. *"Hola,"* she whispered. *"¿Como va todo?"*

"Hola," Alex returned. The woman didn't look away. From beneath the veil, her dark intent eyes held Alex's gaze. Alex had the strong sense that this meeting was not a coincidence.

Alex turned back toward the front of the church but — instinct again — continued to feel the nearby woman's eyes on her. Alex looked back. Their eyes locked again for a few seconds. *"Mas tarde,"* the woman said softly. Later. Then the woman looked away, retuning her gaze forward. *"Por favor."*

Alex wasn't sure whether the woman had mistaken her for someone else. Who, after all, even knew who Alex was within this group, other than Mejías's widow?

The man who had accompanied Señora Mejías down the aisle took the pulpit. He was a nephew, not a son. He delivered the eulogy, then a priest performed the final part of the service. The woman down the pew from Alex never moved, other than to kneel on two occasions to say a prayer, one of her own and one in unison with the other mourners.

Afterward, as people left the church, Alex scanned the crowd, wondering when the woman in black was going to approach her. But she seemed to have disappeared, and women in black were everywhere, many with hats and veils.

Alex circulated through the crowd, wondering what other vibes she might pick up. The celebration of Mejías's life proved resonant with Cuban exiles. Some shed tears as they waited for friends and transport outside Saint Michael's. Alex tuned into various conversations. They were mostly older people, but there was a cross section of the young. Some denounced Castro and communism. Alex didn't disagree with the sentiments but tried to tune out the political diatribes. She had had enough of extremists on both sides. Nor did she feel that a funeral was a place for a political statement.

Then again, Mejías's life had been defined by politics. Without the extremes, he would not have lived the life he had. So maybe it was a proper summation after all.

Alex made a decision. She would continue on to the cemetery. She didn't know what sort of insights she would pick up about Mejías and his death there, but she knew she might come away with a better understanding by going to the burial than by walking away. She scanned again for the woman in black but didn't see her. She wondered who might be watching her. But nothing happened. So Alex struck up a conversation with some of the mourners and cadged a ride to the burial grounds.

FOURTEEN

The long motorcade — Alex counted at least two dozen cars before leaving the church — moved slowly through the warm streets of Little Havana. The trip through Miami took twenty minutes before the hearse pulled into a Catholic cemetery called St. Juventos on the fringe of the city.

Alex followed the mourners through a verdant burial ground that reminded her of the sprawling Colon Cemetery in Havana, where Paul Guarneri had mined a grave during their clandestine visit to Cuba earlier that year.

At the gravesite, Alex stood with a small knot of people. Alex didn't recognize anyone. The sun was high, and the heat was oppressive. The convocation was strangely quiet.

The funerals I've been to in the last two years! thought Alex. Her fiancé's, three other casualties in Kiev, Yuri Federov's. Now this. She bowed her head but kept her gaze lifted. Seeing God's plan amidst such sorrow was not something she could easily accomplish. Bit by bit, day by day, sorrow by sorrow, she had felt her once-strong faith being shaken.

The presiding priest, a middle-aged man named Sotero, was tall and heavy with a puffy face. He conducted the ceremony in Spanish and English, clasping a Bible, as the coffin rested above the open grave. The priest's words were succinct. The attendees shuffled uncomfortably. Alex tried to count them. At least a hundred and fifty, many of whom had arrived on foot. Then the service was over.

Alex waited a few minutes for the crowd to thin out. Turning, she started to retrace her path to the exit when another thought occurred to her. This might be her only chance to corral Juanita Mejías, even if it was a terrible time. She worked her way toward

76

the gravesite. The area was crowded, and people were moving slowly. Many of them were elderly. It was difficult to get near the bereaved family.

Alex persisted, however, and moved to within thirty feet, then twenty. Closer, then close enough to call to the widow.

Immediately, a ring of protectors emerged out of the crowd and formed a barrier around the widow. They looked like more than family. While Juanita Mejías was lithe and mocha-skinned, her ring of protectors was burley and white, professional bodyguard types with what appeared to be, from Alex's experiences over the last few years, an ominous CIA glow to them.

"Juanita?" Alex called again.

But either the widow did not hear or did not choose to hear. Her protectors moved her quickly to a waiting Lincoln. Alex was about to call again when she noticed something that she had missed in the church. Seeing Juanita from the side, Alex noticed that the dark glasses concealed more than tears. Juanita looked as if she had a black eye on the right side. Looking more carefully, she also caught a quick glimpse of what could be a bruise above the woman's left eye.

As Alex watched the guards hustle her into a car, which pulled a quick U-turn and took a side path out of the cemetery, she understood what Lieutenant Woodbine was up against. There were powers in this world that didn't want Juanita Mejías talking to anyone.

Alex started to head back to the car she had come in, but before she had gone several steps, she heard a soft distinctive female voice nearby.

"*Señorita?*" the voice asked.

Alex turned. The woman in black approached her. Alex's gaze dropped quickly to the woman's hands. She held a purse on her arm and a small piece of paper in her left hand. No weapon: Alex had learned to scan for weapons first.

Alex stopped. "*Si?*" she asked.

From beneath the hat and the veil a cryptic smile. "*Venga*

veme," the woman said. Come see me. *"Soy Hermana Ramona."* I'm Sister Ramona.

She pushed a business card into Alex's hands. In part, it read:

Botánica Ramona
Santería
Por todos los Espiritos Ramona Suárez, sacerdotista

The woman in black was a priestess, it explained. A *santera* or *sacerdotista* in the Santerían faith.

"Santería?" Alex asked, unable to conceal her surprise, but able to contain her suspicion of it.

"Santería, sí," the woman said. "We have something to discuss. Come see me soon. Before the time is no longer good with Olodumare and the other spirits."

"Who?" Alex asked.

"We believe in one god, Olodumare," she said. "Olodumare is the source of *ashé*."

"Ashé?"

"The spiritual energy that makes up the universe, all life and all things material. We will do a *mediación* and you will find what you came seeking in Miami."

"How do you know I came to Miami seeking anything?" Alex asked.

"Because I know who you are."

"And how do you know *that*?"

"Magic," the woman said. She nodded toward her business card again. "So you will come see me for *un mediación*."

Alex glanced at the card. She saw an address in one lower corner and a telephone number in the other.

"What's a *mediación*?" Alex asked.

When there was no answer, Alex looked up, but the woman had disappeared. Alex was stunned at how quickly she had melted into the crowd.

She shuddered and wondered. What was going on that she was missing? What did everyone else know that she didn't? What had just occurred this morning right before her eyes that she had perhaps missed?

Was all hell going to break loose again? Was she in another lull before a firestorm?

After the funeral, as she was driving her rental car back to the hotel, she realized the clasp on her earring had finally broken. She had lost the left earring. She pulled off the highway and searched the seat, the floor of the car, and her clothing.

Nothing. No earring anywhere.

She thought of going back to the church and cemetery and retracing her steps and seeing if she could find it.

Then she decided against it. Even if it was still where it had fallen, such a search would take forever. And probably someone would have picked it up by now anyway. What the heck, she reasoned. Two million bucks in the bank, what's an earring? Yet it was another annoyance, another small thing out of place.

On her way back to the Park Central, she had a miserable feeling about all of this. She wondered what she was picking up on, and what she was missing — aside from an earring. There was an overall mood she was picking up that she deeply disliked.

FIFTEEN

In the hotel café — a swanky Bogart-themed affair — Alex watched the people around her. Her eyes settled on a couple of black men in suits who were knocking back Coke-and-Barbancourt cocktails, the dark bottle of rum sitting between them at their table. They were a few years older than Alex, midthirties, maybe. They were alternately watching Alex and having an animated conversation in Haitian French, which Alex found challenging, if not impossible, to understand.

On her cell phone she called De Salvo in New York.

"Mejías had something to tell us, and someone got to him first. Beyond that, it's hard to see where we are," Alex said, speaking softly.

"Okay, but there's other, more immediate business at the moment," De Salvo said. "Let the Miami angle drop, after all. At least for now, okay?"

She sighed. "Hey, boss, look," she said. Alex had already worked that question. "I'd like to stay with this," she said. "My gut is telling me there's something important here. I can't prove it yet, I can't make a logical case, but the alarm bells are ringing all over the place."

"You've finally gone crazy, in other words. Cracked under the pressure."

"Don't even joke about it," she said. "I don't trust the Miami police to keep us in the loop, and the CIA people here seem intent on keeping the widow away from me."

"CIA? Why?" De Salvo asked.

"Because they can. Turf. Their usual bullheaded tactics." She paused. "You're on a secure line now, right?" she asked.

"I am. You?"

"Yes. Listen, I have a friend named Laura Chapman. She works in Washington in government security, used to be with the Secret Service at the White House. She has a friend here in Miami named Rick. I mentioned him before."

"I remember," De Salvo said.

"Maybe I can get a favor or two. Unofficially, if you follow."

"The Alex Network again," De Salvo said, sounding pleased.

"Call it that if you want. I've been in this line of work long enough to have made a few friends."

"Lucky you," he said. "Some people spend a lifetime in this work and make nothing but enemies. Including me."

"I have a few of those too," she said.

"We all do. Wouldn't be doing our jobs if people weren't trying to kill us. Anyway, speaking of enemies, I need you back in New York tomorrow afternoon."

"What? Tomorrow?"

"You need to be here as soon as possible. Frat Boys Investigating — FBI. They want to talk to you on that Russian stuff."

"I thought we had more time."

"I didn't get any advance warning. You know that."

She crunched the numbers: "That means I have to fly back tomorrow morning. Early."

"Brilliant deduction. That's why we pay you the big bucks."

Alex grumbled. "Can't you put them off a week? I've barely scratched the surface here."

"FBI," De Salvo said. "I doubt it."

Before her, the two Haitian men continued to make their rude racket. The echoes of Haitian French, louder now, carried with them echoes of the old Duvalier regimes and their security goons, the Tonton Macoute, the Haitian paramilitary force created by President François "Papa Doc" Duvalier.

"Can you hold for a moment?" Alex asked softly into the phone.

"Sure. Go ahead," De Salvo said.

Very briefly, Alex tuned in the Haitian conversation to see

if it was about her. It didn't seem to be. Then the two Haitians noticed that they had drawn Alex's attention. Alex turned away from them.

"Okay. Continue," Alex said.

"FBI," De Salvo repeated. "You know what they're like. They don't enjoy being put off. They're not smart, but they're stubborn as mules. We need to appease the beast or it'll look like we're stonewalling."

"Okay, okay," she said.

"See you soon," he said. He rang off.

Alex put her phone back in her purse, where she found the business card that Ramona had given her. She reread the address: 146 S. Mariposa. Well, that seemed as good a start as any, she reasoned.

She looked up. The two young Haitian men had stopped and were watching her. One smiled. The other waved. One of them got up and wished her a good evening in French. Alex was having none of it.

"I was just leaving," she said in English. "I don't speak French."

She paid her bill, gathered her things, and went back upstairs.

She went online to book her flight from Miami to New York, stopping by a weather website. She groaned — two ominous weather patterns between Nassau and Cuba had collided to give birth to a sudden late-season storm that was kicking up and heading toward Key West. She would be wise to leave as early as possible to beat the storm. If it hit Miami too quickly it would shut down the airport.

"Maybe a good thing," she muttered to herself. This FBI thing was already a pain and a half. If she couldn't get back, who could blame her?

Nonetheless, she rebooked her flight for an early departure, finding a business-class seat to La Guardia at 7:10 a.m.

7:10 a.m. Ouch!

She knew that meant she would have to be up before 5:00 and out the door. She sighed. Should she pray for a storm? Well, she had enough to do this evening. No point worrying about the next morning just yet.

She changed into jeans, sneakers, and a lightweight Windbreaker for the evening. The latter would have been unnecessary except it concealed her Glock. Hence, she felt, it was entirely necessary.

"Okay, Ramona," she said to herself, "now is your moment."

SIXTEEN

She pulled away from the hotel, alternately checking the roadway in front of her, the rearview mirror, and the sidewalk.

She still couldn't shake the feeling that she was under surveillance. Few people in her line of work failed to develop that sense of paranoia. And from time to time, they were right.

Traffic was a nightmare, cluttered and mean-spirited. Everyone was on their way somewhere to watch the sunset, she supposed.

She saw early diners and drinkers weaving through the pedestrian traffic, stumbling up to standing signs with menus on them. Tinny music blared out of open-front bars, each with a pretty girl posted in front to lure the suckers in. Tourists spun postcard racks, tried on baseball caps or straw hats, and gawked at some of the younger, beautiful people, skimpily clad, who snaked past. She saw klatches of perfectly groomed, remorselessly fit young men in pretty pastel shirts, a biker couple in chains and tattoos, and a woman in a chartreuse miniskirt with an enormous mouth painted deep red beyond the real contours of her lips. Her companion was a small Chihuahua who did stiff-legged pirouettes whenever the woman stopped walking. The reflected sunlight was muted now, but the palms that lined the route barely moved.

Gradually, as she moved away from the tourist areas, traffic slackened. She was able to make several green lights and break free. Using her GPS, she found Mariposa Street in Little Havana. Mariposa was not busy; few cars were parked there. No pedestrians. The neighborhood was lower-middle-class commercial with some grunge. Stores were closed. The streetlamps were sodium vapor and cast sharp shadows, even though a bit of daylight remained. Alex drove with one hand. As she neared her destination, 146 S. Mariposa, she pulled out her weapon and laid it across her lap.

She had another bad feeling and couldn't have explained why if asked.

Her car slowed to a crawl. A Toyota van was jammed on a hydrant, a pair of parking tickets on its window. Nothing more along the curb between her and the corner. Number 146, a dark storefront with a grate drawn, nestled between a hardware store and women's apparel shop, both with Spanish names.

Across the window, hand-painted letters spelled out "Botánica" in blue, white, and red. Cuban colors. A dim light glowed from within. A sign that said "Cerrado," closed, was stuck to the interior of the door with heavy tape. The posted business hours were 10:00 a.m. to 7:00 p.m.

Outside, an enormous banyan tree stood like a giant sentry, shading the store. The trees roots were dangling and exposed, lifting up the sidewalk as if to suggest some force coming up from hell.

Alex stopped. She backed her car to a position in front of the van. Her body tingled with anxiety. She looked past the tree and watched the storefront for movement but saw none. She watched the van for movement and saw none. She wished she had a backup. It wasn't so much being a woman alone as much as being *alone*-alone. Four eyes were always better than two. Her pulse was starting to flutter into higher gear.

The curb space in front of the botánica, she realized, was a no-parking area. Much of the block was the same way. Alex backed her car down the block about a hundred feet and into a legal space. She drew her weapon and stepped out. She kept her right hand low, her arm down, her gun concealed. She took a half dozen casual steps forward, turned, checked behind her, saw no one, and continued.

Still no traffic. No strollers. The street remained dead, the evening air druggy, wet, and heavy, an evening sky turning to a yellowing black. Shop windows behind grates: Latino spice shops.

Bodegas. Car-part emporiums. A shop for musical instruments, mostly second hand. A travel agency that also sent money by electronic transfer. Another hardware store and a *libraria Cristiana*, a Spanish-language Christian bookshop. Well, that was a good sign. Maybe.

A scrawny gray cat sprung from a doorway and stopped, arching its back. Alex recoiled. The cat gave her a disapproving look, hissed, and sauntered off. Alex caught her breath. She returned her Glock to its holster. A moment later, she stood in front of the Botánica Ramona. There was a two-step stone stoop that led to the entrance.

The light within was dim, and the window was streaked from within. Alex climbed the steps and leaned forward. She tried to peer past the grate through the glass of the front door and scan the aisles as best she could. She had heard of Santería and knew a little about it. She knew it was a distant spin-off of Catholicism. She had her own opinions, however, and didn't wish to be judgmental, but she also wanted to keep her wits about her. She shifted position slightly, shielded her eyes from the sodium vapor lamp above her, and peered past the window at a better angle.

Facts. She wanted facts.

What was she looking at and who was Sister Ramona?

Facts: it was a traditional retail store, peddling folk medicine, religious candles, and statuary. She saw displays of amulets and other products regarded as magic or alternative medicines. All the signs in the store were in Spanish. There were also displays of oils, incense, perfumes, and scented sprays. Handwritten signs in Spanish suggested that each had special healing properties. Oddly, there were various other brand-name health-care products, as if a shipment from a Walgreens had somehow gone astray.

Alex knew the stores were common in many Latin American countries and flourished among communities of Latino people in the United States. When she had taken a course in comparative religions at UCLA, the students had visited a botánica as part of a field trip. She was in the midst of that recollection when a gravelly female voice from nearby said, *"¿Señorita?"* and she felt a hand on her elbow.

Alex recoiled sharply, pushed away, and turned. Beside her was a small plump woman in a tattered but colorful dress. The woman's skin was the color of mahogany. She had an old, kindly face, which creased into a smile. Her teeth were discolored and not straight. A few were missing.

"Sorry," Alex said, recovering. "You surprised me."

The woman spoke Spanish. *"¿Estas hechizada?"* Did someone place a spell on Alex, she wanted to know.

Alex switched to Spanish. *"No, no. No me han hechizada. Estoy mirando, nada mas."* No spell, just looking.

The old woman smiled and nodded. She produced a key to the iron grate and unlocked it. "Come in," she continued in Spanish. "You are welcome here. The friendly spirits are present. I hear them: they welcome you."

A beat, and then Alex answered. *"Claro,"* she said. Sure. No harm in taking a closer look. In fact, a closer look would be a good idea. The old woman struggled with the steel grate. Alex, with a free hand, helped push it. Rust came off in Alex's hand. She brushed the rust away. The old lady nodded thanks. She unlocked the door, pushed it open, took a step in, and threw a light switch. In three steps, three banks of lights switched on, illuminating the *botánica.*

"Doña Elena," the old woman said, introducing herself. "Come in if you wish." She smiled again and beckoned. After a moment's hesitation, Alex stepped in.

The old lady made herself busy at an old cash register at the checkout counter. The woman fascinated Alex. There was something strange about her, almost otherworldly, that Alex couldn't quite place, yet something strangely familiar at the same time.

Alex found herself in a compact mini-Walmart of spirituality, its brightly lit aisles teeming with hundreds of varieties of perfumes, cleaning liquids, air fresheners, oils, candles, and incense powders, offering solutions for a host of specific problems. Alex looked at the items with growing incredulity. There were jinx-removing powders and spell-breaking oils. In case Alex was haunted by evil spirits, there were Go Away Evil bath salts and Run Devil Run floor soap. If Alex were broke or destitute, she could buy some Bad Luck Out, Good Luck In oil and freshen up the house with Mr. Money aerosol spray. No one to love? Shower with Attraction soap, dab on some Come to Me perfume in strategic places, and light a Tame Him candle. The more expensive one was purportedly coated with dragon's blood to boost the potency of the charm. She hoped no dragons had been seriously harmed in the making of the candle and that the blood had been extracted from the dragon humanely by a licensed veterinarian, perhaps one who specialized in mythical beasts.

Alex moved to another aisle. This one was given to statuary, from four-inch-tall dashboard figurines of St. Anthony and St. Barbara to a three-foot-tall Grim Reaper molded in translucent plastic. An herbs-and-roots section at the end of the aisle presented preparations for teas and baths, including mugwort, devil's shoestring, and wahoo bark.

Then there were voodoo-doll pincushions, perhaps for the boss back in New York or those pesky FBI agents who were coming to see her. Then in a small green can there was a product called *Dinero Rapido*, quick cash. Alex picked up a few items, examined them, and carefully put them back on the shelves.

Alex continued to peruse the store. Doña Elena noisily emptied the coins from the cash drawer onto the counter and began counting them. Again, Alex wondered why the store had opened that evening. Strangely, as if reading Alex's thoughts, the woman spoke.

"My customers," Doña Elena said. "Any problem they have, they come here; then they go to the doctor. I have a lady who called me this night. She is coming in a few minutes. It is an emergency. That's why I open. Her son thinks he's a water moccasin, a snake. I say to her on the phone, 'What do you mean?'

She answers me, 'I put the food down on the ground and he slithers along the floor and darts his tongue in and out.'"

"That's awful," Alex said without missing a beat. "Does that happen a lot in Miami?"

"In Miami, yes."

"So what do you do for a condition like that?" Alex asked.

"I will sell her something to put in his shoes. A silver charm."

"And that will cure the problem?"

"If Ocha is pleased."

"Who's Ocha?"

"One of the gods," she said. "The one who controls such things."

"Not Olodumare?" said Alex.

The plump old lady shook her head dismissively. "There are many gods," she said. "Just as there are many saints."

"I see," Alex said. "And this snake situation, have you treated that condition before?"

Now the old woman was distracted. She was counting nickels. She nodded.

"Did it work?" Alex asked.

"The previous patient is no longer underfoot," Doña Elena said.

Alex moved away, feeling a little wave of sadness. The spiritual hocus-pocus was all about pleasing a small army of gods, hoping to please them with trinkets and tricks. But Alex didn't believe that the gods were angry. She believed that God was love — and that everything she had was a result of God's grace.

Alex turned a corner and approached the cashier's counter where the old woman now seemed to be working some monetary figures with a pencil and paper, mumbling to herself at the same time. To the side of the counter a flight of stairs was cordoned off.

In front of the cash register was another useful display, this one for alternative medical treatments addressing arthritis, hair loss, diabetes, and menstrual pain. There were also a few more small products — impulse buys — designed to attract love, bring good luck and financial prosperity, or deflect jealousy. If any of this stuff worked, it was more useful than any Home Value hardware store she had ever been in.

On the counter were some small vials priced at $9.95. One was marked Hurricane Lotion. Alex picked up a vial and examined it. "May I open this?" she asked.

The woman was now counting dimes. She nodded.

Alex opened and sniffed. The scent was pungent and made her recoil. Alex took it to be a mixture of turpentine, wood sealer, and cheap perfume. The directions said a homeowner could use it to ward off bad spirits during hurricane season. Just spread it on your doorstep. For further protection, the label suggested, spread the entire contents at the front door and another bottle at the back door. For complete protection, sprinkle a few drops on each windowsill.

"Every time there's a hurricane, people rush in to buy that," the old woman said. "So right now, it sells a lot."

Alex screwed the top back on and placed it back on the counter. "Does it work?" Alex asked.

"Many who have used it have been spared damage from the *huracánes*," the woman said.

"Right," Alex said, finally growing a little weary of the merchandise. For a moment, she surveyed the shop. "I'm actually looking for a Sister Ramona," she said. "Do you know her?"

"Of course. She's my granddaughter," said Doña Elena.

"Ah! Then maybe you could tell me how I can find her."

"Someone put a curse on you?" Doña Elena asked again.

"Would you have Sister Ramona phone me?"

"Sí," the old woman answered.

Alex pulled one of her Fin Cen business cards out of her wallet. She wrote her cell number on the back. She handed it to Doña Elena.

"When will you see her?" Alex said.

"Pronto."

"How soon?" Alex asked.

"Muy pronto." Very soon.

"This evening maybe?"

"If the gods wish. Maybe you should buy an amulet to Olodumare for five dollars. Keep it in your bra, next to your heart."

"Let's try the telephone first," Alex said. "I often have good luck with that."

"As you wish, señorita," Doña Elena said. "But the amulet would guarantee success."

Alex sighed. Seeing no alternative, she pulled out her wallet and bought a small silver trinket. Doña Elena smiled and put the money not in the cash register but in a cigar box. She packed the amulet in tissue paper and bagged it.

Alex was about to leave when Doña Elena spoke softly. *"Señorita?"* She reached and latched onto Alex's arm with a surprisingly strong grip. "Perhaps this would be a *buena* idea also."

From under the counter, she pulled a narrow glass container about the size and shape of a can of tennis balls. She handed it to Alex.

Alex read the label and felt another surge of anxiety, plus something extra that she recognized as fear.

Contra los Cartuchos, the label read. Bulletproof.

"Did someone tell you to show this to me?" Alex demanded.

"Si, señorita."

"Who?"

"Los espiritos," Doña Elena said. Spirits.

Alex smoldered. "Tell Ramona I want to see her," Alex said sharply. "Now."

"The powder is magic, señorita," Doña Elena said.

"I'm doing fine without it."

Alex turned. She had had enough of this place, maybe too much.

As she walked toward the door, a short, thin man in a white hat and a western shirt came in. He gave Alex a gracious nod as he passed her. Alex ignored him.

Alex caught part of the ensuing conversation. The man said

something about joint pain and heat flashes and being haunted by bad spirits. Doña Elena recommended herb-infused baths, plus a good-luck candle called *La Madama*.

"Or this is an after bath powder. You dust your body with it. It will give you protection," Alex heard Doña Elena explain as Alex hit the sidewalk. "Against bad spirits."

Bad spirits. Gunshots. Alex muttered angrily to herself as she walked down the uneven sidewalk toward her car. The heat remained heavy. Her mood was starting to match. She patted her Glock, a nervous habit that was getting worse these days, just to make sure it was still there. A squadron of bugs swarmed above the sidewalk as she walked. She went around it, waved the fringe of it away, then was startled when something on the ground moved: a cockroach the size of a dollar coin. It zipped away and disappeared into a grate by a storefront.

She quickened her pace.

As she neared her car, she stepped from the sidewalk into the street, her hand instinctively on her gun. Then she froze. A small plastic bag hung from the door handle on the driver's side.

An advertisement? A free sample? A full doggie-poop bag that someone had placed there as a piece of anonymous mischief? Or maybe an incendiary device?

Alex held her ground and looked all around her. She saw no one. Calculating quickly, she realized she had been in the botánica probably less than twenty minutes. So the delivery had been swift. Intended for her? Or random?

Open the bag? Call the bomb squad?

Feeling lucky tonight? Or sensing doom?

She decided she was feeling lucky. Or at least not completely unlucky.

She went to the bag and peered in. There was a small canister. Her brow furrowed. She recognized the product. There was a small piece of paper on top of it, a note.

She reached into her skirt pocket and pulled out a pair of

latex gloves, a tool of the trade she always carried. She pulled them on, then reached into the bag.

The note on the top, handwritten in English, said, "Open me."

A chill went through her as she pulled the canister from the bag and opened it. It was identical to what Doña Elena had tried to sell her. *Contra los Cartuchos.* Bulletproof.

Then, seeing the lid was slightly ajar, she followed the brief instruction. She opened the bath powders, and there, on top of the powder, halfway submerged, was the gold hoop earring she had lost at the funeral.

Her fear ebbed. Her resentment surged. She turned back toward the botánica, oblivious to the heat now, and marched boldly toward it. She was within twenty feet when her eyes told her something that couldn't possibly be true.

The store was closed again, lights cut almost completely, only the bluish florescent that had greeted her. The iron grate was pulled and closed. The front was padlocked. She looked in every direction and saw nothing. No one. In her hand, she still held the protective bath powder.

Okay, someone was playing with her. Mind games. But they were good at it. Alex was freaked. Spooked.

Open me.

A breeze kicked up and slackened. Then leaves of the banyan tree overhead gave enough of a rustle for Alex to look up. Again, nothing. Okay, she told herself, she had had quite enough.

She quickly paced back to the car, listening to the sound of her footsteps on the sidewalk. Enough for one day. She unlocked her car door by remote and slid in quickly. She was out of the neighborhood within two minutes.

SEVENTEEN

Tommy Vierra, unlike James Kevork and Nick Skypios, was the recipient of what appeared to be good tidings early in the evening. Like Kevork and Skypios, Vierra was in the orbit around some powerful, wealthy people who had provided the financial underpinnings to his business. He understood who they were, what sort of multinational operations they ran, and that they were not to be taken lightly. He understood that there were insulation levels, keeping him from the very top, about five levels as he understood it. And he knew that the people at the very top were under siege by do-gooders in various governments, including the American one.

He also understood who their enemies were, and he made a point of evading all cooperation with them. His allegiance was not in doubt to himself and should not have been in doubt to anyone else. Thus he was flattered when he received word that he was to be promoted in the Miami organization. He had been summoned to the manmade Palm Island, a wealthy fortressed enclave across the causeway in Miami Beach for a predawn breakfast that next morning. At that time, he was told, he would learn the specifics of his promotion and receive his new assignment.

The air was heavy in the parking lot on Northwest 75th Street, but Tommy Vierra was walking on it. He closed the warehouse and got into his car. The humidity was so thick that he could hear the tick-tick-ticking of wet leaves dripping onto other wet leaves on the scraggly palms in the parking lot.

It was, however, like music to his ears. Unlike the unfortunate Nick and James, Tommy was alive and well and feeling good about everything.

After dinner in her room and having regained her composure, Alex phoned Laura's boyfriend, Rick McCarron, another time. Again, she got no answer. She thought of the events of the day and tried to make some order of them. She failed.

Before going to sleep, she unwrapped the other bag from the botánica. She held in her hand a small silver charm, the offering to Olodumare. It reminded her of something midway between the face on an old Roman coin and a trinket from a Cracker Jack box.

She had no idea what to do with it but didn't feel like tempting luck by throwing it away. So she found her key ring and tagged the token onto it. At least she had an interesting conversation piece.

She looked at East Coast weather online. The indications now were that the sudden late-season storm was accelerating. Some of it would hit Miami overnight. The storm added to Alex's sense of anxiety. She glanced outside and saw no stars; there was a thick cloud cover. A few moments later, a light rain began to fall.

She hit the sack but had trouble even getting into a short night of sleep.

EIGHTEEN

Shortly after 6:00 a.m. the next morning, the pre–rush hour traffic was stopped cold in a steady, annoying rain on the General Douglas MacArthur Causeway, a six-lane that connects Downtown Miami to South Beach. It was blown hard by the storm coming in from the Keys. The wind whipped wickedly, and the rain blasted everything sideways.

The big storm was now four hundred miles away, meaning less than three hours' time according to local Miami television. The storm was not a hurricane yet, but was not a peaceful patch of sunshine either. Below the causeway, Biscayne Bay was green-ish-gray and turbulent with high nasty waves.

An interstate bus had stalled in the center lane halfway across the causeway. Passengers in the stopped cars pressed their faces against windows to see what was going on. Others stepped out to take pictures. There was a crashed car at the front of this mess, not far in front of the stalled Big Gray Dog.

Two cops, a tall white woman and a shorter Latino male, stood a hundred feet on the South Beach side at a point where a taut dirty rope hung over the side of the barrier, tied to a steel railing. On the other end of the rope hung a body, presumably dead, but one couldn't be sure just yet. It was still moving, swing-ing upside down in sort of a pinwheel effect. The top leg pointed to the sky, the other leg at a right angle and the arms descending toward the bay.

It was undulating in the winds, twisting slowly and unpleas-antly, and suspended by a noose not at the neck but at the left ankle. Unfazed, oblivious to the cops and everything else that was going on, a bearded shirtless crazy man in dirty shorts and military boots dug crumpled beer cans out of a shopping bag, and threw them at pelicans and gulls down the bridge in the opposite direction. A few people ventured out of cars to snap pictures with their camera phones.

Lieutenant Woodbine emerged from an unmarked Miami police car fifty car lengths behind the bus. He braced himself against the sideways-sweeping rain and quickstepped down the block.

"What happened?" he asked when he arrived where the two cops stood above the rope.

The male cop turned and indicated the crashed car.

"About thirty-five minutes ago, someone pulled in front of this guy on the causeway and stopped short." "This guy" meant the man on the rope. "They pulled him out of the car, someone said they heard a shot, then they roped him by the leg and threw him over the side."

Woodbine blinked. "They? How many?"

"The nine-one-one report said four. There were three calls. They stopped the driver's car, went for him, and got him."

"Road rage?" the female cop suggested.

"Sounds more like a hit."

"New MO to me," he said. He looked over the rail. A trio of ambulance attendants arrived at the same moment.

"Okay," Woodbine said. "Let's get him up here."

Three attendants and three cops. It took seven minutes. Behind them, traffic slowed to an even more miserable crawl. Brake lights winked. Water continued to sweep. There was a struggle with the body. He was a heavy man, porky, paunchy, and with gray hair. The hair had been pulled back in a ponytail, it looked like, but every part of him was soaked.

The attendants had a stretcher and a bag. No pulse. They positioned the body. There was blood. Woodbine pulled on gloves.

The man had been shot three times in the gut. It was a hit, all right. They had stalked him, crashed a car, pulled him out, and then hung him out, not so much to dry, but to make an example. That's how Woodbine read it.

The dead man's wallet was still in his pants pocket. Woodbine grabbed it, opened it, and prowled. About two hundred dollars, plenty of cards and licenses.

According to a work ID, the man was a warehouse manager in a so-so neighborhood in North Miami. The driver's license was from Florida. Woodbine compared the face on the license with the face of the corpse.

An easy match. Then he went for the name.

Tommy Vierra.

NINETEEN

Alex arrived at her office at 12:41 Wednesday afternoon and walked through the metal detector into Fin Cen's suite. Her assistant, Stacey, was waiting.

"Better go straight to the chief's office," Stacey said. "FBI."

"Already?" Alex asked. She grimaced.

Stacey shrugged. "Two of them," she said.

"I'm not in much of a mood for nonsense this morning," Alex grumbled.

"Are you ever?"

"No. Not these days," she said. "Not with a principal from Párajo freshly murdered. Should I be?"

Stacey shrugged to indicate sympathy. Then she handed Alex the morning message slips. Alex riffled through them as she walked to her desk. She didn't see anything of urgency. She emerged from her office again.

"Okay," she said low to Stacey. "Let's see what these birds want." Stacey smirked.

Alex walked to De Salvo's corner suite. The chief's secretary, Elsa, sat guard outside in her usual spot.

"Go on in," Elsa said without looking up.

"Can't wait," Alex said.

Alex opened the door and stepped in. She could smell trouble. De Salvo sat at the center of his mahogany desk; to his right sat a man and a woman she had never seen before.

"Ah. Here's Alex now," De Salvo said. "She'll bring you up to speed on everything."

Both De Salvo and the visitors stood. Alex summoned up her highest kilowatt smile.

"Hello, Alex," De Salvo said. "This is Special Agent William

Foreman, FBI, Washington, DC, office, and Special Agent Marilyn Wei, also of the Washington office."

Foreman was dark haired. Stocky, maybe forty, in a dark suit. He greeted Alex with a solid handshake. "Nice to meet you, Alex," he said.

"Likewise, I'm sure," Alex answered cautiously.

Marilyn Wei was a tiny, owlish Chinese-American woman with pulled-back hair. She wore glasses and a dark size-two suit, skirt perfectly to the knee. Wei offered a hand, shook, and said nothing. She looked to Alex like a newbie: the suit was too new and she exuded a quiet jitteriness, as if she hadn't been out of her office much and this was something new.

They all sat. Instinctively, Alex scanned her visitors and picked out their artillery. Both were wearing pistols on the right side. A silence dropped upon the office.

Alex broke it with convincing cheerfulness. "Well," she said. "Don't keep me in suspense. Who are we going to talk about this morning?"

De Salvo answered slowly, "Well, actually, Alex, you."

Alex turned toward Special Agent Foreman. "Me? Well, at least I'm an expert on the subject," she added amiably. "What do you want to know?"

"Just needing some answers about a few things, Alex," Special Agent Foreman said. "There's a special investigative unit of a House subcommittee looking into organized crime activity by Russian émigrés in the US. The reports you filed on Yuri Federov came to the attention of some lawmakers."

"It's refreshing to hear that they're concerned about such things," Alex said. "Enough at least to have their aides read the reports."

De Salvo, sensing hostilities, looked away.

"Well, they are," Foreman said.

"And?" she asked.

"We're on the record here," he said, "just so you're aware.

We're looking into the possibility that a crime may have been committed, so be sure to answer all questions truthfully and as completely as possible."

"Truthfully and completely is how I like to do things. So no hang-ups here." Alex was smart, because they could always get her on obstructing justice, Martha Stewart–style — no actual provable crime committed, just poor answers to informal questions.

"We can delay this, although that wouldn't be my choice. You can request to have an attorney present," Foreman said.

"Not necessary," Alex said. "And I'd just as soon get this over with. So again, how may I help you? What do you want to know?"

"Yuri Federov," Foreman said. "The whole case. Your whole involvement."

"That would take quite a bit of time, Mr. Foreman," Alex said. "Surely you've read transcripts of the entire operation, against the late Mr. Federov, his companies, his finances."

"We have. I have."

De Salvo was watching and listening carefully but keeping his own counsel. Wei sat and listened like a little terrier.

"It was quite an assignment," Alex said, "lengthy and complicated."

"I'm sure it was," Foreman said.

"Then if you know the basics of the case, what are your questions?" Alex asked.

"How did you happen to be assigned to the case?" Foreman asked.

Alex looked at De Salvo again to confirm that she sensed something accusatory in the line of questioning. She read something she didn't like in her boss's eyes. She looked back to Foreman.

"If you've read the dossier," Alex said, "you know the answer to that."

"I'd appreciate hearing it from you."

"At the time, I was reassigned by my boss in Washington,

Michael Gamburian, to assist a man named Michael Cerny, a liaison officer between Treasury and the CIA. There was a presidential visit to Kiev, as I'm sure you'll remember. Someone needed to be assigned to keep track of a Russian-Ukrainian gangster named Yuri Federov. I was selected because they wanted a female agent, because I speak Russian and appeared capable of learning Ukrainian quickly, which, by the way, I managed to do. I also had experience in fraud units, and I think there was a notion floating around that Federov had a soft spot for educated Western women. Federov was a fugitive from US justice at the time and had major tax issues in arrears. So it was proposed that I get as close to him as possible, on a social level but not a personal one, if you follow, for the purpose of gathering intelligence. My main assignment, aside from close surveillance, was an assessment of how the Treasury Department might continue its case against him."

"I follow," Foreman said.

"The shoe fit, so it was given to me to wear. Those are the basics. What else?"

"Your relationship with Yuri Federov," Foreman asked. "Not at the outset but as it evolved. You'd categorize it as completely professional?"

"Are you asking me if I slept with him?" she asked icily. De Salvo and Wei kept quiet.

"No, I'm not. I'm asking—"

"I didn't. So put that in your report, anyway. Yes, I would categorize it as completely professional," she said. Wei continued to gaze at her silently, arms folded. Alex now wondered if she had guessed wrong about Wei being a rookie, and she wondered which of them outranked the other.

Alex continued. "Everything that happened between the late Mr. Federov and me is included in the final report that I filed following his funeral. If you read that, you know as much as there is to know."

"Doesn't mean we might not have a question or two," Foreman said briskly.

"Such as? Federov has been dead for several months. There's not much trouble he can cause from where he is now."

"Oh, I beg to differ," Foreman said briskly.

"How so?"

"The part of the investigation that I'm overseeing, Alex, is an anticorruption one. We're looking into how Russian organized crime money may have influenced American law enforcement. So if I asked you if you knew of any instances where Russian money was advanced for some sort of favorable treatment, you wouldn't be able to alert us to anything?"

She thought quickly, running through everything that had happened since Kiev, plus before and afterward. "No, I wouldn't have anything to add," she said.

"And, hypothetically, would you be willing to testify before Congress if the point came up? Say, if we were seeking expert witnesses?"

"You're asking me to testify before Congress?"

"Hypothetically."

Alex glanced at De Salvo and looked back. "I wouldn't have issues with it per se," Alex answered.

"Thank you. That's good," Foreman said. "That's good." He paused. "Let's visit the corruption theme again," he said.

"Okay."

"Why did Mr. Federov include you in his last will and testament?"

"Excuse me?"

"You were included in his will, Alex," Foreman said. "Very generously. Don't be so surprised that we know. It's a matter of public record. The FBI came across it when we were trying to reconstruct his financial affairs for the last few years."

"Is that what this is all about?" she demanded.

"Two million dollars," Foreman retorted, his voice heavy with suggestion. "It takes most of us a long time to make money like that."

"It would take me a long time too," she said.

"Did Federov expect any favors in return?"

"Do I need to remind you it was a will?" Alex asked. "Federov was dead. What sort of favor might he have expected at that point? That I have him stuffed and mounted and put on display at Grand Central? That I lobby the other branches of the government to get him a first-class postage stamp?"

"Alex ...," De Salvo said soothingly.

"There's no need for sarcasm," Foreman said. He paused, then twisted the knife. "A lot of these mobbed-up Russian guys, you know, they take care of mistresses and friends after the fact. It's a power thing."

Alex stared at him and managed to control herself. "I think I answered your question already," she said tersely. She looked to her boss. "Do I have to sit here and listen to this?"

"I withdraw the question," Foreman said.

"And I answered it anyway," Alex snapped. "Even though it was just a plain stupid question. Obnoxious too."

"So?" Foreman pressed. "What about his estate?"

"What about it?"

"Are you, were you, in a position to do any favors for his estate, his heirs?"

"Again, I'm insulted that you'd ask."

Foreman, in rapid return. "I have to ask."

"Well, I just answered," Alex said.

"Alex ...," De Salvo said again, trying to soothe.

Foreman consulted a sheaf of papers. He made a quizzical expression. "Here's what doesn't look good Alex," Foreman said. "Mr. Federov was in debt ten million dollars to the IRS. He apparently walked away on that one. Got his whole tax bill torn up. You were overseeing his case. Then, upon his death, you come into a huge sum of money directly from him. Do you see how that looks?"

"I see how it looks."

"No quid pro quo. No tit for tat?"

"None!" Alex said sharply. "We also had an ongoing situation with a defector and a turncoat. If you get the proper clearance you can see those files also. Releasing Mr. Federov from his tax liability wasn't my idea; it came from higher up. I did not initiate it."

"Were you in favor of it?"

"I had no opinion. Generally speaking, people should pay their fair share of taxes. But it's an imperfect world. I don't set Treasury policy."

"Did you approve it, though?" Foreman asked.

"I had no voice in it. It was policy. I conveyed the offer, and Mr. Federov chose to work with us for his own reasons."

"That's absolutely the case," De Salvo chimed in.

"But you orchestrated it," Foreman said, looking at Alex. "You helped make it happen. Why do you suppose he left you all that money?" Foreman asked.

"I have no idea. He also proposed marriage to me. Before he died, of course. Be sure you get your dates straight on that part."

"I guess he liked you," Foreman said. "Felt he owed you, maybe? For some kindness, some consideration?"

"Kindness? Consideration?" she said. "Not the type that you'd probably understand."

"Try me," Foreman said.

Methodically, Alex let loose.

"Yuri Federov spent about fifty years walking this earth," Alex began politely. "During most of that time, I think we'd all conclude that he was a vile human being, a pretty bad example of humankind. But you know what? Self-professed atheist that he was, in his last years I started to see a spiritual side of him develop. He asked me questions about my faith. I got the sense that there was some small shred of decency there, waiting to develop maybe, waiting to show itself. We had conversations, adversarial maybe, but conversations anyway, about faith and grace and forgiveness, things that many of us struggle with. When he was terminally ill, in his final days, he was looking for forgiveness and salvation. I went to Switzerland for reasons that I don't entirely understand myself, except possibly to show Yuri Federov that forgiveness and grace are always possible. It seemed like the decent thing to do. So I did it."

"And there was no discussion of money?"

"It was a private conversation. I went to Geneva as a private citizen, an acquaintance of a man in a hospice, if not exactly a friend. He alluded to his net worth. He asked me to marry him. I declined. A day later he was dead. Several weeks later, I was informed that he had left me a gift, taxes paid, no strings attached."

"You weren't obligated to accept it, you know," Foreman said. "You could have declined it."

"Is that what you would have done?" Alex asked.

"I'm just saying."

"And I'm just asking."

"When this first arose several months ago," De Salvo said, "the fact that Mr. Federov had chosen to bequeath something to Alex, she sought counsel here. We examined the proper protocols and statutes and didn't find a problem."

Foreman shook his head. "It's got a hoary appearance, Alex," Foreman said. "That's not necessarily me talking. It's what my bosses down in DC are saying. If it were up to me, or if I were in your position, I should say, maybe I would have eased up on him and taken the money too."

"Excuse me," she said. "But the first I knew about it was when his attorney contacted me in New York."

Foreman looked at some notes. "But you knew he was sick," he asked, "as you concluded your business with him?"

"Anyone with two eyes knew he was seriously ill," she said.

Foreman grimaced. "Okay," he said, sounding as if he was ready to conclude. "Mr. Federov liked you," he said, "maybe a little too much."

Alex held him in a long gaze. "I guess he did. Is there any-thing else we need to talk about?" she asked.

"No," Foreman said. "There isn't. Just be available if we have further questions. That's all for now."

Foreman gathered his things, rose, and gave a nod to both Alex and her boss. Wei rose, having said nothing the entire time. Then they both were gone.

Alex and De Salvo watched the door close; they waited for a moment before either spoke.

"Should I be worried?" Alex asked.

De Salvo sighed. "I have a feeling," he said, "we haven't heard the last of this. Worried, no. On your toes, yes. Leave it to Wash-ington to make something out of nothing." De Salvo shrugged and shifted gears. "Anything new on Mejías? Miami?"

"I'm working my contacts," Alex said after a pause. "All of them. And overtime."

"Go get 'em," he said in a tone that suggested he needed to get back to his work.

"Before they get me," she muttered as she got up to leave. When she reached the door, she stopped and turned. "What about you?" she said. "I might as well ask since everything's out on the table."

De Salvo, who had already been back to something pressing on his desk, looked up, baffled. "What about me?" he asked.

"Why aren't you suspicious of me too?" she asked. "After all, it's two million bucks. Maybe I'm not quite the employee you think I am."

De Salvo pursed his lips and shook his head. "You came and ran the whole inheritance episode past me when it happened. You seemed quite ready to refuse to accept it if warning flags went up. And I recall quite well that I urged you to take it. If I were suspicious of your motives, I might equally be suspicious of my own."

She nodded. "Okay," she said.

"Alex?"

She waited. "I've been in the government nearly forty years," he said. "I've been in a chair like this one for more than twenty. I've seen a lot of employees come and go. I think I'm a pretty good judge by now." He leaned back. "I'll impart something to you, Alex. Sometimes in this world, you just need to walk away from things, maybe for a day or a weekend. Maybe for a year. I've seen young people who are whiz kids at thirty crack before they're thirty-five. You find them at their desk one morning, slumped down, tears running into their laptops. Or you find them in the bathroom with a gun to their head. They lock all the pressures away, pretend the stress isn't there, forget how to relax or how to walk away for those precious few days. They let the job destroy them. Some others? They look like they'll be gone in six months, blown away by the first adversity, the first big case that goes gloriously down the crapper. In the end, though, some of those are the ones who are left standing at the end of the big storm. For forty years I've been watching this, Alex. It's the ones who know how to take the knocks and walk away from them who are the survivors. No one bats a thousand here. Few of us hit three hundred. But the three hundred hitters are the ones who know how to take that 'walkaway' moment. Does that make sense?"

She nodded. "Yes. It does."

"If you remember anything from today, remember what I just said. Not anything from that FBI ditz." He paused. "End of sermon."

Alex smiled.

"Thanks," she said.

"De nada," he answered, looking down again as she closed the door behind her.

TWENTY

Alex worked through dinner and far into the evening, not unusual after such an inauspicious start to the day. By 10:30 p.m. she was finally caught up from her visit to Miami. Through a secure car service for Fin Cen employees, she arranged a ride to a gym in the Wall Street area, which was open till midnight. She grabbed the gym bag that she kept at the office and went off to run some laps, shoot some baskets, work with some weights, and smack a punching bag.

Total de-stress.

After the much-needed workout, she called the car service again and caught a ride home, arriving shortly after midnight.

Entering her building, she felt exhausted, spiritually and physically. As she walked through the lobby toward the mail room, her thoughts wandered from Miami to Kiev, Washington to New York. The more she thought about the FBI intrusion, the less she liked it. Frankly, she was seething.

In the mail room, she moved her shoulder bag onto her back for balance, juggled the gym bag to her shoulder, found the mailbox key on its chain, and unlocked the box. Just as she was picking a few pieces of mail from the box, a man cleared his throat. "Hello," a voice said.

Alex jumped. She knew that, burdened from fatigue, she had dropped her guard and made herself vulnerable. Someone had followed her into the mail room and now had the drop on her. If he had a gun, there was no way she could access her own weapon in time. Sayonara, baby. She was as good as dead.

Uncharacteristically, she blurted out a vulgarity. She jerked around clumsily, dropped her mail, and faced her would-be assailant. He was about six two, dark haired, in an expensive leather coat. The face was rugged and handsome, blue eyes that were set intently on her. His hands were empty, his arms folded.

He smiled. "My apologies," he said. "I didn't mean to startle you. I tried to clear my throat, to let you know I was here. Really, I didn't mean to scare you. I'm sorry."

It was Eric Robertson. Yes, she had seen him around this time before. His show ran till almost 10:25 each night. That plus a late dinner and he too was just getting home.

"Here," he said, "let me help you with what you dropped."

Alex's pulse rate began to descend from somewhere in another solar system.

"I'm sorry. I should have noticed you," she said, flustered.

"My fault entirely," he said with utmost courtesy. "Really."

"Sorry about my colorful language," she said. "That's not how I really am."

"I'm so shocked," he said with a wink. "In my line of work, I never hear anything like that."

He stooped and with the dexterity of an athlete picked up her mail. Kneeling to help him, she made things worse. Her bag overturned.

"I've had a bad day," Alex said.

"No harm, no foul," he said, amused. "Working late?"

"Yes. Very late. You?"

Her keys and key chain slid forward onto the floor. He picked it up and, in handing it to her, noticed the silver skull amulet from the *botánica*.

"Sorry!" she said quickly. "I'll take that."

"Mean looking little gremlin," he remarked.

"Yes," she said, packing it back into her pocket.

"I'm sure there's a great story behind it."

"Yes. For another day."

"Let me guess. You're heavily into voodoo. That and tae kwon do, which is what you were doing at the gym."

She continued to gather the things on the floor, reaching awkwardly and unsteadily, hoping her pistol didn't tumble out of its holster.

"How did you know I was at a gym?" she asked.

"Your gym bag. It's open. Wet towel. Damp shirt about to fall out. Sports bra, light blue, also damp, if you're not offended that I notice you're not-in-use intimate apparel."

Further flustered, she reached backward to rezip her gym bag. "Do you notice everything?" she asked, piqued.

"Sometimes."

The zipper on the gym bag jammed. She gave it a second tug and it still resisted. She tugged it hard a third time and threw herself off balance just enough to start to fall forward toward him from her crouching position into his.

Eric's two hands came up quickly, strong, quick, and supportive, one taking her arm and the other steadying a shoulder. She gasped and found herself looking eye to eye with him from about eighteen inches away.

"Hello again," he said.

"Hi," she said, icily this time.

He steadied her and quickly released her. "You okay?" he asked. Somehow his amusement defused her anger. He had, in a funny way, the comforting aura of a goofy protective big brother, combined with an obvious physical strength and an evident presence.

"Yes, yes, fine," she said, recovering.

"Late days," he said. "They kill you, don't they?"

"Yes. They do," she said.

He rose to his feet. She grasped her two bags and hooked them onto her shoulder, the mail under one arm. He graciously extended a hand to help her to her feet. She thought twice about accepting it but not for long. She stood.

"Thanks," she said.

"Any time."

"I'm such a klutz."

"I don't think so," he said, amused.

"Were you working late too?" she asked.

As soon as the question was out of her mouth, she realized how foolish it was.

"Regular hours," he said. For a moment their eyes met again. There was a one-second hitch, then he added, "But it beats an honest job, you know. Acting. Singing. Generally making a spectacle of myself for pay."

"Yes, of course. I know. Sorry. You're in a Broadway show."

"Only for as long as people keep buying tickets," he said. "And the show is the star, *South Pacific*. Not me. It was around before me and will be around when I'm drooling into my mashed potatoes. I'm just lucky enough to be living in it for a few weeks."

"It's doing very well," she said. "I've heard the buzz."

"Seen it?" he asked.

"Sorry. No." She shrugged. "Work, you know."

"Ah, well, of course," he said. "But New York has been very kind and generous to us. We're appreciative."

Moving away from her, he reached to his own mailbox, opened it, and removed a large clump of letters, bound together with a rubber band. He closed the box without examining the mail and looked back at Alex.

"You sure you're okay?" he asked, amiably. "You seem a bit shaken."

"I'm fine," she said.

"Yes, I can see that."

"I mean, I'm okay."

"That part I'm not seeing."

In the back of her mind, she was now processing the surreal nature of this encounter. She had come home late from work, scattered bills and catalogues over the mail room floor, and Mr. A-List-Broadway-actor had stooped to help her clean up the mess. Wait till she told Laura and her friends at the office.

"Well, look," he said, "I assume you're not planning to spend the night in the mail room. So I'll see you to your door, may I? You're on three, correct?"

"I am. How did you know?"

"I've seen you before," he said. "I keep an eye on who's around, if you know what I mean. Can never be too careful. So I know which faces belong in this building and which don't."

"I do something similar," Alex said.

"You should if you come home at odd hours," he said as they moved to the elevator. "Simple urban precautions."

"Exactly," Alex agreed.

"You never know what degenerate members of the New York acting community could be lurking in a public area, after all," he said. They stepped into the elevator and rode it to the third floor, bypassing his floor. "I also happen to know that you live right over my head," he said. "You're in three zero six, I'm in two zero six."

"How did you know?" she asked.

"Well, I always check to see who lives nearby when I sublet an apartment. The owner said it was a professional woman, single, very pretty, no-nonsense type, who carried voodoo charms and worked in the financial sector. That seemed blasé enough to keep me happy."

The elevator arrived on three and the door opened.

"Oh, and I quickly discovered you're very quiet, which I appreciate," he continued. "Despite what you hear about hell-raising actors, I treasure my peace and tranquility. I like to read, listen to music when I'm home, and rest. So the lack of intrusion and annoyance is much coveted."

"I do the same," she said, stepping out.

"I'm Eric," he said. He offered his hand. With the other hand he pressed the elevator's Hold button.

"Yes, I know," she said. "I'm Susanna."

"Ah. Like the song by my friend Leonard Cohen. The girl who takes you down by the river and feeds you tea and oranges that came all the way from China. Well, almost anyway: Susanna as opposed to Suzanne. Close enough?"

"Perhaps," she said cryptically.

"I'll watch you to your doorway," he said.

"It's not necessary."

"I know. But I'm afraid you'll trip over one of the scuff marks on the floor."

"Thank you," she said, laughing. "Some days I need someone watching over me."

"We all do. Every day," he said.

She turned, walked to her door, and unlocked it. Scanning quickly to see if there had been any illicit entry, she found none. She looked back to Eric at the elevator.

"Good night," she said.

"Have a pleasant evening," he answered

She gave him a final wave and a small smile. As she closed her door, she heard the elevator door close as well. Then, standing in her foyer, she remained perfectly still, waited. In approximately half a minute, she heard the distant sound of the door closing to his apartment just below hers. Then she remembered her own alarm system, bolted toward it and switched it off seconds before it would have erupted.

She set down her bag and collapsed onto the sofa. Final lines of her conversation with Eric went on instant replay in her head.

"Some days I need someone watching over me."

"We all do. Every day," he had said.

How true. What a day, indeed.

TWENTY-ONE

How a man with the work ethic and automotive skills of Luis Rivera could have become moderately wealthy by middle age was not a mystery to his friends, and certainly not to his family. After six years of military service in the United States Army, including tours of duty and combat in Kuwait and Afghanistan, the immigrant from Panama returned to Jamaica, Queens, a New York City neighborhood not far from Kennedy Airport. He invested his own money in buying and running a neighborhood garage, which was part of a row house in the middle of a mostly commercial block, bordered by a residence and a bakery.

Rivera's business was modest at first but eventually prospered, thanks largely to a steady stream of what he referred to as "old army buddies." They often came and went at odd hours, pulling their cars into his garage for brief repairs. Invariably, the cars would roll out a few hours later, looking fresh, shiny, waxed, and sparkly. In the neighborhood Luis Rivera was known, with a grin, as *El Lavandero de Carros*, the washer of cars. Or simply, *El Lavandero*. The cleaner.

As years went by, Luis expanded his business. When the bakery next door went under financially, Luis bought the building, knocked down the common wall, put in a new façade, and expanded. He built himself a small office in the back. It led to the residence on the other side of the garage, which, by this time, he now owned also. The office was a small room, twelve by sixteen feet, with all the modern security devices — antibugging and antitheft — that money could buy. The office was spare. A desk, telephones, a computer terminal, a few chairs for visitors. Behind Luis's chair, a pair of flags stood in stands, one of the United States, the country he had served, and one of Panama, where he had been born. On his desk was another one of his personal objects that spanned his two nations: a small statue of his name-sake, Mariano Rivera, the great New York Yankee reliever — no relation, but a fellow countryman who had also found great success in New York.

When Luis was in his early twenties, he had held a job as a busboy at a resort in Montauk, Long Island. Things had not been going well for him at that point in his life. In fact, they had gone badly. He had entered the United States illegally, and the stubborn troublemakers at INS were coming after him. Luis wished to stay in America.

The owner of the resort had taken a liking to him and fought the INS on Luis's behalf until he could think of something. That "something" came about one day while the owner was dining with a US senator. When Luis came to clear the table, the owner introduced the young Panamanian to the senator. Luis knew the man from the television news. The two men shook hands. The senator was the most famous person Luis had ever met, so he was favorably impressed. This was what America was all about, Luis thought to himself, where a kid like him could shake the hand of a powerful man like the senator. Luis was about to get a second lesson in civics.

"Luis is a good young man and an excellent worker," the resort owner told the senator. "Unfortunately, I may lose him. He's having trouble with Immigration and Naturalization."

The senator smiled and scoffed. "Those clowns," he muttered in his distinctly New York accent. "What exactly is the problem?"

"When he was young, Luis made some careless mistakes in his immigration procedures," the owner said. "The proper forms got lost and were never filed."

"That doesn't sound so serious," the senator said, turning toward the young Panamanian. "Happens all the time. Do you have a clean police record, Luis?"

"Yes, sir," Luis answered.

"If we check it, we won't find anything bad?"

"No, sir. Nothing, sir."

"How long have you been here?" the senator asked.

Luis hesitated. The owner gave a slight nod to indicate that this was a rare moment for truth. "Seven years, sir," Luis said.

"How did you really get here?" the senator asked.

The owner nodded. "I jumped ship in Brooklyn, sir."

The senator, whose public stands against illegal immigration were fearsome, laughed and grinned. "And you're not even Chinese, Luis!"

"No, sir," Luis said. "And I'd like to join the US Army, but there's this immigration problem and—"

The senator turned to another table. There was a man in a suit sitting there whom Luis hadn't noticed, a personal assistant of some sort. The senator motioned, and the man in the suit came over.

"This young man is having some problems with INS," the senator said to his aide. "Who do we know over there?"

The aide mentioned a name.

"Let's take care of it." The senator winked at the young busboy. "These things can be arranged if you follow the right procedures," he said. "It's as easy as getting a pothole fixed. You just have to call the right number."

The aide gave Luis a business card, noted his name in a small black notebook, and instructed him to phone in two days. Luis followed instructions and found himself on the path to citizenship within four weeks. Within another eighteen months, he was in the United States Army.

In the Army, Luis did his automotive training but also revealed a talent for lethal tools. Weapons, for one example. Explosives, for another.

When Luis received his honorable discharge in 2004, it was no surprise that he would use his skills to build his personal fortune. Cars in the front room, weapons in the back. Explosives . . . for special customers via special arrangement.

By 2010, Luis had earned his nickname of El Lavandero a

second time. Within a twenty-block radius of Queens, Luis was the most dependable dealer of illegal firearms to be found, many of them smuggled into the port of New York on freighters from Honduras, Panama, and Guatemala. But he didn't have just firearms. Luis had lethal weapons that were guaranteed "clean." Their registry was nonexistent, their code numbers were removed, and they were free of fingerprints. Luis guaranteed it. His rates were high, but on the street it was known that you would never go to jail using one of his weapons, if you used it wisely.

The New York City police were aware of his businesses, mostly the late-night auto business, but also the armaments industry. There were those on the police force who wanted to close him down, notably a couple of busybody detectives named Bill Chen and James Rocco who worked out of the 115th Precinct in Flushing. Chen and Rocco were both bucking for promotions and saw Luis as a major case.

Once, Chen and Rocco arrived with a search warrant and trashed not just Luis's garages, but his residence. They found nothing. Luis wished them well as they left. Later, he lavishly tipped the formidable network of spies he had in the neighborhood, the girl who worked in the Baskin-Robbins on Astoria Boulevard, the Paki guy who sold newspapers, and a seemingly dopey kid named Martin who drew coffee at the Starbucks. All of these people watched the block for Luis and knew detectives when they saw them. It was never a surprise to Luis when he hit the radar screen of the precinct cops.

Most of the important people in the local underworld knew Luis. They used his services for both cars and weapons and thus offered him a piece of their protection.

Over the past decade, he had played his contacts within the NYPD wisely. On three occasions when major cases were stymied, and the public, the police commissioner, and the politicians were clamoring for arrests, Luis had offered small bits of information that he knew from his double life as an urban arms merchant. The small bits had led, as he knew they would, to other larger bits of information. Eventually, these tips led to major breaks in major cases.

The contacts went much higher than Chen and Rocco. On such information from this cherished and highly discreet informant, certain current captains, lieutenants, and senior detectives had acquired their promotions, promotions that helped them send their kids to college and own vacation homes. Thus it was an unwritten rule among the captains who ran several district commands in Queens that Luis be left alone — illegal weapons, hot wheels, and all. There was a further understanding that Luis's weapons were never to be used on the street against any police officer. Use them against other members of criminal society or against private citizens; that was fine. But if anyone from the shady side of New York criminal life ever used a Rivera weapon to threaten or harm a law enforcement officer, retribution would swiftly follow from sources far more brutal and inevitable than anything any district attorney could imagine.

So Luis was valuable to the police, the same way he was valuable to organized crime. From such an equation, the immigrant from Panama led a good life. Day to day, he tended to meet interesting people with peculiar needs. He prospered and regularly sent money to his extended family and old friends in Panama. He was known both in his neighborhood and in Panama as a true success, even as he operated in the gray area of the law.

But gray had many shades. On the big canvas for Luis, life was proceeding nicely, if a little nerve-wracking. He lived comfortably, and in the year 2012, his other dark art, a genuine talent for bombs and explosives, went largely ignored by everyone.

Almost everyone.

Luis, a cautious man in a dangerous business, was used to keeping his blinds drawn at all hours of the day and night. He was also, at random moments, in the habit of barely parting his window blinds to survey the street. There was a drizzle this autumn night, one that had an eerie warmness and humidity. The weather, and the malaise that went with it, had him on edge and seemed almost tropical. Were the tropics sending him other problems? He wondered. He was a victim of unsettled suspicions more days than not. He had spent too much time on both sides of the law, dealing with too many disreputable people.

This evening, after midnight, he spotted a car across the street, down the block, its engine idling. With the binoculars that he kept by his bedroom window, he looked more closely. Inside the car: a lone man, unfamiliar, sitting, engine running, windshield wipers going. He spotted the orange glow of a cigarette.

Luis cut the lights in his bedroom, returned to the window and looked again.

Ford Focus, New York plates, ending in 825. Standard-issue rental. The front part of the plate was obscured by another car.

Then he watched as the driver stepped out — a man, obviously waiting for something or someone, or just watching. He was dark, wore a cap, a sweatshirt. He was a little bit like Lou Ferrigno, hulking on a smaller scale, normal colors not green. He looked like someone whom Luis could handle, maybe, but would get bloodied in the process. He'd prefer to avoid contact.

The man was gazing in the direction of Luis's home. Coincidence? Paranoia? Or had Luis picked up the first sign of some sort of surveillance? Cops again? Feds? Something unofficial and worse?

The Focus hadn't been there when Luis had returned home. Who sits in a car and smokes, steps out for a walkabout in the mist, then, as this visitor now did, gets back into his car and sits again for time without end?

Who, except someone who's watching or waiting?

Luis kept some of his field artillery at home. He made friends with a real blockbuster, a Browning .45 automatic.

He checked his doors. Steel reinforced and locked tightly. He also had an early warning system: a big ninety-pound bull mastiff named Max who would slow down anyone coming through a door or window.

The car was still there at 4:30 a.m., when Luis rose to check.

But it was gone by 6:15, the first light of dawn. Luis kept rising from his bed to check. But it was replaced by an independent cable van in the same parking place. New Jersey plates this time. An out-of-state repair vehicle made no sense at this hour. Nor did the fact that there was another smoker in the driver's seat: sitting, waiting, puffing.

Luis smoldered, an inner combustion to match the many cigarettes consumed on this unofficial watch tonight. *"¡Tranquilo!"* he told himself.

He went back to bed and waited for the next installment. Something was up.

TWENTY-TWO

Sam Deal clicked in on the second ring of his cell phone. It was Friday afternoon.

"Hello, lovely Alex," he said softly, having checked his caller ID. "This is Sam. Who do you want shot? Give me a name and an address."

"Sorry, Sam. It's just information I need today."

"Pity. I'm feeling ornery."

"You're always ornery, Sam."

"Sure, but you must need something unofficial. Why else would you get your hands dirty with poor old Sam Deal?"

"Maybe because I secretly enjoy it," she said.

"Ha! You finally admitted it. That's what you love about me, LaDuca. I'm ornery and a sneak. I'm everything you're not. It works for you."

"You bet it does," she said. "How are things?"

Alex had been buried in her office the day after the FBI had departed, spending the back end of the previous day and the top half of this one cooling down. Wasn't there enough to do in this job without having to fight a rearguard action against people trying to question how you did it?

Then, gathering herself again, working on both instinct and hunch, she had picked up her cell phone and dialed the nefarious old acquaintance who was becoming an old friend: Sam Deal.

There was the bustle of a busy retail store behind Sam's husky voice. Sounds of shoppers, animated New York conversations, a clerk rapping on a jewelry counter. The symphony of money being spent.

Deal was a former CIA guy who'd been integral in a covert group called the Nightingales. Sam's guys had done dirty work in

Central and South America for the past several decades. Sam was currently enjoying genteel "retirement," so to speak, as the head of security of a pricy New York jewelry store on Fifth Avenue. Alex assumed he was busy stalking shoplifters, but as was his habit, he always checked the caller ID, and he never refused a call from Alex.

Sam was a guilty indulgence for Alex, bordering these days on being a guilty *pleasure*. Alex's friend Laura knew Sam, had dealt with him, and frequently joked that one should always have a tetanus shot before contacting him.

"Things are all-out hunky-dory," Sam said. "I'm on the second floor of one of the most famous buildings in Manhattan, stalking shoplifters with mid–double digit IQs. There's a guy in a cheap baggy raincoat who's been circling the silver tableware for fifteen minutes. It's a sunny day, in case you didn't notice — and this isn't a cheap store. So who dresses like a Goodwill version of Colombo, doesn't look like he's got a couple of nickels to rub together and circles five-hundred-dollar silver? Do they think I'm as stupid as they are? If I drop you suddenly, you'll know why."

"I get it," she said. "I'll cut to the chase."

"Why not?" he asked. "When I flirt, you never take the cue anyway. But I love you, anyway, Alex. The guy's fingering a gravy ladle right now. How's tricks?"

"*Santería*," she said.

"What?"

She repeated.

"What about it? A lot of Caribbean gobbledygook if you ask me. Blood sacrifices of chickens, worshiping of sacred stones, and the ritual use of herbs and plants. You thinking of converting? I'd advise against it. I'd stick with New England Episcopalianism if I were you. Makes more sense. If anything you'd be going for the money and the power."

"I'm working a case," Alex said. "Want to meet for a drink so you can give me a crash course on Santería?"

"Affirmative on the first suggestion," Sam said, "but what do you want to know about that West Indian mumbo jumbo for?"

"I was in Miami just in time to see the aftermath of the murder of a principal in a case I'm working. Then I get approached by a woman at his funeral who claims she's a priestess. I went to visit, but she'd flown the coop. I'm getting the feeling there might be an angle, so I'd like to know what I'm dealing with."

"You're dealing with a lot of toads, goats, magic potions, hot air, and two-bit con artists," Sam said with his usual charm. "But if you insist, Old Man Sam can set you up with an old buddy of mine named Danny Suarez. We used to go to the racetrack together in San Juan to play the ponies on days when we weren't reading other people's mail and romancing dark-eyed beauties."

"Which San Juan?"

"The good one. Puerto Rico."

"Where's Danny now?" Alex asked.

"He's a cop. On the job here. NYPD. Brooklyn. Good man. Used to be assigned to the Community Affairs and Child Exploitation Unit. Current assignment is with the Criminal Intelligence Bureau. Expert on ritualistic crime investigation — in Brooklyn; that means Cuban, Dominican, and Haitian. Not so much the Puerto Ricans. They're still good Roamin' Catlicks, most of them. Still listening?"

"Intently," Alex said.

"How 'bout I give him your phone number? I'll have him call you."

"That would be excellent."

"You owe me a drink," Sam said.

Alex agreed that she did and added, "Enjoy yourself, Sam, shadowing your prey."

"It's a living," he said with too much enthusiasm. "I don't know if it's an honest living, but it's a living."

"Is it legal, Sam?"

"Of course, it is, LaDuca."

"You get paid?"

"Obviously. Pretty well, in fact."

"Then it's an honest living."

"Ah, here we go," Sam said with a laugh. "The bozo in the Peter Falk outfit just dropped two silver serving pieces down his sleeve. Time to rock and roll."

"Have fun."

TWENTY-THREE

At Carabinieri headquarters on the Via de Sebastipoli in Rome, Gian Antonio Rizzo was nearing the end of his workday. He sat at his antique desk with his feet up, an empty porcelain espresso cup to one side and the phone cradled between his left ear and shoulder. His free hand fiddled with a silver fountain pen, turned over to him by a trusted colleague. The pen bore an engraving, the name of a friend and associate: Alejandra LaDuca. The writing instrument, once a gift to Alex from her boss in New York, had disappeared from her possession months earlier.

He picked up the phone and called Alex at work. They spoke in Italian. He had nothing to report personally on the Dosis, but — in response to her request — he had begun to initiate his own inquiries. He had also burrowed deeper into Italian intelligence files and come up with a few tidbits. "I will get to those in a moment," he said. "But I must preface: I have travel plans to visit your country soon. Will I find you in New York or Miami this week?"

Alex expressed her pleasure to hear that she would soon see her friend face-to-face. "It's day to day right now. I expect to be in Miami from Tuesday to Friday. Maybe longer. After that, I suspect I might need to commute back and forth. It's more instinct than anything right now."

Rizzo replied that, with its lack of firm logic, her plan made perfect sense. He also promised to shake up a few contacts of his own. "Tell me where you are on this Párajo," Rizzo asked. "May we violate the normal standards of security and speak openly? You tell me what you have, and then I will reward you with a small lead that I've uncovered."

Alex thought about it, then decided that yes, they could violate the normal standards. This was a man she had learned to trust, after all.

She explained in detail. Alex had some operatives on the ground in Morocco, she said, people whom she was paying to keep an address under surveillance. A local CIA contact had spotted the venue: a high-walled compound overlooking the sea but not accessible from it. There were a dozen guards around the place, macho young bucks with Israeli machine guns who rarely left the complex. "Lowbrow dumb guys with high-tech smart weapons," a CIA analyst had described it to her.

"Curious," Rizzo said. "And fascinating."

"The security squad is foreign, my contact said," Alex continued. "The leader speaks good Arabic and is also believed to be foreign. A telephoto had snapped him reading a Spanish language newspaper on occasion, which gave further credence to this being a Dosi operation imported from the southern half of the western hemisphere. A man and a woman who match the Dosis' description occasionally come and go in an armored Cadillac SUV, and the Dosis are known to have had at least three of those vehicles. The Dosis are doing their part in General Motors' recovery.

"In addition to agents on the ground," Alex said, "the American taxpayers were financing the rental of a little crow's nest of an apartment two blocks away, from which agents can see the entrance of the compound and the end of the street as well as a quarter of the yard. Surveillance photos are inconclusive, but there, beyond American extradition, is where I think the Dosis are hiding, based on what my two sets of operatives told me."

That information, Alex explained, jibed with the Dosis' recent trip to Rome. The two people who lived in the compound had left on Saturday, almost two weeks ago and had gone to the airport. Alex had a list of passports she believed they could be using. Two of the names on the passports connected with a passenger manifest for an Alitalia flight from Casablanca to Rome.

A local CIA contact had trailed them from Leonardo Da Vinci

Airport to the hotel. It had taken two laborious days to gain the proper Italian court orders and assemble a raiding party. By that time the couple had been tipped off. So the "capture" operation fell apart.

"So you feel the betrayal was where?" Rizzo asked. "In North Africa or in Europe?"

"It was in Rome, I'm sure," Alex said. "If the betrayal had been in Morocco, the Dosis would never have set foot in Italy, from where I could extradite them. It was after arrival in Rome that they were tipped off."

There was a lengthy silence on Rizzo's end. In his office, the door opened. Entering the chamber was Captain Cabrini, leader of the raid at the hotel in Rome. Cabrini wore a headset with which he had been listening to the conversation in the next room. Rizzo held a finger up to his mouth to suggest continued silence.

"So your 'watchers' back in Morocco?" Rizzo asked as Cabrini eased into a deep leather chair. "You still trust that part of your network?"

"Per adesso," she said. "For now. Until proven otherwise."

"Capisco," he answered. Understood.

He also grimaced slightly. Another silence followed as he considered his next words. In his hand, he continued to finger the silver pen that Captain Cabrini had retrieved in the raid — the one with Alex's name engraved on it.

"Are you there, Gian Antonio?" she asked.

"Yes, yes," he answered. "Of course."

On this previous operation, Alex explained, she had been forced to use other people's operatives. Not so this time. Off her conversation with De Salvo she had a budget and authorization to form her own alliances. If it was a game of chess, this time she would capture the opposing queen and checkmate the king. Rizzo said he liked the chess analogy.

"Then you'll be my white knight," she said, teasing him. *"Sei il mio prode cavaliere!"*

"I prefer the role of queen's bishop," he said in suddenly high-spirited return. "*Il alfiere!* The player who starts at the side of the queen he worships wields tremendous power both in the court and on the battlefield, can defend his monarch from anyplace on the board, moves lethally and diagonally for an unexpected attack, carries a powerful sword, and can administer the final fatal blow to the opposing king and queen without the queen placing herself in danger."

"I should have known better than to ask," she said.

"You knew perfectly well. And I'm flattered that you asked."

"Well, I can use such a man, as always," she said.

"And as always, as long as I have a pulse, you will have one."

From his position in the leather chair, Captain Cabrini gave a thumbs-up. He smiled.

"Now I will tell you something," Rizzo continued to Alex. "Your friends who are hiding out in North Africa, the ones we just missed in Rome . . . there is some new intelligence, some calls monitored. My *amico*, Captain Cabrini, who administered the raid in Rome has come by these from an excellent source. The Dosis are seeking to minimize any help you may get from any potential informants in the United States. Accordingly, murderers have been hired. Informants, people who may have had any contact at all with American law enforcement, are to be eliminated. You might follow this thread. Particularly in the Miami area. They are probably already on the ground in the United States and at work."

From across the room, Cabrini nodded again.

From three thousand miles away, as Alex assimilated this; her voice was silent.

"And you consider this reliable?" she finally asked.

"Highly," said Rizzo.

Alex rang off moments later. Rizzo's expression was grave as he clicked the line dead on his phone. For several moments, he stared in silence at Captain Cabrini.

"She is going to get herself killed. And what can we do to stop it?"

Cabrini shook his head to indicate nothing, if that's what the fates had in mind. He joined his peer in remorse. Neither had any good answer for that question. Rizzo's gaze returned to his desk. He picked up the silver pen with Alex's name on it and popped it back into his pocket. It was safer there than anywhere else.

TWENTY-FOUR

Back in New York, Alex laughed as she signed off her call to Rome. Rizzo was a dear friend and a man for all seasons, all occasions, and all centuries including the fifteenth. She looked forward to seeing him and assumed he would bring along his young squeeze of the past year, a twentysomething techie named Mimi.

Alex returned to her monitor. Responses were now coming in from the other cohorts she had queried in Europe and Asia. Nothing yet from Peter Chang in China, but that was to be expected due to differences in time zones as well as the hypersensitivity of many of Peter's assignments. She already knew that she might not hear from him, or not for a while.

But reading the responses, she could count on help from contacts in England, Spain, Switzerland, and France in addition to Italy. The positive responses were heartening. A network of operatives she could call her own had quickly emerged out of the ether. Such things were two-way streets: these people wouldn't have rallied to her assistance if they didn't feel as good about her as she did about them. She would follow up with personal phone calls to all of these men within the next week, after going to Miami again, she reasoned.

Then Alex turned back to Rizzo's tip. Methodically, she accessed her FBI list of all potential contacts and informers who had had business with the Dosis or their various companies. Digging more deeply into other FBI files and police records, she began an arduous task of cross-referencing the names into any crime reports of the last two weeks.

She came up with nothing on her first five attempts. But something told her to attempt a sixth and final attempt. Suddenly, the computer screen came alive with three matches.

Kevork, James
Skypios, Nicholas
Vierra, Thomas

An unholy trinity, a trifecta of homicides.

She stared at the screen for several minutes, then spent an hour accessing everything on all three cases. Not by complete surprise, Lieutenant Woodbine's name turned up in two of the three investigations.

Kevork, Skypios, and Vierra. It sounded more like a law firm or the top of a batting order, rather than an unhappy trio of victims. But what about Mejías and Ramona? Where was the link? Here before her was a suggested corroboration of Rizzo's professed intelligence, something that linked the ongoing Dosi operation to events in Miami within the last month. James Kevork, Nicholas Skypios, and Thomas Vierra, all small-time bit players in the Miami underworld, all had had links to the Dosi organization. And all had been murdered within the last month. Tracks were being covered and potential informants eliminated as quickly as possible.

Alex took the occasion to spend another half hour in Andrew De Salvo's office, arguing for an immediate return to Miami the following week. She won the argument.

Then, back in her own office as the afternoon faded into evening, she logged on to her other secure net connection and made a business-class flight reservation for her return to Miami Tuesday morning. She bought the last business-class seat for an 8:00 a.m. flight out of Newark, or at least the American taxpayers did.

Things were falling into place.

TWENTY-FIVE

The venue for the meeting with Danny Suarez of the NYPD was a restaurant café on Sixth Street near the aging Waverly movie theater. Alex arrived first and selected a table where she could sit with her back to the wall and watch the comings and goings. Suarez arrived a few minutes later. She spotted him right away: a ruddy, small unshaven man but with a fireplug physique on top of a shuffling gait. They established eye contact from twenty feet, and Suarez came to her table. He moved with a low stride that favored one leg, as if he had been badly injured at one time and all the bits and pieces hadn't quite knitted back together perfectly.

"Alex?" he asked, more as an affirmation than a question.

"That's me," she said.

"Sam described you," he said, sliding into a chair at the table. His accent was pure outer borough. "He said you were bodacious. Hot. A knockout."

"Sam tends to flatter," she said.

"Sam's opinionated but rarely wrong. Certainly not wrong here. Plus, let's face it, Sam's got a thing for pretty girls," Danny responded.

As if cued, a perky waitress in snug jeans and T-shirt appeared. Danny Suarez addressed her as "beautiful," ordered a beer, and unleashed a big smile. Alex already had an iced tea going. The beer arrived, Suarez knocked back a third of it with his first gulp and then played verbal table tennis with small talk for a few minutes. None too soon, Suarez finally said, "So? What can I do for you?"

"There was a homicide in Miami a couple of days ago. A recent Cuban émigré."

"Nothing newsy about that. I'd be more surprised if some recently arrived *cubano* hadn't been whacked."

"This one was part of a case I'm working," she said.

"If you don't mind my askin'," Suarez replied, "since when does Treasury in New York get mixed up with homicides in Florida? Not enough bad stuff here on your doorstep to keep you busy?"

"We get mixed up when it touches on one of our investigations."

"Got it," said Suarez. "That's the answer I was lookin' for."

"There might be a *Santería* link," Alex continued.

"How so?"

"At the funeral, this little woman came up to me, started talking," Alex explained. "Called herself Sister Ramona. She gave me the impression that she might know a few things that I might want to know. But she wasn't ready to talk yet. Kept hiding behind this Santería stuff. Said I needed to get in touch with Olodumare."

Suarez snorted. "Good luck with that. Olodumare is one of their gods."

"I know."

"He's a big man in the Santería community."

"A big man or *the* big man?" Alex asked.

"Depends. Sometimes Santería has as many interpretations as it has people making interpretations. It goes heavy on the saints, mostly prominent saints that they swiped from traditional Christians. Not much mention of God. None of Jesus. Olodumare resembles Jesus in their pantheon. It's a gutter religion in my book, but that's not what you're here askin'."

"Bring me back to Olodumare."

"You can get directly in touch with him, Olodumare, if you have the right *madrina*," Suarez said with evident cynicism. "Or the right *santera*, or *sacerdotisa*, or if you buy the right amulets from a good *babalawo*, sure. You can be in touch that way too. Cash is always preferred. Cross the palm with silver, and you can be in touch with anyone you want. Your Sister Ramona was probably just tryin' to hustle some stuff on you. A funeral is a business

opportunity for these people. Ever deal with this stuff before?"
Suarez asked. "On any level?"

"I grew up in the Los Angeles area," Alex said. "I know a lot
of this spin-off religion goes on there in the immigrant neighborhood. The recent arrivals from the Caribbean mostly. Some from
Central America. But I've never dealt with it close up, never had
a case involving it. Sam said you've dealt with it a lot."

"Oh, yeah. Too much, maybe," Suarez said.

His first beer was dead. He raised the empty bottle to the
waitress who spotted it from across the café and gave him a nod.

"That's why I'm here, Danny," Alex said. "Can you familiarize
me a little? Just from your own experience?"

"Can do," Suarez said. "Okay ... Olodumare. He's the big
honcho to most of these chicken-slaughterers, the god of spell
casters and hunters. Olodumare is also considered a god of justice. How do you like that? Often, he's associated with the police,
the prisons, and the entire legal system."

"Busy man," she said.

"Oh, yeah," Suarez said again. "Olodumare has got his god-
like work cut out for him these days, there's so much to do. But
he gets around, this dude." Suarez leaned forward. "Look, sometimes when you're working a case, the strangest stuff can come
from the most unexpected quarters. Your Sister Ramona — she's
probably a priestess. Self-appointed, self-anointed."

"That's what she says she is," Alex said.

"Sure. They all are. It's not like they went to Union Theologi-
cal Seminary or sang in that there big Utah church with all the
Mormons." He paused. "What you're dealing with here is an Afro-
Caribbean religion that has spread to the US. Comes in the door
with the immigration from the Caribbean and Central America.
Hang around here and you'll see it every day in some communities," Suarez said. "The practices of Santería are toked-out by the
normal Christian standards. Like the other Afro-Caribbean cults
practiced here. Haitian Voodoo, Obeah, and Candomblé. That's
Brazilian. All of it blends African religions with Christianity, with

some magic and a scramble of spiritual stuff tossed in. Officially they claim it's not magic, but then the first thing the practitioners do is start talking about magic."

"I noticed that."

"Okay, I'm gonna go nonpolitically correct. Does that bother you?"

"Nope," Alex said. "Go for it."

"The Spanish, French, and Portuguese introduced illiterate African slaves to Christianity. The local priests in the New World baptized the slaves and tried to sell them God and Jesus. The slaves bought it only halfway and depicted the various African deities with likenesses of Roman Catholic saints. The gods and goddesses of Santería come from West African bush origins, mostly from the Yoruba area in southwestern Nigeria. That's where the slaves came from. With me so far?"

"So far."

"Since the slaves weren't allowed to worship their native gods, they incorporated their own traditional stuff into the Catholic saints. The slave owners thought they were practicing Catholic stuff, when, fact was, they were worshiping African gods and goddesses. When the Spanish settlers noticed that the slaves had developed an excessive devotion to the saints rather than to Christ, they called the practice Santería. That means, 'the way of the saints.' More?"

"Sure," Alex said.

"In Yoruba tradition there was one creator. God. They called him Olodumare. Jesus became part of the same figure. Holy Trinity and all. But this god was too busy and important to get messed up with the everyday affairs of mankind. So the worshipers were forced to pay tribute to other entities called *orishas*, who were sort of like manifestations of Olodumare. The orishas converted into Catholic saints because anytime a worshiper needed a special favor, he would turn to the orishas for help. One orisha called Elegua was converted into Saint Anthony, owner of all open doors. Saint Anthony helps people find lost articles, Elegua opens up all hidden knowledge. An entity called Oggun was converted into Saint Peter because he controls life and death. Know how Saint Peter holds the keys to the kingdom? Oggun holds similar rights in the netherworld. Orunmila was converted into Saint Francis of Assisi because he was the only orisha who witnessed the creation of the universe. Weird Al Yankovic became Michael Jackson, because they could both sing and could be made to look alike on MTV. Or maybe it was the other way around, I'm always forgettin'."

"What?"

"Just making sure you're payin' attention. I'm not borin' you?"

"I am and you're not . . . ," Alex said.

"Good," Suarez said. He winked again.

". . . so far," Alex said.

The second beer arrived. Alex and Suarez fell silent until the waitress departed.

Alex sipped her tea as Suarez put a big dent in his second beer, straight from the bottle.

"According to Santería," Suarez began again, "each one of us is born under a particular guardian saint, an *orisha*. You worship your orisha throughout your life. That's your guardian saint. Your guardian saint is central to all rites and magic of Santería. A big part of those rites involves the use of herbs, roots, flowers, and plants. The Santeríans buy most of their religious paraphernalia from botánicas. Want to visit one in Brooklyn?"

"Miami," Alex answered, shaking her head.

"Good. Formal Santería rituals also require the use of sacrificial birds and animals. Each of the saints is 'fed' his or her favorite food or sacrifice. The blood of roosters, turtles, and goats is the most common offering. Pigeons, canaries, and hens are used in rubbin' rituals where the practitioner is cleansed, the evil supposedly passing from the victim to the animal. Go to Borough Park or Park Slope any Sunday morning and you always find decapitated birds from the Saturday night services."

"What's the point?" Alex asked. "Of the sacrifices?"

"Good question. The Santeríans kill the birds to resolve conflicts. Got a problem inside you, kill a chicken. Got a spat with a family member, chop the head off a pigeon. Mets on a losing streak, dismember a frog. Then the Mets win a game they would have won anyway and the 'santies' think the frog sacrifice did it."

"How much criminal activity is involved?" Alex asked. "Aside from the animal cruelty?"

Suarez scoffed. "Gray area. Complicated answer," he said. "You hungry? I am. Want some food?"

"I'm okay," Alex said.

Suarez signaled the waitress again and ordered a burger without looking at the menu. Then he turned back to Alex without missing a beat.

"The Santeríans get taken to court all the time on the animal-cruelty rap. They usually beat it. God forbid a court crackdown on a minority sect, right? But ignore me, I'm old-fashioned and have old-fashioned white-man ethics. Anyway, Santería does not promote malevolent or criminal activities by itself. But it does have an element of malevolent sorcery, I'd say. Criminal individuals use it for their own gain."

"How so?"

"I get drug dealers in Brooklyn who are often busted with elaborate statues and other depiction of Santería in their homes or their safe houses. The god of hunting and owner of traps, Olodumare, for example. He's a popular guy, as well as being the head guy in their pantheon. He gets honored by Latin criminals in order to avoid incarceration or to obtain release from jail. Or just to ward off the pigs. That's us, you know. The pigs, the police. Do you think your priestess was involved with drugs?"

"I don't know yet."

"Well, keep an eye out," Suarez advised. "Santería doesn't have a built-in moral code like you'd find in Christianity. Or Judaism or even Islam. So, absent that, Santería is used to power up the criminal enterprises of those who may use its magic for personal protection and good fortune. I try to be fair-minded, you know? But every time you start scratchin' the surface of some Santería stuff, you find somethin' funny. And it's not like you got people with PhDs practicing it. So you go to one neighborhood and it's a little different than the next or the last. I only can report on the spins I seen." He shifted gears. "Look, nutty as this crap sounds, the cult keeps growing. Why do I think so? The number of botánicas throughout Brooklyn. Just Brooklyn. I mean, right now. There are more than two hundred in the one borough. Someone's money is keeping these places open; otherwise they wouldn't be here."

"They're not fronts for anything?" Alex asked.

"Not that we've seen. Not yet." He paused. "Your lady friend, she said she was a *santera*?" he asked.

"That's what she said."

"All the priests and priestesses in Santería religion are known as *santeros* or *santeras*. The high priests are known as *babalawos*. Men and women can become priests but the babalawo is only reserved for males. The priests predict the future and interpret omens in the consultant's life. The Santería practitioners organize themselves under what is known as *casa de santo* — the 'house of the saint.' Most of these people don't have much money, so they work out of their homes. Each new initiative is sponsored by a *padrino* or *madrina* — think of it as a godfather or godmother — who's responsible for teaching the secrets of the religion. This same godfather or godmother has numerous other individuals who've become full-fledged practitioners under their guidance as well as individuals who have consulted them once or twice for minor problems. Love magic, prosperity, health problems, gambling debts. You name it."

Alex sipped her tea. "What's a *mediación*?" she asked.

"Where'd you get that one from?"

"The lady I'm dealing with," Alex said. "She wants to do a *mediación* to help me find some answers I'm looking for."

"Do the answers involve somebody who's dead?"

"Yes, they do," Alex answered, feeling a little creepy that Suarez had hit that one on the head.

"A *mediación* is like a séance in a gypsy clip joint. Your santera wants to communicate with the dead for you." He paused. "But what's really gonna go down is that she wants to sell you some information that she has but wants to channel it through her spooky santera scam. She might have info that you want, but be prepared to spend a few bucks to get it."

"That's what I figured," Alex said. "A lot of mumbo jumbo and hocus-pocus around the table and then she's ready to talk."

"Maybe," said Suarez. He eyed Alex. "Sam says you're a smart kid. Give 'em a little and get what you want. You know how it works. You don't go into anything like that without your own plan on how to take control of the situation. I've heard of people sitting too close to a curtain or a sheet hung behind a chair and they get swatted over the head — or worse. Got a backup?"

Thinking ahead of Miami, Alex thought of Rizzo or Rick McCarron. "Probably," she answered.

"It's always a good idea," Suarez said.

Suarez's eyes drifted to some college girls at a nearby table. Violet NYU sweatshirts, jeans, and a lot of laughter. Danny seemed to know one of the girls and gave her a wave and a nod. Then he came back to Alex.

"She's in New York or Miami?"

"Miami. It's one of the elements I need to address when deciding whether to go back down."

Suarez grimaced. "Close call," he said.

"You'd advise against it?" Alex asked.

"No. No," he said, shaking his head. "I'd advise you to go. These people are clever, con artists, most of them, but they always want you to feel like you got your money's worth. She's probably got a little something. Like I said before, you never know where the little something's gonna come from that makes a case. It's a wheel of fortune. I'd give it a spin," he said. "Check it out. Like I said, you never know."

TWENTY-SIX

Alex left the café and walked to Greenwich Avenue.

All right then, she said to herself, she'd been briefed on Santería, had four possibly related murders on her hands, and was on her way back to Miami as soon as possible, which meant Tuesday.

She would spend two or three days there, talk to Lieutenant Woodbine, scare up Sister Ramona, see what the cops and the CIA had to say, then come back to New York and reassess. Heaven knew, she could only be in one place at one time. Simple physics.

It would not be a bad idea to put a few things in her refrigerator for when she returned. She strolled into Balducci's specialty supermarket on 14th Street. Well, she felt healthy enough after a four-mile run earlier in the day. What was on the shopping list? Oatmeal, fruit, yogurt. Maybe some lean sliced meat and a few pieces of produce. As long as no one shot her, she was dedicated to a healthy lifestyle.

She grabbed a basket at the door. She browsed and found a few items. The prices they charged were borderline outrageous, but, well, life in Manhattan had its price. She made good money and spent good money. She was thirty years old, single, and might as well enjoy it.

She had played hooky from church that morning. Not good. She would hit Saint James at 71st and Madison the next weekend, she promised herself. It was out of her neighborhood, but she liked the feel of the grand old place. She felt connected there, connected to a faith larger than just New York, connected to the faith of her parents and grandparents before her. It reminded her that God's grace was more than just for her, for now.

She picked up a plastic produce bag, selected a tomato, then a second. She wanted a couple that weren't quite ripe. She would put them in the colder part of the fridge and they would be fine by Friday when she returned.

A man moved into position next to her, his hand near hers, intruding on her space. She gave him some extra room — it was New York, after all. Too many people, not enough space. But he remained close. Peripherally, she saw that he was big and trim, like an athlete, with a long arm and a rangy body, wearing big dark glasses and a navy and white Yankees baseball cap with the bold white NY logo pulled low, obscuring the top portion of his face.

Then she was aware of him stepping back and glancing toward her. She could feel his eyes. Well, she wasn't much in the mood for a clumsy pickup attempt or small talk with strangers. She put the tomatoes in her basket and turned away.

"Hey!" he said suddenly. He tapped her shoulder. "Susanna, right?"

She whirled. Was she about to be shot? Her hand started to move toward her weapon.

"Hi," the man said, innocent as a schoolboy. "Didn't mean to startle you ... again." He raised his hand and lowered the dark glasses that had obscured his face.

"Oh!" she said, recognizing him. "You!"

"Me. Sorry. Hello. And you're Susanna of the third floor," Eric Robertson said. "Unless I'm mistaken."

"Yeah, that's me," Alex said.

He laughed. "I have this deplorable knack of startling you," he said. "I apologize."

"Not a problem," she said. Then she was curious. She glanced at her watch. "Don't you have a matinee performance?" she asked.

"I did, yes, but I decided to blow it off."

"What?"

He laughed. "No, silly," he said. "We do our Sunday performance in the evening. Two matinees a week, Wednesday and Saturday. Monday we're dark while we all recover from the previous week and grit our teeth for the next one."

"Oh, I see."

"You're smiling again. I'm glad I'm entertaining someone on a free afternoon."

But then Alex's professional instincts kicked in. The circumstances of this encounter passed in review. Coincidence? Why would an actor of his status have her in his sights? He was glamorous and from a world she would never be part of. She thought of herself as a working girl, a woman in a job more dangerous and unusual than others, perhaps, but in the end she was a plugger, a clock puncher, a government slogger.

Could he be stalking her? Or was this just a coincidence, that two people who live in the same building would shop at the same supermarket?

"If you don't mind my saying, every time I see you, you seem overstressed and overworked. Whatever you do for a living is taking its toll. I hope you realize that."

"And why should that matter to you?" she countered.

"It shouldn't. But it does. Sorry."

A surprisingly awkward moment followed.

"It's that obvious?" she finally said. "The stress."

"To me it is. Obvious, I mean. And I don't even know you."

Another strange moment followed.

"Why are you even talking to me?" she asked.

"What do you mean?"

"We don't know each other; I'm not in your profession. We've passed on the street twice. That's our only history."

He paused, then said, "I'm unaware of any law against talking to you, correct me if I'm wrong, and you are my very quiet and secretive upstairs neighbor ... so I thought I'd say hello since out of all the people either of us could run into on a Sunday afternoon in Balducci's, we've stumbled, by chance, into each other. What a titanic coincidence."

"Yes. What a coincidence," she said.

He smiled. "There's a saying my mother always used. When she didn't know why something had happened, good or bad, she'd say 'All things work together for good,' and just go with it and try to make the best of it."

"That's a good thought," she said. "I like it. I suspect I would have liked your mother."

"I know I do," he said. "Lovely lady. She lives down in Florida now and plays tennis, golf, and poker."

Alex laughed again, adjusting the shopping basket in her arm.

"Okay, then," Robertson said next, "I will admit that I was lying about the titanic coincidence and that this meeting isn't entirely by chance."

Alex's heart started to pound.

With a flip of the head, he indicated the other side of the store. "I saw you on the street. I was across the way, going the other direction. I saw you walk in. So I waded through traffic, made lifelong enemies of several cabbies, and wandered over to say hello. I suppose that's not serious stalking, and it's putting a mild charley horse in the long arm of coincidence. But for 2:30 on a Sunday afternoon, it'll have to do."

"I guess it will," Alex said.

Another beat, then, "So, listen," he said, "I wanted to ask you something. I don't know very much about you, but I've seen you a few times. I pick up on some lively vibes beneath the terminal stress and fatigue. So I thought I'd ask you a favor."

Still anxious, she answered, "Go ahead."

"Okay," he said, lowering his voice to exclude any eavesdroppers. "I was wondering . . . let me, let's say, make up for scattering your mail the other night and for startling you here today. Let me take you to lunch sometime. Or brunch on a weekend. How would that be?"

Alex looked at him appraisingly, then in near disbelief.

"You're inviting me to lunch?" she asked.

"Yes, I believe I am," he said. "I don't have the patience to wait for you to invite me."

Her response was out of her mouth before she could even think it through. "Sure."

"Yeah?"

"You're surprised?"

"Well, yes. But good. That seemed easy."

"And that's unusual for you? Don't make me laugh."

"It's my job to make people laugh, depending on the role."

"What role is this?"

"Me. In person, regular guy. Being quite serious. You'll meet me for, let's say, brunch next Saturday. Giacomini's Trattoria. A nice little Italian place on West 44th, not too far from Broadway. I have a show at 2:00 p.m., so it'll have to be a little early, but 11:15 works for me. What about you?"

"I have a business trip to Miami this week," she said. "I expect to be back by Friday. If I'm not ..."

"If you're not," he said, reaching into his pocket, "call me and let me know. We'll reschedule." He wrote out his phone number and handed it to Alex.

"I would. I mean, I will. I mean, I don't expect to, but I will."

"You will what?" he asked, raising his gaze as he wrote.

"Phone you if I can't get back."

"And if you don't get back, you get a rain check. How's that? No pressure, okay?"

"Okay," she said. She took the number.

He didn't move. "Well?" he asked.

"Well, what?"

"Maybe, if I'm not being too nosey, you could give me a contact number for you?"

A beat. A second beat.

"Yes, of course," she said. She wrote out her cell phone number and handed it to him. He folded it and tucked it into a pocket.

"See you Saturday," he said.

"See you then," Alex answered.

He turned and left the store without buying anything. In disbelief, she watched him go.

TWENTY-SEVEN

On Monday morning, Laura Chapman returned Alex's call. They spoke business first. Alex summarized where she was in the Dosi investigation and asked if she could contact Rick McCarron in Miami and run some information past him — Fin Cen business that might impact the CIA, for whom Rick worked.

"No problem. I'll give him a call and have him phone you," Laura answered.

"Thanks. I appreciate it."

"How are things in New York?" Laura asked.

"Hectic. Busy. But under control."

"Have you seen the star again?" Laura asked.

Thinking Laura was asking a question associated with work, Alex blanked. "Who?" she asked.

"In your building. Eric Robertson."

"Oh," Alex said, relaxing for a moment. "Him." She gave a moment's thought to whether or not to fill Laura in on the latest. She decided she would. "Yes. He asked me to lunch."

"What!"

"Yeah. I ran into him in the produce section of Balducci's, for heaven's sake. We got talking, and he asked me to lunch. Or brunch. Or coffee. Or something."

"When?"

"Saturday. It's no big deal."

"No big deal? Are you kidding me? You run into this guy over carrots and turnips and you say it's no biggie when he asks you out?"

"Actors are actors. Flakey, erratic. And often far out in left field, you know what I mean?"

"You said yes, I hope."

"Yes to what?"

"Yes to going out!"

"Oh, Laura. Stop acting like a teenybopper. Yes, I said yes, we're going to some Italian place in the theater district if I'm back from Miami in time."

"Do you know how many million women would crawl to the airport with two broken legs and scratch and claw their way onto the airplane to make sure they got back?" Laura asked.

"Well, I know you would," Alex answered.

"Heck, yes! And you should too! Has he invited you to *South Pacific* yet?"

By now Alex was sorry she had mentioned it. "Laura, you're jumping way ahead. And no, he hasn't."

"Wouldn't you like to see the show?"

"I suppose I would."

"Well, he will, if you play things right," she sang. "How can you be so blasé?"

Alex drew a breath. The fingers of her free hand drifted unconsciously to the small gold cross that she wore. She fingered it and sighed. "It's just brunch, Laura. Come on. Friendly. That's all. I'm curious more than interested."

"Uh-huh." There was a silence. "Alex, is this the first time you've dated since Kiev?"

"Laura, it's not a *date* date."

"Then what is it?"

"It's a friendly brunch, okay? We're neighbors. It's like I was having lunch with Mrs. Stein from the fourth floor."

"Eric Robertson is not Mrs. Stein. I've never met Mrs. Stein, but I'm sure she's not a hunky guy who's in movies and on Broadway. Alex, repeat after me, Eric Robertson is not Mrs. Stein."

By now Alex was laughing. "Okay, he's not Mrs. Stein."

"Admit that he's an A-list star and he's gorgeous and he asked you to brunch."

"Okay, I admit it."

"Thank you," said Laura.

"I'm just not as impressed with it as you are."

"That's all right. At least now we're getting somewhere." Laura paused. "When will you admit that you're in denial, Alex?"

"What's that mean?"

"You're interested. But you won't admit it. Not to me, not even to yourself."

"Laura—," Alex began.

"Just promise to tell me all about it afterward," Laura said, "and I'll let it go for today."

"Thank you," Alex said. "And you'll phone Rick?"

"I'll phone Rick."

"Soon?"

"Now."

"Thank you."

"Mrs. Stein," Laura mumbled again as a farewell.

Shortly before 6:00 p.m., Laura's friend Rick phoned from Miami. He would be happy to see Alex in person on Wednesday or Thursday, he said. He sounded amiable. And he had also done some initial spadework on the case.

"Señora Mejías is in protective custody," he said. "Not the police. She's at an agency safe house. She's still in shock, after all, and they're babysitting her pretty tightly. The plans are to get her out of the country as planned and as soon as possible."

"To Spain?" Alex asked.

"I wasn't told where."

"Can I see her?" Alex asked.

"Might be possible, might be a problem," Rick said. "There's a case officer here. Lionel Dickey."

"His name has come up already," Alex said.

"Where and how?"

"There's a very unhappy homicide lieutenant in Miami who claims Dickey swiped his best material witness."

"Yeah, figures. Dickey's a piece of work. Manners and personality of a chain saw. I know him a little. He's handling her protection. I already put in a word for you."

"Thanks," she said.

"I can't promise it will get you any brownie points with Dickey. He's a tough bird."

"I appreciate that you tried," Alex said.

"Sooner you get here the better," McCarron said. "I'm getting vibes that this situation is highly fluid. Twenty-four hours could make a difference."

"I'm flying down tomorrow morning," she said. "May I send you some files on a case I'm working. Secure email by attachment."

"Okay. I'll take a look," McCarron said. "I'll also email you an address for the place we should meet. Don't come to my office, we should be able to talk freely first. So there's a place called El Rincón Cubano in Little Havana. Little family place with some local color. Pleasant and cheap."

"What more could I ask for?" she answered.

"May I send a car to the airport for you?" he asked.

"Thank you, but no. I'll rent one. I need to get around the city."

"It's still warm," he said. "And potentially wet. Dress accordingly."

"Thanks for the warning," she said.

Alex's eyes snapped open in the middle of the night. She looked at the clock by her bed. It was 3:12 a.m. Sleep had been sporadic and troubled, pockmarked with creepy images. Then another feeling, a sense of not being alone, was upon her.

She lay still for a few minutes, wondering if what she was sensing was some impending danger. After all, over the past couple of years she had been shot at more than once, including one time in her own apartment; and she had been drugged and abducted one night in a Swiss hotel. So who could blame her if her imagination had caused her to break out in a sweat in the middle of the night?

She knew she had been under surveillance several times. The CIA had done it once and obviously the Dosi organization had too, which had led their sniper so close to his target. Was someone at it again? Was that what she was sensing?

Slowly, she allowed her eyes to adjust to the dim light of her bedroom. She scanned. No one there. Slowly, she moved her hand to the Glock that sat in its holster on the bedside table. She took it out. Still no movement, no sound from the next room. Nothing. She rose and decided to look around.

She moved to the door to the living room. She had left a small light on for exactly this reason. The door was still bolted and chained from within. Okay, she told herself, she was imagining things. She checked the kitchen, the other bedroom, all the closets.

Nothing. Okay, everything was fine.

On a whim, she moved to the kitchen window, leaving the kitchen light off, pushed the shade slightly to the side and peered down onto 20th Street. No one lurking. Cars parked, hard to the curb, bumper to bumper. Nothing unusual.

Then she saw movement. There was a man sitting on the stoop across the street, smoking a cigarette, a bottle in a brown paper bag parked next to him. She had never seen him before. He was partially obscured by the leaves of a tree, so she couldn't see his face. If he was a watcher, he was pretty low tech.

She moved back to her living room and froze. Now she was convinced. She was hearing something. It was faint and distant, innocent building noise maybe, but it was there.

In her living room, she went down to one knee and could hear it better, though it was still very distant and audible only because the rest of her surroundings were so quiet.

She got down flush on the floor and put her ear to the floorboards. Music. Music from down below. Things fell into a logical pattern. It was her building buddy, Eric, the actor, downstairs.

She listened and listened. No voices. Was he simply an occasional insomniac too? A little devil appeared on her shoulder: she should grab a bottle of champagne from her fridge, slip into a lacy peignoir, and go down and knock on his door and—

The music went off. As for the champagne and peignoir scenario, she didn't have a bottle, didn't own said peignoir and didn't do that type of thing anyway. Ah, well.

With a quick movement, she was up on her feet again. She checked the door, still locked, and went back to her bedroom. She resettled the gun next to her radio and climbed back into bed.

She slept. The alarm jarred her at 5:15 a.m. What a night. But she crawled out of bed, dressed quickly, and was off to the airport by 5:45. The homeless man across the street was gone, but that creepy feeling of being on someone's radar screen, however distant, was not.

It traveled with her to Miami.

TWENTY-EIGHT

On the flight, Alex sat in a window seat with her laptop open, up and running. But she barely consulted it. Fettered by an uneven night of sleep, her eyes kept closing. Yet she could not quite knock back and nap. Too much was on her mind. Air travel always gave her too much time to think, sometimes involuntarily, and this flight was no different.

She gazed out the window, her eyes aching with fatigue. Clouds covered the east coast. Sometimes she thought there were clouds across her life too, or at least over the last few years.

She was a woman of deeply shaken faith these days. Might as well admit it to herself. The trust in God that she had been raised with had left too many questions unanswered. Since the tragedy of losing her fiancé in Kiev, she tried to stay with what she believed in. But it wasn't easy. The old quote from the American theologian Reinhold Niebuhr came back to her. She closed her eyes, let her right hand drift to the gold cross she wore and muttered it as a prayer. "God, grant me the serenity to accept the things I cannot change, the courage to change the things I can, and the wisdom to know the difference."

For Alex, trust in God was an increasingly elusive proposition. Whatever the merits of her faith, right now it did not seem to provide an easy answer for hard times. She tried to use it as a strengthener, a bright light and motivation with which to face life's problems. She tried to affirm that no tragedy, even what happened in Kiev, was without some meaning.

"Faith is a two-way street," she recalled from a recent sermon she had heard. But was God being faithful to her? Right now, at twenty-eight thousand feet, she did not know. All she knew was that she prayed for light and wisdom for her journey. And she was not sure she was seeing it. When would she see an indication that

God really was looking after her, was really on her side, really had a plan for her? So many people who had been raised with a faith in God lost their faith as the years piled on, only to desperately cling to it in their old age.

Was she starting to see why?

Another quote came back to her: "Faith is a knowledge within the heart, beyond the reach of proof."

A flight attendant passed by with a drink cart. Only 10:00 a.m. and the booze was rolling. The man next to her ordered a Bloody Mary. The flight attendant looked to Alex. She went with a second shot of coffee. Much too early for alcohol, and she was trying to stay away from the stuff anyway. There had been too much of it in her life as a crutch after the loss of Robert. In her case now, cold turkey might work better than cold beer.

She shifted positions in her seat to get comfortable. When she moved, the attention of the man next to her moved briefly in her direction. She donned headphones to avoid a conversation. Her eyes sagged with sleepiness.

She thought ahead to Miami. Her trifecta of assignments: Rick McCarron, Clarence Woodbine, and Sister Ramona. Dreamy doggerel pursued her. Manny, Moe, and Jack. Curley, Moe, and Larry. Harpo, Chico, and Groucho. Huey, Dewey, and Louie. She sipped more coffee to throw off the goofy, dreamy sleeplessness. McCarron, Laura's boyfriend and Alex's local CIA contact. Nice contact — but why should he give Alex any special treatment? Well, Alex had been in her job long enough to see how the moral compromises crept into one's life. If the CIA didn't respond to her through normal channels, and she increasingly had a feeling that they wouldn't, she would have to offer something to McCarron in exchange for a peek at his computers.

Was she ready to do that? She already knew she was. At the same time, she asked herself how long she could stay with such a lifestyle, compromising ethics for greater short-term gain. Did good intentions obviate dishonorable methods? She knew which road was paved with good intentions and where it led.

The next thing she knew, she was opening her eyes. She had

dropped off for an hour. The pilot was announcing their descent into Miami. The flight had been smooth and easy, and Alex had even caught a few winks. A godsend. The flight even arrived on time.

In the airport, she checked her phone messages. Nothing of immediate significance. She went to the rental agency where a reserved car was waiting. She intentionally got something nondescript: a dark blue Ford. Easier to blend into traffic and parking lots.

She left the airport and took her usual route into Miami on the expressway, which passed the sprawling old Orange Bowl, then along the congested causeway to South Beach. Traffic was heavier than expected. But within an hour, Alex checked in again at the Park Central. She had a comfortable corner room with a view of the Atlantic Ocean on one side and another view up Ocean Drive with its art deco buildings on the other. Better, there were no dangerous sightlines for another sniper. She pulled the shades anyway.

She changed clothes, freshened up, and tucked her Glock into a small holster on her right hip, concealed by a light navy sports jacket. She would go by Lieutenant Woodbine's office at Miami police headquarters first. Or so she planned until her cell phone rang.

She answered. "Alex LaDuca," she said.

"LaDuca?" a male voice said.

"Yes. Who's this?"

"Lionel Dickey," returned a voice. "We communicated earlier."

"That's correct," she said. "We're still on, I hope."

"We're on for a meeting. Slight recalculation though."

"Go ahead."

He said, "I thought it would be best if we met for the first time outside the agency offices. We can speak more freely."

"When and where?" Alex asked.

"I'm in the hotel lobby," he said. "I figured you'd be here by now. They said you'd checked in."

"You are a spy," she teased.

"Just a tech guy and a case officer," he said without humor. "Can we meet now? Let's get this done."

"Where?"

"Casablanca," he said.

"Huh?"

"That's the hotel bar," he said. "I thought you were a detective."

"I just checked in. Sorry. I didn't notice."

"Whatever. I'm downstairs. How soon can you get here?"

"I'll be in the lobby in five minutes."

"See me in the bar," he said. "I can use a drink, and it's private."

He rang off.

TWENTY-NINE

Three minutes later Alex stood in the doorway of the bar, next to a potted palm. The bar was pleasant enough, with dim, low light and dark furniture. The subdued walls had framed pictures of the movie of the same name. Bogie with Bacall. Bogie with "Sam" at the piano. Bogie with Victor Lazlo at the airport with that old Hollywood airplane prop in the background. That made Alex smile. A friend in the film business had once explained how the prop had been made to seem bigger and farther away by using midget extras nominally servicing the plane.

Alex's gaze swept the room. Her eyes hit a bulky man seated at a side table. He was leaning back with arms spread over two adjoining chairs, dark suit and open collar, staring at her with two beady brown eyes beneath a receding hairline and above an ample chin. On the table was a tall glass with ice cubes, a clear liquid, and two slices of lime. It was already at half mast.

He gave her a slight nod, split between supposed recognition and a signal to come and sit. She came and sat. "Lionel?" she asked.

"Who else?" he answered.

"I'm Alex," she said.

"Yeah. I guessed."

A waiter appeared. Alex ordered iced tea. Lionel Dickey wasn't much for small talk. His eyes were small and dark and piggish and he had an aura to match.

"Look, there's nothing I can do for you," he said after less than a minute. "So stop being a pain."

"Excuse me?"

"You're here on the Mejías case," he said in a low voice. "Or 'Gemini,' as we're to call him now. Did you know that? We don't say or write the M-name again."

"If you say so," Alex said.

"I do," he said. "And I say even more. We can talk freely here in this bar. The agency installed a baffler about a year ago."

"I suspect if they have a baffler in here they can probably listen in on any phone conversation too," she said. "If you're going to drop a bug on a place, why not go all the way, right?"

"Who knows?" he said. He eyed a small bowl of nuts that sat near his drink—he had a look of trying to resist it, but the willpower was fading.

"Are you the primary case officer on Gemini?" Alex asked. "And his survivor?"

"I speak for all concerned." His stout fingers came together and lifted his drink. He drained it. A second arrived at the same time as Alex's tea. He gave the waitress a thin smile and watched her go, his eyes working her over rudely. Meanwhile, Alex's eyes were doing the same with Lionel Dickey but going in a different direction.

The man's name suggested English-Irish but the face was more Mayan-Guatemalan. He came off more as one of the CIA's street guys than a university-educated case officer. But who knew these days? The ham-fisted guys got their promotions too, usually until they reached their highest level of incompetence.

Dickey's brown eyes dumped the waitress and came back to Alex.

"So when can I interview her?" Alex asked, picking up the pleasantries.

"Who?" Dickey asked.

A pause and then, cordially but icily, "Mrs. Gemini."

"Negative on that," Dickey answered.

"Negative on what?"

"You can't talk to anyone. Nor can we share any information with you. There's a steel curtain drawn over this case. It's ready to drop on your toes—or maybe even your neck—if you make any more of a pest of yourself. No one gets to see anyone, hear anything, read anything. That's what I'm here to tell you. The whole thing's off-limits. So take a hike, wise up, and let it go."

"You're forgetting, I brought her out of Cuba."

"Well, that's fine, that's good, but that's also yesterday's news, all right already? That and a buck and a half will get you a stale ptomaine-laced tamale over in Little Havana. You don't get to see her no matter how much you kick and whine. My advice to you is go out and do some salsa dancing tonight and take a flight back to New York in the morning. Can I put it to you any more forthright?"

"When is she going to travel, Señora Gemini?"

"You hard of hearing? Is that it?"

"Is Spain still the destination? I also heard something about Portugal."

Lionel Dickey sighed. "I'll only tell you one thing as a favor so your boss up in Washington — "

" — New York — "

" — doesn't get after you about the cost of your plane ticket and hotel — "

"I'm here for a reason," Alex said. "I spoke to Gemini right before he was murdered. He had information for me. A list of names. I want them."

"Why?"

"They have a bearing on a major case I'm working."

"That's *your* problem, and the list probably doesn't exist anymore. Or — who knows? — maybe it never did. So forget it."

"I can't."

"You can and you will," Dickey said. "The individual you spoke to is dead. The other individual you're seeking isn't even in Miami. So you're wasting your time kicking around here."

"Well, I might waste some more by hanging around and asking some questions."

"Not a good idea," he said as he worked through the upper half of drink number two. He finally reached for the mixed nuts on the table, emptied a third of the bowl into his palm, and knocked them back with a single toss. "A very bad idea."

"Do I hear a threat?"

"You hear advice." He glanced at his watch. "And that's pretty much the last thing you're going to hear. From me, anyway." He then rose heavily to go. On his feet, he was even more of a Humpty Dumpty–shaped guy. "I've got another appointment. I don't have time for this. Play it anyway you like, LaDuca. But don't step on the wrong feet or you'll regret it for the rest of your life. Get it? There you go. That's as blunt as I can get and still be polite. Don't say you weren't warned, all right? You're welcome."

Alex rounded on him, at last prepared to let go with her own indignation and anger. But Dickey was barely conscious of her reaction. He threw thirty dollars on the table and lurched unsteadily toward the door, taking his hostility, arrogance, and unique charm with him.

THIRTY

Alex met with Lieutenant Woodbine halfway through that same hot afternoon at Miami Homicide Headquarters. He kept her waiting in a gray anteroom for forty-five minutes, had her ushered into the office, then spoke on the phone for another ten minutes before he hung up, looked up, and, with no apology, acknowledged her presence.

"So?" he said. "You're back in Miami."

What was your first clue? she almost blurted out but instead said, "Yes, I'm back."

"What's going on?" he asked.

"I'm here to ask you that question," she said.

"What question?"

"What's going on in the Mejías case?"

"Why should I tell you?" he huffed. "Even if I knew."

"Professional courtesy, maybe. Maybe because I'm from another law-enforcement agency and might be able to return a favor someday."

"Feds don't return favors," he said.

"Ever met me before last week?"

"Nope."

"Then don't assume anything," she said.

Woodbine took advantage of the lull in the conversation to rub the side of his nose. "Well, I ain't here to answer no questions," he said. "If you're looking for help from this department, I'll tell you right now, you ain't going to get it. So why don't you take whatever you're selling and hustle it somewhere else."

He took it as his cue for her to leave. She took it as her own cue to stay exactly where she was. "What is it that you don't like about me, Lieutenant? I'm from the north? I work for the feds? I'm a woman?"

"Yes, yes, and yes," he answered. "And what's worse is that you're here, bothering me. I got plenty to do, so look, don't take it personal, but why don't you be on your way?"

Alex drew a breath and tried a tactic that she presupposed was doomed: reason.

"Come on, Lieutenant," she tried. "I have my job, you have yours. In some senses our purposes overlap. So why don't we overlap our resources too, and we can both get a job done?"

"Why don't we, huh?" he said, mocking her.

"You don't like the idea?" she said.

"No, I don't," he answered angrily. "I also already got more interference from you people than I need. Last thing I need is more, okay?"

"CIA is not my people," Alex said. She wondered if Dickey himself had been in the same chair where she sat just a few hours earlier, wondered but did not ask. Nonetheless, a pattern was emerging.

"Whatever. You're all the same to me," said Woodbine.

"Where do they have her?"

"You tell me and we'll both know."

"You can't get at her, either?"

"No," he said.

"How about if I find out, I'll share with you, and we can go at them together. And you share with me, of course."

"That ain't gonna happen."

"It will if you let it."

"Like I said, lady, be on your way. I don't need your help, and you ain't getting mine."

"If I told you I was investigating some Santería links to the killing, would it surprise you?" Alex asked.

Woodbine took on a surprised look, then a skeptical look, then grimaced. Alex had the reaction that she had told him something he hadn't known, which meant he hadn't explored the case very far, for whatever reason. Now she wondered if he was just stubborn and stupid, or was he stonewalling for a larger reason — he had been told to.

"Well, it would and it wouldn't," Woodbine said. "Santería crap pops up so much on the crime stats around here, I ain't surprised." He paused. "There's always a level of violence not too far away. Maybe it's linked to immigrant communities, or maybe it's linked to their crackpot religion. Want a couple examples?"

"I'd listen to that," Alex said.

"Our officers often run into ceremonial sites in homes when we serve warrants or conduct investigations. A lot of times, we end up making further arrests: animal cruelty, you see that a lot. They do ritual animal sacrifice, these Santa-nut cases. Then there's other crap. Last week we had this Cuban guy who died from multiple gunshots after being chased down by a Dominican gentleman. The victim was wearing a shirt and pants covered with silver glitter. Same stuff was in his shoes. He also got this here silver-plated hammer and a silver-plated flashlight. So what's this all about? Our investigation revealed the victim was a Santerían. He would often wear silver shoes, a silver shirt, and eyeglasses with silver lenses. But here's what broke the case. Three days earlier he had threatened to cut off the head of his eventual assailant and offer it to the saints. That was the actual motive for the shooting: self-defense, or so he said. Then earlier in the week, we had a thirty-five-year-old Cuban man who was a primary in a grand-theft-auto conspiracy trial. He visited his madrina, that's a Santería godmother, one evening for a ceremony to cleanse his spirit. The ceremony to cleanse the spirit implies appeasement to his personal god, or orisha. The failure to make the orisha happy results in punishment, such as bad luck. Getting caught by the police is considered bad luck. The dice throw is a divination ritual. So they did this dice throw in front of a statue of his orisha to see how his trial would go. The dice were carved out of coconut shells from Cuba. The dice didn't bode well: double threes. So shortly after midnight he gets dressed all in white and leaves the room as a concluding phase of the ritual. He was found dead the next morning. A postmortem examination was performed. His death was attributed to a heart attack. But all through the community, the natural practitioners of Santería attributed supernatural powers to the wrath of his orisha." Woodbine paused. "Your guy, Mejías? Your santera is probably going to tell you that he wasn't in favor with his orisha. That's fine. If she can tell you why, then maybe we're in business."

"So should I give it a shot?" Alex asked, even though she had already decided to.

"It's on you. I'm out of it, at least in this angle. It won't go nowhere."

"At the funeral, a woman sought me out and said she was a santera. Said the spirits were upset. Obviously, she wanted to sell me some information. Whether it's good information or a two-bit con job remains to be seen."

"You got that part right."

"Why do you think she came to me, not you?" Alex asked.

"They hate cops, the Santería people. The cops are the authority, the people who bust them down. Why come to us?"

"The other reason is that she might think the information is worth more to me than to you," Alex said. "Or maybe I'm hyperanalyzing."

"Doing what?"

"Thinking too much."

"Could be," Woodbine said. "Got a name? Of this woman?"

"Yes," Alex said, without offering it.

Woodbine got the message. "Okay, what do you want from me?"

"I'll give you the name, you tell me if you have anything in the Miami PD files on this lady. Then you wait, let me visit her first. If I come away with anything that will help you, I'll slip it to you on the q.t. How's that?"

Woodbine thought about it for several seconds. "No," he said.

"What's your problem with that?"

"I told you. Too much interference already. We'll push our own plow. I only got one thing to tell you."

"What's that?"

"The door is over there," he said, indicating.

"Thanks," she said, "for nothing."

THIRTY-ONE

Late that same afternoon, back in Queens, a thousand miles to the north, Luis Rivera waited for a visitor who had been referred to him by a trusted friend from Panama, a second cousin named Carlito, with whom Luis had served in the US Army.

The visitor was a wiry little man, dark, with narrow brown eyes, who gave his name as Manuel Ortega. He turned up at 3:00 p.m. as prearranged. Luis warmly greeted the visitor and led him to the bunker-style office in the rear of his shop. The men spoke Spanish.

"I believe my friend Carlito spoke to you and vouched for me," Ortega said.

"Claro que si," Luis replied. Yes. Of course. "Otherwise the garage door would not have opened for you."

"What did he tell you?" Ortega asked.

"Only that you are an emissary from a powerful person in Central America and need an explosive device."

"I need a small but powerful device," Manuel said. "Something that would devastate everything within close range."

Rivera settled in. He looked at his visitor for several seconds. Yes, he was used to dealing with people who used explosive devices for nefarious purposes. But usually they were used to destroy or intimidate. He studied this little man carefully for an extra few seconds. He almost wondered if he was an imposter of some sort. He had a harmless, almost casual feeling about him. If he hadn't come with such stellar credentials, Rivera might have thrown him out. Rivera did not like dealing with fools or amateurs.

"Everything and everyone perhaps?" Rivera asked, bringing his visitor along.

The visitor shrugged.

"The ordnance must be the top of the line," he said. "But I should be able to get in close to the target. I intend to equip a small vehicle with a high-power explosive, park it, and wait for my target to be exposed on the street. Think of a tiny car. Easier to park and leave, don't you think, in the city? Rather than a larger one?" He didn't wait for an answer. "I want you to create a device for me that might pack into a shoe box and yet have a lethal range within fifty feet, say from a backseat or a trunk. Can you do that?"

"I can do that," Rivera said.

"I will need a dependable remote mechanism that will trigger the explosion and I would ask for the explosives to be of a powerful but common variety. Hence, more difficult to trace. I assume you can do that too."

"I can," Rivera said.

"I need it no later than one week from today."

"You will have it."

Ortega continued. "The important thing is the potency," he said. "It needs to be high quality so that any explosion is lethal to anyone within fifty feet. It does not have to be technically sophisticated, in fact I prefer it not to be. It just needs to be one hundred percent effective."

"I can create for you what you want," Rivera said.

"How much would your services cost?" Ortega asked.

"Five thousand dollars."

"How long would it take to deliver?" Ortega asked. "You can work in less than a week's time?"

A beat and Luis answered. He glanced at his watch. "Come back here four days from now, this exact time, and I'll have your device. It will be broken down and in a duffel bag. Reassembly would not be a problem, I would guess?"

"Not at all," Ortega said.

"I will give you instructions on how to prime the timer. We would probably use a cheap telephone. It's not difficult."

"I'm sure it's not," the visitor said. "So then? We have a deal?"

"We have a deal," Luis nodded.

Ortega reached to the wallet inside his suit jacket. He opened it and peeled out fifty one hundred dollar bills and laid them on Rivera's desk. Rivera gathered them up, but without his usual smile.

Rivera eyed him closely. Then he smirked. "And maybe even you should be careful of your thumbs and your fingers," Rivera suggested. "Have you ever planted a device before? You seem a bit like a fish out of the water, my friend. Are you sure you know what you're doing?"

Before Rivera could suggest that the visitor run along, the little man stiffened. He gathered himself to respond, turning on Luis, fixing him with a burning gaze.

"Do not take me lightly, Señor Rivera. Many people before you have made that mistake and many of them are dead. I know who you are, where you live, where your family is. I also know who your relatives are in Panama, where your father goes for coffee each day, where your mother chats with her sewing circle, where your nieces operate a bodega. You are going to provide me with services and goods here in New York, and you have been well compensated in cash. But you will never speak to anyone about this. Not one person. If you do, you will be murdered as quickly and methodically as a man steps on a spider. Further, your parents will be murdered in Panama, and your house here will burn to the ground with your family in it. Your nephews will be tortured and executed, and your young nieces will be sold in Asia as whores. If anything should happen to me during this assignment, such as if I am arrested, it will be taken as faith by the people who employ me that you called in your friends in the police department, the ones who normally protect you. In that case, the same horrible misfortunes will befall you and your family. Is all of this clear?"

Luis Rivera broke a sweat faster than he ever had in his life. "Perfectly," he said.

"Good," said the visitor. "Then we will proceed with business."

THIRTY-TWO

El Rincón Cubano was a small family restaurant, bustling with activity, on Xavier Street, not quite in Little Havana but on the periphery. There was an indoors and an outdoors. A cute girl in red shorts and a blue-and-white T-shirt, which bore the restaurant's name, greeted Alex with menus.

"I'm meeting a gentleman," Alex said, somewhat wishfully after her two earlier encounters that day. "I know him only from a photo. May I look around?"

The girl smiled and said that would be fine.

Working the front outdoor area, Alex took only a few seconds to spot a trim man of about six feet, slender and athletic, with dark hair. He wore a dark suit, with a pale blue regimental tie. Laura had shown Alex a picture of her boyfriend on the beach during a visit to New York.

No doubt about it: Richard McCarron. Her unofficial CIA contact.

Richard spotted her, and their eyes locked. He waved gently, then stood and beckoned. Alex smiled, went to his table, and slid into a seat.

"Alex, right?" he asked.

"That's me," she said.

"I'm Rick. Nice to meet you."

"Likewise. Laura has told me so much."

McCarron laughed. "Only the good stuff, I hope." He offered his hand. They shook.

"According to Laura, there's nothing but good," Alex replied.

"Laura lies," he said as they sat.

"I'm going to order food," he said. "Join me?"

"I'd be delighted," she said.

"Have a drink?"

"Just some bottled water would be fine. Sparkling, maybe."

"It can be done," McCarron said. It was the first time Alex had encountered that concept all day.

McCarron had a boyish face, though he must have been forty. His shoulders were broad and powerful. He wore a gold Movado watch with a leather band; no bracelet, no rings. Alex frequently noticed a man's hands if the man was attractive. They expressed so much. There was a beer parked in front of him.

Alex ordered the sparkling water and made some small talk. After the water appeared and the waiter vanished, McCarron finally got around to asking, "So? Why are you here in Miami, Alex, and what can I do for you?"

"Here's the crux of it," Alex said. "Laura probably mentioned, or you got this much from the files I sent you: I'm working a long case against a very bad couple who operated out of Panama and who have now fled to North Africa. The project is called Operation Párajo. I can share a verbal overview of the files with you."

"You can. But I took a quick read of what you sent me. Just to acquaint myself."

"Thanks."

"No problem. Run through it quickly in case I missed anything."

"They, the individuals in Panama, hired a gentleman to see if I could be taken off the assignment permanently. I got a message through my window one night in Manhattan when I came home."

"I heard about that," McCarron said softly, the din in the outdoor café — loud conversation and a zippy new track from the Spanish pop star Ana Torroja on the sound system — now proving exceptionally useful.

"The fellow who was buried the other day contacted me in New York in his final days. Gave me the impression that he had something to discuss before his departure. He implied that it touched upon my Panamanian operation. Of course, the departure the gentleman was looking forward to was to Europe, not to a cemetery here in Miami. Anyway, I want to know what he had for me. I think it was a list of names that I would deem useful. He alluded to such. Speaking to the widow might be useful."

"Okay. Got it," Rick said.

"And you know what it's like going through the 'proper' procedures," Alex said. "Takes you a month to find the right person to ask, another month to get all the proper authorizations, and that's if you're lucky. By the time you're in business, your bird has flown."

"Tell me about it," McCarron said.

"I get down here to Miami, and the next thing you know I'm at the funeral and I start picking up traces of a Santería connection in the case, complete with a woman named Ramona, who may or may not be some sort of spiritualist and may or may not be involved. Says she wants to talk to me but then pulls a vanishing act."

"Ramona, huh?"

"Yes. That mean anything?" Alex asked.

McCarron shook his head. "Nope. Just wanted to get the name right." He paused. "That narrows it down to about fifty thousand women here. It's a popular name in Miami, a little old-fashioned in the rest of the world."

"Yes, well," Alex continued, "I'm sure she's Latina of some sort."

"No doubt."

"And meanwhile," Alex continued, "it looks like I'm being stonewalled by the police and the local CIA case officer, that Dickey thug they sent over to the hotel. So I thought I'd see whether anything back-channel was possible. You know what I mean."

"I do," he said. "That's why we're taking our first meeting here and not at my office."

She laughed. She waited. "You're a quick study, aren't you?"

"I try to be," he said. "If nine years with the agency is a quick study."

The waiter reappeared. Alex ordered a fish salad, and Rick ordered man food, some sort of Cuban delivery system for ground beef and cheese with some *cerveza* to chase it down. The waiter departed.

"So?" Alex asked. "We can work together a little, if I need to call on you? I'm having a rotten day so far, so I'm hoping you'll say yes."

"Well, here's the thing," Rick said, dropping down an extra few decibels out of instinct. "Sharing information with someone in another agency who doesn't have full authorization could get someone written up. Or fired. Or sued. Or something. Or all of those things. So one has to be careful."

"Obviously," Alex said.

"Laura speaks well of you," Rick said.

"We're old friends. Spent a year at the same boarding school in New England. Same one Glenn Close went to. Michael Douglas too."

"Ah. That place. Of course. Incubator of presidents, if I recall."

"One of them," she said with a smile. "One that was tightly involved with Cuba."

"I'll be blunt. I can share things unofficially, bend the rules a little. You can come to my office, and I can open some computer files, show you what's around. I've got an upper-echelon security pass, middle level. I can see everything except the very top stuff."

"That's what Laura indicated," Alex said.

"But I have to cover my backside too. If it ever gets around that I let classified information loose, I better be ready to show that I had a darned good reason. I imagine it's that way for you too."

"It is," she said. "These days I'm a woman of very firm principles, but the foremost principle is that of flexibility."

"I like that," Rick said. He leaned back from the table. "Alex, I'm in a hard place on the Mejías case. The FBI has a file on this and so does the Miami Police department. But they're playing it very tight. I've been told by one source that someone high up at the agency has nailed a lid on it. That being the case, it's going to be very hard for you to poke around in it, but I may be able to do something."

"You've asked a few questions?" Alex asked.

"Yes. And I got my hand slapped, so to speak. When I tried to access higher than my security clearance, I got an inquiry generated by the deputy director of something-or-other asking why I wanted to know. I told them, 'Just curious.' I read the papers and like to know the rest of the story, same as any other earnest professional. Gave them a cyber shrug. I haven't heard back."

"But you could show me what you've seen?" she asked.

"If you come by my office. No one told me not to show you, so that means I can. You have a parallel security clearance in another agency, so that should make it hunky-dory, at least until we get caught. You'll need to sit quietly and read. Don't say anything, don't verbalize questions. Can do?"

"Yes," she said.

"Then that's what we'll do. Tomorrow."

"I appreciate it," Alex said. "Has anyone linked Laura to me, and, thus, me to you?"

"No," he laughed. "Hey, they're paranoid, but they don't catch everything."

"I know," she said.

"And don't rattle Lionel Dickey's cage again," he said. "If he doesn't see you again, he'll think you took a hike, which is good. Was he as nasty as I think he might have been?"

"Yes, he was."

"Must have been meal time. He was probably extra cranky," he added as half a joke.

"Should I change hotels? Make him think I left Miami?"

"Wouldn't be a bad idea," Rick said. "Then again, if you're only staying a few days, that will keep him happy too. Let him know you've left. He'll probably check. How long do you plan to be here?"

"I'm leaving Friday morning unless something big happens."

"You should be okay. Also, I'll give you my office cell phone number," he said. "Secure line, scrambled on a two-second delay. You know how it works." He wrote out the number. "Memorize it, please."

She looked at the number and worked it into her head. She handed it back. "Got it," she said.

"That fast?"

"Numbers don't lie."

"True enough," he said. "Do you have a city map of Miami?" he asked in a slightly louder voice.

"In the car," she said.

"I have a better one," he said. "Very up-to-date."

He reached to his inside jacket pocket and pulled out a city map, one of those tourist things. He slid it across the table to her, face up.

"Take it, don't open it here," he said softly. "You'll find a flash drive taped to the center of the map. Open the flash sometime next week or whenever you're back in New York. CIA has an interest in some tax records of a chap in New York. Last name of Frederickson. Jonas Frederickson. Jonas Frederickson and his wife, Jenny."

"Address?" Alex asked.

"Don't have one. That's part of the problem."

"Lives in the continental United States and, in our opinion, he has too many friends in some bad places. Has a little shrew of a wife fifteen years his junior. He's fifty. Her name is Jenny. From Jennifer. We're just starting to get a focus on him. They were involved in some dirty stuff in the Bahamas. Money, bribes, drugs, and maybe a murder. You'll see all the key information there: birthdays and Social Security numbers. The sets of numbers should give you a quick match even if the names are common. This is what I need in return. I'm wondering if you can maybe help me with something through Treasury. Think that's possible?"

"One hand washes the other?" she said.

"Pretty much," he said. "You help me with this one, and you're in line for some big-time favors out of my office, okay?"

"We won't even discuss the ethics, right?"

"What are ethics?" he laughed. "Listen, when those Navy Seals went into the bin Laden compound, we're they wondering about the ethics of putting some bullets into one of America's enemies. You didn't have problems with that, did you?"

"None," Alex said. "Mind if I run it past my boss?"

"Not at all," Rick said. "And if he asks, assuming your boss is a he, tell him I want them for 'inventory.' Follow me?"

Alex followed. Inventory meant for sale or exchange with a foreign intelligence service. The agency conducted a healthy commerce in such things, with always a few prize items stashed away for a rainy day. And according to Rick, it was raining. She knew Fin Cen policy on such things, and it wasn't much different from other security agencies. Sometimes the rules had to be bent a little, or even twisted, for the greater good.

She slid the map into her purse. "I'll take a look when I can," she said softly. "And I suspect I'll be able to pass it along."

"Perfect," he said. "There's even a long shot that this might have a distant impact on what you're working with."

"How's that?" she asked.

"The Bahamas. Banking. Your pals, the Dosis. They have a presence there, don't they?"

"They do."

"So maybe there's an odd dividend down the road," Rick said. "Bahamas. After all. Luck is the confluence of hard work and opportunity. Right?"

"Sure."

He laughed. "When do you want to come by my office?" he asked.

"Tomorrow morning. Depends on how things go."

"I'm in all week," he said. "Just give me a buzz an hour ahead of time, if you would."

"That works for me," she said. "Thanks."

Dinner arrived. Rick paid. Afterward, they walked outside

together. It was evening, but the heat was still oppressive, just not as oppressive.

"Where's your car?" Rick asked. Alex indicated a meter down the block. "I'll walk you," Rick said.

"Thanks."

"How do you like working in Miami?" Alex asked.

Rick McCarron snorted a small laugh. "It's a weird town. The young people, the old people, the Jews, the Latinos, the old-line WASPs." He shrugged. "You see all the CSI stuff on TV and the old *Miami Vice* stuff that you watched as a kid. Crockett and Stubbs, bikinis and coke. It's like that but it isn't. I grew up in Ohio, family moved here when I was in high school. So I feel a little like a stranger. They've got an NBA team called the Miami Heat. They should call it the Miami Humidity. Here's what it's like: Methodist minister gets called to a Miami Beach Nursing Home to perform a wedding. A nervous old guy meets him at the door. The minister sits down to counsel the old guy and starts asking the man questions. 'Do you love her?' the minister asks. The old man replies, 'I guess.' 'Is she a good Christian woman?' the minister asks next. 'I don't know for sure,' the old man answers. 'Does she have a lot of cash?' asks the minister. 'I doubt it,' says the old guy. 'Then why are you marrying her?' the minister asks. 'She can drive at night,' the old man says." Rick shrugged. "That's Miami. Laugh now, but someday you'll want your dinner at 4:00 p.m. too."

They were at her car.

"Thanks for the help," she said.

"I have a couple of other questions," Rick said. "A couple of final things. Is now a good time ...?"

Alex's eyes drifted over Rick's shoulder as he was in mid question. Her gaze smacked directly into a solitary figure standing maybe thirty feet down the pavement, a woman in a subdued blue dress, half obscured by a potted outdoor palm. The woman stared intently in Alex's direction.

Their eyes locked. It took a second, and then recognition kicked in as Rick continued to speak.

"Ramona!" Alex said softly.

"What?" Rick asked.

"That's her! That's Ramona!" Alex blurted.

Ramona turned abruptly and bolted. Alex grabbed Rick's hand. "Come on!" she said. They gave chase.

Ramona was like a deer, fast and elusive. She darted in and out among pedestrians and turned a corner down the block. Alex was about forty feet behind her and turned the corner in time to see Ramona skid slightly on the wet pavement.

Rick caught up to Alex. Alex thought Ramona was going to fall, but instead she bumped off a yellow cab that was pulling to the curb beneath the blue awning of a French restaurant.

"Ramona!" Alex shouted after her. "Stop! Talk to me."

The lady in blue, however, accelerated. She hit the end of the block and arrived at a small car. A Honda or Toyota, it looked like, maroon and new.

Now Alex slipped on the slick pavement, went down hard on one knee. Rick stopped and steadied her. He helped her up and Alex came up again fast. But up ahead, the fleeing woman grabbed the passenger door of the maroon car and jumped in.

Alex was still thirty feet away. There appeared to be a man at the wheel.

The car backed up sharply, noisily coming into contact with the front bumper of the car behind it, setting off the alarm. Then the vehicle turned sharply, wheels ripping into the asphalt, and pulled out with a screech of tires just as Alex arrived and slapped at the rear trunk.

"Ramona!" Alex screamed at her.

Traffic evaded the fleeing vehicle, a couple of angry car horns punctuating the escape. The car weaved and ran a red light. Alex could only stand and watch. She cursed. She hadn't even had the presence of mind to get the license number. Nor had Rick, who was next to Alex now but hadn't seen the rear of the escaping car.

Given to understatement, Rick said, "I'm not so sure she wants to talk to you."

"Then why was she here?" Alex asked. "Tell me that?"

He shrugged. "I wish I could," he said.

Alex stood by the empty parking place, snarling over the even greater emptiness that Ramona had left behind. Another vehicle stopped on the street and backed into the parking place.

"Come on," Rick said, placing a comforting hand on Alex's shoulder. "Let's get out of here."

They turned and walked back in the direction of the restaurant, only realizing when they arrived under the restaurant's canopy that the humidity had turned to warm drizzle. They were both quite wet. They went a few more paces in the drizzle and were at Alex's car.

"I was in the middle of a couple of other questions," Rick said. "Now that we're back out here under an open sky in God's great band of tropical humidity, let me try to throw them at you again."

"Sure."

"Fin Cen," he said. "I know what territory you guys work. Crimes of a financial nature. So I should think you might have access to IRS records, would I be correct about that?"

She smiled warily. "You might be," she allowed.

"Would you mind sharing with me the methods for accessing them?"

"The white methods or the black methods?"

"Any you'd care to share."

"For me to get a look at IRS records, I ask my boss, get approval from the powers that be, requisition the information, and wait. Or I can nestle a casual look into any ongoing case that I might be working on, Párajo, say, and run a quick glance and see what bubbles to the surface." She paused. "I assume this is vis-à-vis your new best friend, Frederickson."

"You assume right."

"I'll probably need to be back in New York to do it," she said. "I have a more secure portal at my office than on the laptop. The laptop leaves cyber fingerprints. Don't want that."

"No, we don't," he agreed.

"Thinking it through," she said, "I don't suppose it would be very difficult to work it into Operation Párajo. I could send half a dozen numbers to the IRS and ask if any of them clicked with funds issued by any Dosi company. The IRS won't check themselves. Too much trouble. They're mulish, but they're also lazy, some of them. They just send me the last three or five years of the investigated party's federal tax returns and say, 'Here. Don't waste our time. Have a look for yourself.'" She paused.

"I'll try to be back to you by Tuesday or Wednesday of next week," she said. "How's that?"

"Perfect. So one last thing. What kind of cell phone do you have?"

"What 'kind'? You mean, what brand?"

"I need to know exactly what you have," he said.

She pulled an Android out of her purse. She handed it to him.

"A Droid, huh?" he said. "Perfect."

He examined it, critically and carefully, even looking at the portals, batteries, and memory card as she unlocked her car door with a click of her key.

Then he handed it back.

"It meets your approval?" she asked, bemused.

"It more than meets it," Rick said. "Come by my office tomorrow for sure. We'll talk more."

"Should I bring my phone?"

"By all means. Security won't let you bring it in, but carry it anyway. You should always have it with you."

"See you then," she said.

Rick gave her an embrace and held the car door open for her. She slid into the driver's side. She watched him in her rearview mirror. Always a gentleman, he watched her pull out into traffic and disappear.

THIRTY-THREE

Alex took a detour on her way back to the Park Central, stopping again at the Botánica. This time the shop was locked and the grate was pulled. Alex stood for a few moments to see if Doña Elena or even the annoying and elusive Sister Ramona would materialize out of the mist and maybe read a tea leaf or two for her.

But no dice. No one appeared.

Alex went back to the car, did a U-turn, and left the neighborhood just as happy to have not made contact at this hour. She would try again, maybe against her better judgment. Or maybe she would just lie in wait and anticipate the moment that Ramona would reappear. Their meeting outside of El Rincón Cubano had not been a coincidence. Ramona had followed her: *stalked her.* Why?

Alex returned to the Park Central. Being in no mood to go back to her room, she walked out onto the downstairs terrace, where she took a table by herself. It afforded her a good view of the harbor and the ocean beyond. She spent a moment pondering about God and heaven and wondered if she was going in the opposite direction from either or both. She spent another moment wondering if she was a fool to worry about such things. Yet something within her demanded such inquiries.

She watched a trio of yachts exit the harbor and another couple of ships glide soundlessly into it. She wondered absently who these people were, what they did, where they were going, and what it would be like to be one of them, far away from the world of pursuing financial miscreants, poking into murders, exacting information swaps with people in other security bureaus, and rapping on ramshackle doorways to faded houses wondering if she was going to be met by a friendly quack priest-ess or, worse, a barrage of bullets through the woodwork.

She looked at the ocean beyond the harbor and the freight-ers that lay at anchor in the distance. They had come from all over the world and would head out to sea again. She wondered about the ocean of possibilities that lay before her, not just on this assignment but in life itself.

THIRTY-FOUR

The next day, Alex's meeting with Rick McCarron took place in a small conference room on the lucky thirteenth floor. A young female assistant led her in. There was an oblong table with six empty chairs. The walls were light blue with no windows. A series of prints hung on the wall, showing assorted embassies all over the world. In one corner was an American flag in a stand, lest anyone forget who signed the checks.

Alex sat at the table and waited. Two minutes later the door opened and Rick strode into the room. He wore a dark suit and had ID badges dangling in plastic holders across his chest.

He got right to it. "I might have something for you."

"I can use it," she answered.

"Ever heard of anything called 'Operation Gemini'?" he asked.

"I've heard of a Project Gemini," she said. "Wasn't that an early space program? Before my time a bit?"

"Yeah. Part of the race to the moon in the sixties," he said. He added with a wry smile, leaning back at his desk. "If you're willing to believe that man ever got to the moon."

"I don't argue with science," she said. "If God gave us a brain he must want us to use it."

"No, this is a different Gemini," Rick said. "Nothing to do with NASA, but everything to do with the agency. And it's not the sixties. It's the eighties. And it's Cuba."

Then it kicked in: Lionel Dickey's reference from the other afternoon.

"Ah," she said, "keep going. Our pal Lionel Dickey used that word in reference to a matter of mutual interest. Is that where we're going?"

"Probably," McCarron said softly. "I did a little referencing and cross-systems searching. It might touch on your guy Mejías. The time is right and so are some of the reference points. Dates. Information that he mentioned that he was part of. What was the code name that you said you knew him as?"

"Figaro."

"Anything in the files under that name has been deep-sixed. The only reports I can access are things on the fringe, and even those could disappear overnight or in the middle of a hazy afternoon. Sometimes the agency is lazy with files. Or just incompetent. I can access stuff under Gemini, but if I type *Figaro* into the computer, the system freezes me out."

"Typical," Alex said.

"Reports like that probably won't make much sense by themselves," Rick explained, continuing to speak softly. "But if you know some of the guidepost of the Figaro operation, or Gemini, then maybe a couple of scraps or hearsay will make some larger issues fall into place."

"So how can I see these files? Your screen?"

In an even lower voice, he said. "I'm trying to get overnight authorization," he said. "I'm not supposed to print anything out, but there's a way to do it. Don't ask and I won't tell, okay?"

"Okay," she said. "But where does that steer us?"

"Maybe nowhere," he said.

In the afternoon, Alex drove again to the Botánica. This time the place was open and busy. The old woman, Doña Elena, was behind the counter and looked up when Alex entered. She gave Alex a double take, recognized her, then threw Alex a smile and continued with customers.

Alex took the opportunity to explore more thoroughly than she had been able to on her previous visit. Today, a basement workshop was open. There was a small table with a red patterned tablecloth, candles, and four chairs. The chamber looked like a gypsy's parlor. At the table in the center of the space, four ladies were at work, dark skinned and wearing thin dresses from the Caribbean, chattering in what Alex recognized as Creole, a corrupted cousin of French, creating products — amulets, statuettes, and potions — presumably to be sold in the store.

A sign in Spanish said the room was used for communication with the spirits — the dead. Alex wanted to look more closely at their work, but the women at the table abruptly stopped talking and stopped working. All four stared at Alex as if she were intruding on some sacred or forbidden space.

Alex smiled back at them. *"Hola,"* she said.

They ignored her. Having overheard Creole, she switched into French, accompanying it with a smile.*"Bon après midi."*

Again, no one answered.

"What is this room for?" she asked in French.

Silence, then, *"On parle aux âmes perdus là-dedans,"* one of the Creole women replied. *"On parle aux morts."* One speaks to the lost souls there; one speaks to the dead.

"Je peux parler aussi?" Alex asked. Could she talk to the dead also?

Fearfully, the Creole lady shook her head to indicate no. It was not permitted, not for Alex.

"Mauvaise idée, madame," the woman warned. Bad idea.

"Pourquoi?" asked Alex. Why?

"Parce que le diable écoute aujourd'hui aussi." Because today the devil listens too.

Alex looked around. Suddenly the air felt thick, suffocating. She took another glance around the room. *"Qui parle aux morts?"* Alex asked. Who speaks to the dead?

The four women exchanged glances among themselves, as if it were a foolish question.

"Hermana Ramona," one of them answered.

"And where is Sister Ramona these days?" Alex asked. "I'd like to speak with her." In response, the women lowered their heads and worked silently.

"Okay," Alex said, signing off in three languages. "Bonne journée. *Que le vaya bien.*"

The women put their heads down and ignored her.

Back upstairs, Alex also discovered that the botánica had leased the second floor to an organization called the Pagan Center of South Florida, which proudly announced upcoming witchcraft rituals that would be overseen by a wiccan high priestess named Lady Rhea. Alex climbed to the second floor to have a look. A mischievous voice inside her wondered whether Lady Rhea and Sister Ramona were the same woman. Who knew in an establishment like this?

She fell into a conversation with an employee, Arturo Lopez, who said he had worked there since 2007. He described himself as "an underpaid therapist."

"The other day, this guy come in," Lopez said. "He asks me, 'Do you sell iron pots? Big ones?' 'Yes, we sell iron pots,' I answered. 'How big you need?' 'Big enough to fit a person?' he asks. This go on all the time," he said. "Who knows what's cooking these days, right?" He winked. "You like to cook, lady?"

"Yes, but I think I'll stick to casseroles."

"Wise," the man said.

A short plump man missing half his teeth approached Lopez and rescued Alex.

Alex bided her time. Eventually, when the customers in the store had thinned out, Alex again approached the old woman.

"Ramona, ella está aqui?" Alex asked. Is Ramona here?

"No, señorita."

"Did you give her my message?" Alex pressed.

"Sí, señorita."

"Will she be in tomorrow?"

"I don't think so, señorita. There are many problems." Over Doña Elena's shoulder an electric Creole god with a moving head and penlight eyes grinned like a gargoyle, as if enjoying the way the old lady strung Alex along. "Family problems." Her excuses came in a liturgical monotone, with an undercurrent of scorn.

Alex had had enough. She felt a flash of anger. Doña Elena turned away and prepared to walk away. Impulsively, Alex lunged across the counter and grabbed the old woman's wrist.

"Well, *señora*, I'll tell you what," Alex said, speaking in brisk Spanish. She was angry but courteous. "I'm having problems too. Big ones, okay? One problem is that I saw Ramona last night, and she ran from me, which I didn't appreciate. The other problem is that some enemies of mine are murdering people in this city. I don't want Ramona to be next, which might be why she doesn't want to be seen talking to me. So that's our problem. And Olodumare has been telling secrets recently. He indicates to me in no uncertain terms that you know where I can find Ramona and probably even the hombre who drove her getaway car last night. So why don't you share that with me before there are even worse problems?"

Doña Elena's eyes went dark and cold, as if they had gone into some deep freeze, ironic for Miami in the still-sweltering season. As for Ramona's whereabouts, she said as Alex released her wrist, she might know and she might not. It depended.

"On what?" Alex asked.

For the first time, the old woman spoke English. "If I mention an address, will you promise to not come back?" Doña Elena asked.

"You don't like me here?" Alex answered, also in English.

"You're bad for business."

"Then make sure I get a good solid address," Alex said, "and I won't need to come back."

"*¡Bueno!*" Doña Elena said. The old woman reached to a note pad. She wrote down something and handed it to Alex. "*Qué le vaya bien.*"

Alex took the paper and read an address. 165 South Arroyo. Another address, not exactly in Little Havana, but adjacent.

"*Su casa,*" the old woman said. Ramona's home address.

"*Gracias, señora,*" Alex said. "*El placer es todo mío.*" The pleasure was mine.

THIRTY-FIVE

Back at the hotel Alex plugged in her laptop again, trying to manage several aspects of the Dosi campaign almost by remote control.

Waiting in her secure email was another message from Rizzo in Rome. He had booked a flight to New York with his girlfriend, Mimi, and expected to arrive at Kennedy the following Tuesday. Writing in Italian, he said he also had another "observation" that he wished to share with her, but it was one that he wanted her to read and destroy immediately, secure line or not.

She took the hint. Alex fired back a message that reassured him that she hoped to be back in New York by his arrival but might possibly still be in Miami. She was also standing by, she said, even though it was near midnight in Rome.

She waited. Nothing. And all this time, the notion of Gemini was running wild through her head. "Gemini?" she asked herself. Alex tended to examine code names carefully. The more one examined them, she always felt, the more one found tiny fragments of clues. Of course, one could also misinterpret tiny clues and scramble them in the wrong direction.

Gemini. An astrological sign. In college, Alex had had a one-term roommate who had been heavily into astrology and was in the habit of going on and on about her favorite subject. The pre-Christian ancients believed in so-called "wisdoms." Gemini had always been considered a highly masculine sign, almost excessively so, Alex remembered, kicking over a mental wastebasket in her mind and rummaging through the contents.

Buzz phrases returned: The dominant Gemini characteristic was versatility. Gemini was further considered an "air" sign. The planet Mercury rules Gemini. People born when the Sun was in

Gemini were considered Gemini individuals. Attributes: intelligence, cleverness, wisdom, high education.

Then there's the Greek Gemini. She had studied classics at her hotshot boarding school. The Gemini were the twin brothers in Greek mythology, Castor and Pollux, the sons of Leda by Tyndareus and Zeus respectively. They were also the brothers of Helen of Troy and Clytemnestra. Involuntarily, her memory riffed: Helen who had caused the Trojan war, and Clytemnestra, who had murdered her husband, Agamemnon, commander of the Greek forces at Troy, to give his throne to her lover Aegisthus. At the school where she had gone, the classics were forcibly pounded into the student so thoroughly that there was no hope of ever forgetting them.

Gemini. The twins. Two for the price of one.

"Heck of a family," she remarked. Castor and Pollux. Leda who had a swan as a common-law husband, or at least a casual acquaintance. Ah, the Greeks. They all had crazy families, but Alex loved their culture, swagger, intelligence, and intensity.

Same as the Italians. And with that segue, she jumped back to her emails.

Her loyal and dependable amico, Gian Antonio Rizzo, had responded by saying that he would be delighted to assist her in any way while in the United States, if only to watch her back. He would be at her disposal for seven to ten days.

Rizzo was in a giddy but querulous mood, judging by his written message. He almost seemed a little "off," as if something weird was going on. Too much Chianti late in the day? Something more prosaic? Or something more ominous?

His message rambled on, although they often did, with a vent on whatever was on his mind. Often there was a veiled message to the discerning recipient. And Alex knew she was supposed to zap this one after she digested it.

Her brow furrowed. She read carefully. Line by cryptic line and then between the lines.

This time the riff was on the previous morning's traffic in

Rome, which he insisted was getting worse. The streets were overrun, he maintained, by squadrons of small cheap automobiles from India, made by the Tata conglomerate.

In his email, Rizzo complained:

> These little Tata motorized absurdities are spreading their terror and hydrocarbons all over the seven hills of this great city. These cars are itty-bitty and crumple like accordions. Just this morning I saw one squashed like a tin can on the Via Condetti, the shredded remains of its driver hanging out of the front window upside down, the top half of his skull down the block several meters, the rest of him having already oozed into the gutter. The good news is that he reduced, I suppose, his own carbon footprint by a hundred percent. The whole deplorable incident and the cleanup and paperwork surrounding the same quite upset my midmorning espresso, as you might expect. I do not know why any self-respecting Italian would want to drive a car designed by Hindus who believe in reincarnation.

Then his email went around the bend and came back:

> Indeed, on the subject of reincarnation, I must ask you, Carrissima Alexa, if you believe in such. I do not and assume you do not either. With that in mind, would you please be particularly careful. We had a conversation this past evening here with a gentleman—I use the term loosely—familiar with a certain financial enterprise. Word is that they have contracted with a veteran troubleshooter to contract work on a high-priority "signora" involved with enforcement, contract to be exe-

cuted at the soonest convenient moment. Does
this make sense?

    Il tuo caro consigliere.

She immediately sent back her response.

It does. I'll be careful. *Grazie mille.* LaDuca.

She zapped the message and closed out of secure email.

THIRTY-SIX

In the evening, she returned to her rental car and plugged in the GPS. This time, driving even farther off the beaten path, she found herself in a poor neighborhood, mostly Latino, with a couple of scary moonscape blocks, before she emerged into a lower-middle-class neighborhood where windows were barred, most houses were behind steel fences, and many lawns were uncut.

A foggy mist grew into a light rain. Alex used the windshield wipers on their lowest setting. She found the address, 165 South Arroyo, shortly after dark, as she had planned. She pulled to a halt in front of a small single-unit house on a tiny lot. The residence was pink, deco, and compact, with borderline maintenance in a borderline neighborhood. The lawn was unkempt and the lights were off. A glance at a mailbox revealed that no one had picked up anything for maybe a few days.

For several moments, Alex sat in her car, studying the street.

A teenage boy rode by on a bike. He stopped, dismounted, and pulled open a gate of a nearby house. He walked the bike inside and disappeared. Abruptly, three teenage girls walked by, in short shorts and T-shirts, oblivious to the rain, talking about boys. Their speech was rapid, their accents first-generation Cuban-American.

Alex's gaze continued to work the block. Several houses had fences that crawled with unruly shrubs. Some front gates appeared soft on their hinges. One hinge was broken. Most of the windows on the ground floors were lit, often behind grates and with curtains drawn. Alex scanned for hidden danger. She looked to see if anyone was watching her. She focused down the block. At the far corner, beneath a streetlamp, there was a husky man with two huge dogs. A watcher? She kept a close eye on him. Then he disappeared down an adjacent street.

Several minutes passed. The rain must have driven people inside. The street was empty. Alex scanned the second floors of the surrounding two-story homes. In one, high up, with no curtain, a couple looked to be arguing; in another the blue light from a television dominated; and in a third a man sat just inside the window frame and practiced a guitar. More time passed.

Then for some reason all of her professional thoughts crashed, and the image of Eric Robertson was in front of her. She wondered what it would be like to be involved with a man like that. To date him. To be married. To have a family and children, which was what she wanted someday — right?

She was deeply into this line of thought when there were two loud staccato raps on the passenger's side window. Alex nearly jumped out of her skin.

She whirled. A husky young man with a shaved head and a stubbly beard looked in at her. How had she missed him, how had she let him creep up on her? She couldn't understand. He could have blown a hole in her head with one easy shot.

It only confirmed that her nerves were shot, and so were her powers of attention and observation; she wasn't just slipping professionally, she was free-falling.

Her hand went to her gun and stayed there, poised.

"¡Hola!" he yelled.

"What?" she demanded. "¿Qué?"

"¿Qué sapa? ¿Qué dices?" he asked. "¿Estas disfrutando?" What's up? How are things going?

His accent was distinctly Mexican, not Cuban. Significant? She calculated quickly but couldn't get off zero. She tried to stay cool. She answered, "Todo tranqui'. Espero a una amiga." I'm fine. I'm waiting for a friend.

He grinned and made a forward and back stroking gesture at his mouth. She wasn't sure whether he wanted to bum a smoke or wished to peddle something that she certainly didn't want. She waved him away. She thought it was the latter, that he was selling, but it didn't matter. She wasn't interested and wasn't buying. Worse, she just wanted her palpitating heart to settle.

He continued to stand at her window and grin. She waved him away a second time, watching his hands, waiting for the appearance of a weapon, her own grip tight on her Glock, wondering when this situation was going to explode.

Then he persisted and confirmed his intentions. He was selling drugs.

"¿Quieres fumarte un pito?" he asked.

"No me gusta la hierba," she said, attempting to be polite but firm. *"No soy una fumerla."* I don't like grass. I'm not a smoker.

He laughed indulgently and drew back. *"Si tú lo dices, bonita fumanchera."* He stepped away from the car. To her relief, both his hands remained empty. She gave him a final wave and a grudging smile. Then, in an inspired moment, she reached for her cell phone and made a fake show of punching in a number.

The visitor thought better of what he was doing and moved along.

Her nerves settled. Somewhat. Her pulse still raced. The street settled again. Another ten minutes and mercifully no more movement.

She looked at the house that was supposed to be Ramona's. She saw no movement inside, not much of anything. Lights off, shades drawn.

Alex checked her weapon again. She returned it to its holster and then got out of the car. She went through a low gate in a chain-link fence and walked to the front door. Weeds growing on a flagstone path brushed against her exposed ankles. She could have done without this. What had once been a lawn had turned to tall grass. Within it was the rustle of rats. From it came the stench of stale water. Above it, mosquitoes swarmed.

She knocked at the door, keeping her other hand under her jacket on the back end of her Glock.

She knocked a second time. Did she hear something from

within or not? The door was wooden and flimsy. She moved to the side. Just in case. Training 101. Bullets coming through a door have a wicked tumble and do not do beneficial things to the internal organs. She broke an extra level of sweat. It was dark now, and she could see only from a streetlight a hundred feet away. Time to retreat.

Or was it? Against her better judgment, she tried the door-knob again. It felt as flimsy as the door. She squeezed it and turned it. She felt it stop and hold. Then there was a snap and the lock gave way. The door opened with a creak.

For a moment she stood perfectly still, unable to decide whether to move forward and enter the house or back. Her worst instincts took hold.

The question repeated itself. Forward or back? Go home or maybe move ahead and get killed. Sooner or later, she said to herself, one move would prove a little too aggressive, too asser-tive, too foolish.

Her thoughts and fears ran wild.

Where was God these days?

Would God protect her?

Might as well find out.

She gave the door another push.

THIRTY-SEVEN

She stepped into the small foyer as the floorboards creaked beneath her. A pungent herbal smell assaulted her nostrils, something not too distant from the Botánica, mixed with what she took to be either cleaning solvent or kerosene. Taking stock, she drew her gun and kept it low and close to her, pointing downward. She called out.

"¿Hola? ¿Ramona?"

No answer. She could offer as an excuse, if she ever had to offer one, that she had come calling in response to Ramona's invitation, then had stepped in out of concern since Ramona had gone missing. That argument got her two more steps forward inside the small house.

Then she passed a small Rubicon — no turning back now. Her eyes adjusted to the dim light, and she pushed the door closed. The lock clicked back into its fragile place. She knew that what she was doing was against every law and regulation.

There was a dim light on in the kitchen, and as she scanned she spotted another light upstairs. A hallway light, she guessed. There were also a pair of night-lights scattered, as if the resident here didn't care much for complete dark. Well, who could blame her? And Alex was thankful for such small favors of illumination.

As she stepped forward, the wood beneath her feet continued to groan. The place was like an oven. While the outside had cooled down to the eighties after the sunset, there was no such process in the house. The air was stale, fetid, and overheated. Her blouse was sticking to her ribs.

The floorboards were bare with the exception of a small carpet in the living room. Then Alex noted with distaste the original painting that adorned the floor and the walls and, when she lifted her gaze, the ceiling. There were endless patterns of flowers, insects, birds, snakes, and fish. There was no logic to them. There were fish on the ceiling and birds on the floor. The drawings were in bright hues, some in DayGlo, and in patterns that were twisted in more ways than one, perhaps to match the psyche of the artist.

Alex looked to her left. Through the kitchen door, she saw a cluttered counter and a pile of dirty dishes stacked high in the sink. A garbage pail overflowed.

Keeping her gun at her side, Alex moved through the living area. The place was creepy beyond words. The closer she came to the kitchen, the stronger the stench. Alex stealthily moved to the steps. Her Glock remained out and ready for business; she was the intruder. A voice within her started to scream. Leave now. Nothing good can happen here.

"¿Hola?" she called again. "Ramona? Anyone?"

No one on the first floor. She moved to a back door and undid the chain that held it. She opened it slightly and scanned the small yard. The door offered a potential escape if things went the wrong way. A scraggly cat watched her from the top of a fence.

Alex came back to the living room. She moved halfway up the steps, then to the top of the steps. There was a large open landing, plus three bedrooms and a bathroom.

She took inventory again. The second floor was even hotter than the first. Sweat was pouring now. It was on her face, her arms, her legs, her ribs, her neck. Okay, she told herself, a few more minutes then out, before the roof caves in, literally or figuratively.

She glanced into what appeared to be the master bedroom, which was fed from the outside with light from a streetlamp. It was a shambles, clothing all over, an unmade bed, dresser drawers open, the floor cluttered.

Sign of a struggle? Her training taught her to look. She didn't see one. No blood. Alex was happy for what she didn't see.

She went to the other chambers and peered in. One room seemed to be a stock-and-storage room for items from the

Botánica. The third room was storage also, personal, much in disarray also, as if items like clothes and suitcases and extra chairs had been thrown into it at random.

She made a decision. She went back to the master bedroom. In the back of her mind, she knew what she feared most: finding a body.

Well, if you don't want to find a body, maybe you should leave, said another voice inside her. The same voice that had warned her not to enter? Or was this something different, one of Sister Ramona's spirits talking to her?

Alex shook her head to dismiss that idea. What was going on? Even the narrative of her own thoughts was starting to march in strange directions.

She stood at the door to the bedroom. The room had an odd smell, female fragrances, combined with the heat and the odors from downstairs. It was repugnant. Alex wondered how people lived like this. There was a single air conditioner balanced in an uneven window. A clock radio printed out the time, wrong by twenty minutes by Alex's calculations.

Alex stepped cautiously into the bedroom. She lowered her gun but kept it against her skirt, right side. She looked across the room, letting her eyes adjust. A pile of skirts and dresses lay on the floor. A whole wardrobe of lightweight cottons. Undergarments and shoes were equally scattered. There was also a desk, the top of which was cluttered in the same manner as the room.

Alex stepped to the bathroom. Nothing strange. More mess. The sink dripped. So did the shower. A shower curtain was torn and towels were on the floor. Alex stepped out and used the toe of her shoe to open the only closet in the room, half fearing that a body would roll out. Hangers were full and jammed together. The floor was cluttered with shoes and skirts that had fallen.

No body, though. Thank you, God, for the small blessings.

Then Alex heard something.

She froze. Inside her chest, it felt as if a swarm of wasps had been released. A sickening truth struck her hard: not only did she have no right to be here but she was trapped. She turned her head slightly and saw that a light had gone on downstairs. This was followed almost immediately by a conversation.

Spanish. Two male voices. Husky, muffled, and angry. Alex could make nothing of the conversation, only that two men were engaged in an intense dialogue.

Seconds later, heavy footsteps crossed the groaning floor-boards — a man's footsteps — and hit the stairs hard. They ascended in a rush.

Alex held her weapon straight up and took the only cover available. She went into the closet and pulled the door. It jammed. It closed but not completely; it was caught on clothing that lay on the floor. By now the wasps had buzzed away, and what she was feeling in her chest was a jackhammer that had replaced her heart. Her head throbbed, sweat was rippling all over her body in torrents now, and she was so scared that her vision blurred through the single narrow two-inch crack between the closet door and its frame.

Then it got worse.

A huge man lurched into the open doorway. He was at least six-feet three-inches tall, unshaven, and stout. His weight must have hovered around three hundred. He had a massive Latino face, dark circles under the eyes, and a double chin. He wore dark denim shorts that fell to mid-calf, bulky, loose, tent-like, and hip-hop style. His huge belly filled a black T-shirt. Dark socks and green sneakers rounded out his fashion statement.

On his left forearm was a long deep scar, and on his left hip he had a gun. Cop? No way, Alex figured. No visible badge, anyway. He threw the bedroom light on and stood for a minute as Alex's heart raced ever faster. He looked like a gangbanger, a really nasty one.

She got a good look from maybe twelve feet away, a very good look. Her first impression was that she had never seen him before. Her first fear was that he knew she was there. There was no way she could reveal herself or explain herself. She had entered illegally and she knew it. Careers ended this way and, worse, so did lives.

Alex was afraid to move, even to breathe. It was dusty and she feared she would sneeze. She held her gun hand near her face and brushed her nose, suppressing the sneeze impulse. The man didn't move. Then he looked her way and came into the room, as if suspicious about the possible presence of an intruder.

The old words came back. They had worked before.

Oh, please, oh, please, dear Lord, deliver me from this . . .

How, she wondered, had she been stupid enough to come to this address alone? How had she dared to come into this building without a backup on the street?

Never again!

The heavyset man swelled into her view, out of it and back in it again. He circled the room and once, for one unbearable moment, stood directly in front of the closet, examining the area. He was so close that Alex could feel the heat of his sweating body and the cologne that he must have bathed in. His hand landed on the closet door and Alex knew there was little chance that she'd be able to fight her way past him.

Her only option might be to freeze him at gunpoint and flee. Then again, had he figured out that she was there?

She waited to make the move she didn't want to make. But he turned and lurched away from the door. He seemed to be look-ing for something but wasn't interested in the closet. Not yet. He went to the dresser, pulled the drawers all the way out, examined the contents, and emptied them on the floor. He did this until the dresser was empty.

Then he kicked the drawers away from his path and moved to the desk. Watching him carefully and now having seen him up close, Alex thought he was older than she had first thought. She put him down as maybe fifty, maybe a nickel past that. He had the shape and movements of a stout middle-aged man combined with the menace of a much younger one.

She continued to watch.

He looked angrily at the desktop and made a similar search, discarding items onto the floor as he rejected them. Then he hunkered down onto the desk chair and sat. He started going through the drawers. Still Alex watched, barely breathing, sweat rippling. In a cramped position, she was aware of the sweat all over her legs as her thighs pressed tightly together.

The visitor's attention was now fixed. He had found a trio of cigar boxes in a side bottom drawer of the desk. He was examining the contents. Alex could see him from a three-quarters angle, and she tried to read the expression on his face. The expression suggested that he had found what he wanted.

One by one, he went through the three boxes. He swept everything else off the desktop and piled them one by one. Alex couldn't see what was in the boxes, but it looked like a series of documents: papers, small notebooks, possibly checkbooks, and maybe even a passport or two.

Alex couldn't tell exactly. The contents didn't appear to be cash and didn't look like a gun or any sort of hardware or software. Paper documents, Alex concluded. And they sure were of interest to someone.

Several minutes passed as he riffled through the contents. Then, happy with what he had, he pushed the documents back in the boxes, bunched the boxes in a stack under his arm, turned the light off, and walked from the room.

Alex heard him trudge down the steps. She waited. She heard another distant conversation in Spanish. The conversation sounded congratulatory. She couldn't make out what they were saying, but she was certain there were only two voices. That didn't preclude other presences, however, or backups waiting outside.

Alex remained as motionless as possible, not wanting to alert anyone with a creaking floorboard. Within another minute, however, she heard the front door slam. The house was quiet again.

As best as she could, she exhaled a long sigh. Sweat was still pouring. She cocked her head to be sure that no one downstairs had stayed behind.

More minutes dragged by. Finally, she emerged, every article she wore wet from perspiration. Gingerly, she moved to the front of the room to see if any clue had been left as to what had been taken. She didn't see any. The light was poor. She didn't want to turn a light on that might attract attention. She would love to have tossed the room entirely, to give it a complete search. But that was impossible. She reasoned it would be better to get out before she got cornered again. She reminded herself that she was there illegally.

Gradually, she made her way from the room. She emerged on the landing, gun still ready. No opposition. She took the stairs down. The house was empty again. They had turned the lights off before leaving. Her nerves were starting to settle.

She stood in the living room and drew a long breath. She had never been so anxious to get out of a building in her life. Outside, beyond the front window, the street was shady. An occasional car passed. Nonetheless, she thought better of the front door.

She went to the back door. Using a paper towel to avoid finger-prints, she opened the back door. There was a low fence beyond and beyond that an alley. She went outside and found herself alone. She climbed over the fence quickly and saw that the alley, which was mostly backyards and garage entrances, accessed a side street in two directions.

She put her gun away and followed the alley as quickly as possible. There was a slight breeze. The fog had thinned and the rain had ceased. An early moon shone through a light mist. It consoled her. She found the side street, turned the corner, and walked at a normal pace, careful to survey the street in all direc-tions, her weapon hand not far from her Glock.

She spotted her car, unlocked it with the remote, and went to it at a quick pace. She jumped in, locked the doors, and turned the key.

The engine sprang to life. Heaving a massive sigh, which turned into a full body shudder, she tried to expel as much fear from her wet body as possible.

"Never again," she muttered, almost angry with herself. "Absolutely positively without exception never again!"

She gunned the engine, her fear morphing into anger, cut a three-point turn, and turned toward the luxury and safety of the Park Central Hotel as quickly as possible.

Later that evening, while doing laps to unwind in the hotel pool, she came to a second decision as well. Her rendezvous with Eric on Saturday was a nonstarter. How was she ever going to get out of Miami with so much unfinished business?

Where was Ramona? How would Alex find her?

Alex would phone her boss tomorrow and give him an update, she decided. Hopefully, he would be okay with her staying through the weekend. Then she would phone Eric and cancel. So much for that. So much for a fantasy future. She cursed her job and her life. Well, it had never been real anyway. Just a nice idea that she had played around with.

THIRTY-EIGHT

That next morning in Queens, Luis Rivera walked back to his car and pulled out of his garage. He reverted to his knowledge of the northeastern United States and where he could acquire run-of-the-mill explosives without arousing suspicion. He drove across the Tri-Borough Bridge, Upper Manhattan, and the Bronx until he crossed the George Washington Bridge into New Jersey. Then he picked up Interstate 80 West, followed it till he reached the Delaware Water Gap, and entered Pennsylvania.

A few exits later, he followed a secondary road south and eventually came to a heavily forested area that was used primarily for deer and turkey hunting in the autumn. Years earlier, he had been trained at the US Army base at Indian Town Gap, and it was here in these woods that soldiers came to hunt during the deer season. The memory of hunting with friends calmed him and steadied him, but he was also under no illusion. There were people and powers in Panama that were not to be challenged or questioned. His visitor, Ortega, was such a man. The sooner he had satisfied Ortega and was rid of him the better. He tried to tell himself that sometimes a man had to do distasteful things just to get by. This was true, but it did little to calm Luis this morning.

Morning turned to early afternoon.

Luis continued to drive until he reached a sparsely traveled two-lane highway, which wound by the rock-strewn rivers and jagged hills of northeastern Pennsylvania west of Scranton. When he reached an isolated bend in the highway, he pulled over, waited a moment or two, then left the road completely. On a remote road, concealed by trees, Luis placed a stolen set of license plates on his car. Then he continued until he reached a region of the Allegheny Mountains laced with quarries, forestry offices, and coal mines. He easily found an establishment that sold dynamite. Pennsylvania placed no special regulations upon its use.

The firm that Luis visited was a supply depot located in a single building off the interstate. The clerk was a grizzled, surly old Pole named Sawatski who owned a small hardware store bearing the same name. Sawatski engaged in no unnecessary conversation. Luis attempted conversation, mentioning that he had a number of tree stumps, boulders, and collapsing buildings to clear from his land. Easier to blow them up than to dig them up. He needed five pounds of the most powerful stuff on sale.

Sawatski complied wordlessly. Luis also purchased fuses and detonators, including remotes. Then Luis inquired as to the availability of nitric and sulfuric acids. Sawatski raised his eyes. "Would you be wanting glycerin next?" the clerk asked.

"Sure do," Luis answered.

"I'll getcha some," Sawatski answered, recognizing full well the three components of nitroglycerin.

Half an hour later, Luis placed his carefully separated acquisitions in the trunk of his car. Retracing his route, he drove back toward New York City. He found the same isolated road where he had switched license plates early and returned the proper ones to their place. With pliers, he ripped the stolen plates in half and dropped them in different locations of the Delaware River when he crossed it.

He breathed easier. This part of his mission was finished. But he would not rest comfortably, he knew, until this Ortega pest was out of his hair completely. Dealing with an emissary of the powerful Dosi clan, as he knew he was, a man could never be too careful. They'd kill you as readily as they'd look at you. He would make it a point to carry a gun for the foreseeable future. A funny feeling was sneaking up on him, and he recognized it as fear.

THIRTY-NINE

Alex went by Miami Homicide again early Thursday afternoon. If she thought her previous reception had been chilly, this time it was wintery. She was kept waiting for a half an hour before catching Lieutenant Woodbine emerging from his office with an entourage around him. On one hand, she recognized he was overworked. On the other hand, she understood that he was by nature foul tempered and uncooperative.

She fell into stride beside him. "Lieutenant?" she asked.

He shot her a look and went on autopilot. "What is it you don't understand?" he asked. "I don't help other agencies. I got nothing for you, and your job is your own problem."

She eased off her pursuit and let him swagger down the hall with his acolytes. Twenty minutes later, she was back in her car.

Her next stop was Rick McCarron's office, which was on the twelfth floor and had a view of Miami Beach. Much nicer than the conference room where she and Rick had met before. Rick received her politely. For a moment Alex stood at the window and admired the view. She settled into a leather chair, and McCarron closed the door. "What's up?" he asked.

"I want to tell you about something that happened last night," she said.

"Care for some music?" he asked.

"Sure," she said.

Rick hit his computer keyboard and came up with streaming pop rock from a radio station in Mexico City. He turned it up to a few decibels above their voices. Under it, Alex recounted the events of the previous evening: illegal breaking and entering, hiding in the closet, and the brush with a fat thug near enough to sniff his overpriced cologne.

"Wow," Rick McCarron said. "You were lucky."

"I know. I made a major mistake. I got away with it."

"Understatement of the year," he said.

"And the man you saw in Ramona's bedroom?" Rick asked, leaning back in his desk chair.

"A complete blank," Alex said. "If I've ever seen him before, I don't remember it."

"The Mejías funeral maybe?" Rick asked.

"I thought of that," she said. "I don't remember him, but he could have been there. I'm going to see if I can access some photos. See if I can spot him. If I can, I'll see if I can get an ID."

"You going back to Woodbine?" he asked.

"Just did," she said. "He's worse than useless."

"Knowing who the man was at South Arroyo might help explain why he was there. And what he was looking for," Rick said.

Alex nodded.

"Why didn't you ask me to back you up?" he asked. "You went from here to there, pretty much. I would have gone with you, watched the street for you."

She sighed. "I didn't want to ask," she said. "You don't have any business over there either."

He rolled his eyes. "I could come along as a friend," he said. "No one's going to get on my case for keeping an eye out for a friend. Promise you'll ask next time if something similar arises."

"Okay. I will," she said.

"Promise?"

"It's a promise," she said. "But I can also tell you that if I'm back in Miami in the next two weeks I'm going to have an associate with me."

"Do tell."

"His name is Gian Antonio Rizzo. He's worked in security in Italy. I've worked cases with him."

"He's vetted here?"

"More than vetted," Alex said. "I believe you and he are on different ends of the same payroll."

"I get it," Rick said.

"We worked together in Spain and Italy. He went to Federov's funeral with me in Switzerland. I trust him."

"I look forward to meeting him," Rick said.

"Only if I'm back in Miami," she said.

"You'll be back," he said. "I'm sure of that."

"Why?"

"Operation Gemini," he said in further lowered tones. "You're going to find it interesting."

"For that to happen," she said, "I'd have to have access to the file, wouldn't I?"

"Correct," he said.

He pulled a small envelope from his inside pocket. He opened it and poured into his palm a miniature memory card. It was small and rectangular, about a quarter the size of a dime. He reached out and transferred it into her hand.

"When they give you your phone back out there," he said, nodding in the direction of agency security, "substitute this for the memory card in your Droid. Get the idea?"

He reached into a side drawer again and held up a small digital Nikon. She got the idea very well. He had photographed documents for her.

"I'll do that," she said.

"Don't forget the favor for me."

"I'll try to have something for you by the beginning of next week," Alex answered.

She dropped the tiny card into the change compartment of her wallet and smuggled it out of the CIA offices with little effort.

Alex picked up her Glock and her cell phone at the security desk as she left. She went back to her car, drove several blocks, and found a parking place. She was feeling eyes on her again; maybe it was paranoia, but she felt as if she was being stalked. She watched her rearview mirror. Another car had stopped a few lengths behind her and double parked. But no one got out.

She kept her own engine running, and then, when traffic was aligned perfectly, she shot out of her parking place and drove several more blocks. The double parker never moved. She found another parking slot on a side street and slid into it. This time, she was certain her back was clean.

She sat in her car and fiddled with her phone. Breaking it open, she removed its memory card. She replaced it with the new card. The phone turned into a tiny electronic reader. There in miniscule print, too small for the naked eye, were the bootlegged results of Rick's efforts: CIA files on Operation Gemini. No such thing as information that can't be stolen, she remarked to herself. A modern truth: there was not a cyber document anywhere that couldn't be hacked if someone wanted to do it. This was a small example.

She knew exactly what he had done. He had called up the Gemini document for a one-time viewing by his eyes only, something that would remain on record but probably raise no questions. If he had downloaded it or printed it out, he would have left a record and later someone might raise the question of whom the information had been shared with. But instead, she guessed, he had used the camera to painstakingly photograph every page of the document. Riffling through it quickly with a few clicks of her thumb, she judged it to be about sixty pages, maybe fifteen thousand words.

Operation Gemini.

Okay, what was contained here? How had Rick correlated it to her Cuban connection or the Dosi family? Well, she would soon find out, same as she would phone her boss soon to tell him she was staying through the weekend, and then make another call to cancel out with Eric on Saturday.

She pulled the new memory card out of her phone and put it back in her change purse. She felt exhilarated but still far from where she wanted to be.

FORTY

On that same Thursday, Manuel Ortega, the Panamanian, took the subway to Atlantic Avenue in Brooklyn where he paid a visit to the least scrupulous dealership in the neighborhood, Armen's A-OK Used Cars and Motorcycles. There, he prowled though an area with second- and third-hand motorcycles, battered Indians, Kawasakis, Vespas, and Hondas. A trusted associate had already made a call there for him and had spoken to Armen himself.

He wandered from bike to bike until a heavy, bearded man in a Harley T-shirt appeared.

"Hey," the salesman said.

"Hey," Ortega answered.

"I'm Tomás. What can I help you with?"

"I need something cheap. Not gonna ride it much. Just around my neighborhood."

"Performance doesn't matter? You're not looking for a crotch rocket, huh?"

"Nope."

"Gonna be riding in traffic? Long distance?"

"Just need something to get me from one place to another. Short haul, but need decent cargo bins."

"What do you want to spend?"

Ortega shrugged. "A thousand dollars. Got anything for that?"

The dealer made a disdainful sound. "You ain't gonna get much."

"I don't need much," Ortega said, then added, "Did Armen say I'd be coming by? I'm Cirillo from Panama City."

"Ah," Tomás said. "Sure, buddy." Tomás's eyes gleamed with

amusement. He looked his visitor up and down. "Midnight rides, huh?" he said.

"Of a sort."

"Follow me."

Tomás led the visitor through a scruffy shop with a dirty floor and posters on the wall. There was a manager at a steel desk reading a tabloid newspaper and a girl behind plate glass taking telephone calls and presiding over several bookcases crammed with files. There was noise from a back area, which looked like a repair shop, pneumatic drills alternating with hammering above the din of a small-time Spanish-language radio station.

Tomás passed through with his visitor without acknowledging anyone. He led Ortega through a rear door, out to a back lot enclosed by chain-link fencing with concertina wire across the top. A huge dog on a chain stood up when Tomás appeared. On the other side of the fence was an alley pockmarked with potholes and littered with debris.

A pair of old Hondas were parked near a dumpster. Tomás led Ortega to them and said, almost proudly, "One of these might work for you."

One was red, the other a pale green, both rusted, with worn seats and handle bars. They had many dents, and their odometers bore numbers that were eyepoppers. Ortega spent several minutes evaluating. He keyed the ignition and drove each in a small arc within the pen behind the dealership. Each had a New Jersey license plate with a current, if not fresh, sticker.

The second vehicle, the green one, had a better feel to Ortega. The color pleased Ortega because green was less conspicuous in traffic or in a parking lot. Much of the success of his plan depended on blending in unnoticed.

"Can you open the gates? I want to try this one in the alley," he requested.

"Sure," Tomás said.

Tomás unlocked the chained gate and pushed it open, not

completely but enough to allow the rider and bike to pass. Ortega sat on the old Honda, revved it, and guided it through the gate.

"Have a nice ride," Tomás said, almost as a blessing.

Tomás leaned on the fence and watched as his customer drove up and down the alley several minutes at various speeds, testing the acceleration and the brakes, finally stopping and wheeling the vehicle back into the yard.

"What do you think?" Tomás asked. "Good?"

"Registration?" Ortega asked.

"Valid as a temporary for twenty-one days. You'll be okay if you're stopped. Registered to an empty building in Jersey City."

"VIN number?"

Tomás coughed. "It's clean."

"Clean how?"

"Copied from another bike that took part in a liquor store stickup and got dropped in the river. That's how clean."

Ortega nodded. He opened the boot area of the motorcycle and nodded. There was rust in it, but it was located on the rear of the vehicle and mounted high. It was boxy but had adequate capacity for what he needed.

"How much?" Ortega asked.

"A thousand flat," Tomás said. "And the registration ... no extra charge. It'll take about a half an hour. We got helmets too. Better take one. You don't want to get stopped. Then you can roll."

"Let's do it," said the Panamanian.

They went back into the sparkling showroom. Tomás passed his customer along to the man at the desk, who, it turned out, was Armen, the shop owner. Armen, who knew how to guide these things to a conclusion, handled the paperwork and received the thousand dollars in cash. He took a look at Ortega's Mississippi driver's license and, intentionally, neglected to check it with New York State Motor Vehicles.

"Their phones are always busy this time of day," he said with a straight face. "What's the use? I know your license is good."

"Sure," said Ortega.

Armen, never acknowledging that a prearranged fix was in, signed the bill of sale. Ortega signed the temporary registration.

"Want to leave through the front or the back?" Armen asked.

"The back," Ortega answered.

"Happy motoring," Armen said. "Pick out a helmet on your way."

"Yeah. Thanks."

From a closet, Ortega found a used helmet that fit. He carried it out back and then pulled it on as Tomás slid the back gate open again.

No one said anything further as Ortega slipped out of the dealership, into the alley, and out into the New York evening.

FORTY-ONE

In her room at the Park Central, standing at her window and overlooking the Atlantic Ocean, Alex spoke into her cell phone and asked Andrew De Salvo in New York if she could stay in Miami through the weekend and into the following week.

"Ha! No way!" Andrew De Salvo said, reacting immediately. "Not a chance!"

"What?" Alex asked, stunned.

"Your hearing is good, Alex. You understood the first time. I want you out of America's Medicaid Mecca for a couple of days. You can go back next week after you've caught up on things on this end."

"Why?"

"Why what?"

"Why can't I stay?"

"First, I've been listening to you for five minutes and reading your emails all week. You've got nothing imminent in Miami; you're chasing down a fortune-teller who doesn't want to be caught; your questionable Italian pals from Rome are about to arrive in New York; we're hearing rumors that the Dosis have another bullet with your name on it; and you've hit that 'walkaway' moment. Do I have to run you through the crying-into-the-laptop-left-standing-after-the-storm speech again?"

"No."

"So get your butt on a plane tomorrow."

"Look, Andy —"

"Aaaah, enough! You don't argue with people named Andy, all right? Prince Andrew. Andrew Carnegie. Saint Andrew. Amos and Andy. If you don't mind my asking, what's on your personal calendar this weekend? Anything?"

For a moment it slipped her mind. Then she recalled. "An acquaintance asked me to brunch tomorrow. I was just about to call and cancel."

"Acquaintance?" her boss said. "That's rather cryptic. None of my business, but is this something that you'd just as well avoid? Not anything that could present a danger, is it?"

"A fellow I met," she said.

"Ah. Forgive me for prowling."

"You're not."

"Romantic?"

"No!" she answered quickly. "And I doubt that it will be." On her end of the line, she paused, choosing words carefully. "An interesting guy, a neighbor in my building."

"I see," he said. "Well, it always starts with lunch, doesn't it? Or at least that's what I hear these days. I haven't been out there in the social swirl for thirty-eight years, so what would I know? I'm not sure I even remember how babies get made."

"It sometimes starts with lunch," Alex said, "and by three in the afternoon both lunch and the 'something' are over. So it should be pleasant, if he even remembers that he made the engagement, and I doubt much will come of it."

"Well, by all means, go," Andrew De Salvo said. "Order the most expensive thing on the menu if you think the chap has a credit card that works. What's he do for a living?"

"He's an actor."

"Be prepared to pay for both of you."

"A successful actor."

"Reassure me. Name something that I've heard of that he's been in."

"*South Pacific* on Broadway. Right now."

"Please don't wreck this by telling me you're dating a chorus boy."

"He's one of the leads."

"I saw the show two weeks ago."

"Eric Robertson."

There was a pause as De Salvo dropped his phone and picked it up. "Eric Robertson has invited you to brunch?"

"Yes, and please don't mention it around the office, okay? The fact is, I was about to call him and cancel."

"Do that and I'll fire you! You need the socialization. That's my point."

She sighed.

"I want a verbal report on Mr. Robertson at 9:00 a.m. on Monday," De Salvo said. "Do a Siskel and Ebert: thumbs up, thumbs down. But go, and report back."

"But — "

"End of discussion. Call the airline and book your flight. It's the weekend. Drop by the office late tomorrow if you get in on time. Aside from that, I'll see you when I see you."

He clicked off. When she got past her astonishment, she called the airline and booked the flight.

Early that evening, Alex drove back to South Arroyo. This time she picked up a protected parking place down the block, watched the location, but went nowhere near it. Once a woman on foot stopped in front of the house and seemed to be studying it for some reason. But the passer-by made no approach to it, then turned and went on her way. Alex maintained her surveillance for close to an hour.

She wasn't even sure what she would do if she saw activity, though if Ramona appeared, Alex knew she would accost her and demand a reckoning. But that did not happen.

Later, back at the Park Central, she spent ninety minutes on the software package that Rick had provided. She managed to crack it. Then downloaded the document to regulation size and fed it into her laptop. What resulted were a series of high intensity photographs of a CIA document on Operation Gemini.

Alex worked to scan it further and translate it into a readable document. After another hour, she had what she wanted.

She was also exhausted, more mentally than physically. So she set the document up for in-flight reading for the next morning. She reviewed her email, found nothing more, and left her laptop up and running while she went to the outdoor pool for a late swim at 10:30. She needed the exercise and release.

During the swim, she thought about Eric Robertson and their lunch still scheduled for Saturday. She had heard stories about actors. She wondered if he would remember or even show up.

As she swam, she figured the socializing would be good for getting her away from her work. De Salvo was right about that much.

Walkaway time. Last woman left standing after the storm.

Andy had a way of expressing things.

So she planned on showing up at Giacomini's and hoped Eric would too. If nothing else, it would be amusing to recount to Laura or to look back on as an odd event after she reached retirement, if she was lucky enough to live that long.

She swam twenty laps.

Returning to her room, she made sure she had saved the new Gemini document, and popped half an Ambien. No return calls from Ramona, she noted, checking her phone a final time. No surprise there. She began to conclude that the woman was a crank, as flaky as her religion, maybe involved in some petty scams and the jowly visitor to her bedroom had more to do with the demimonde of petty crime in Miami than with the Dosis, Mejías, or, Heaven knew, eternal salvation via the baksheesh-seeking Olodumare.

She showered and slept. The next morning, she departed for the airport by 7:15, concluding her second visit to Miami in two weeks and not certain whether she would make a third.

FORTY-TWO

After boarding at 9:45 a.m., Alex settled into her usual window seat in business class, waited for the aircraft to hit its cruising speed, then fired up her laptop. Within minutes, she had accessed the opening page of the document she had gotten from Rick McCarron.

"Operation Gemini," it read. "Results of Special Mission in Cuba."

Part of the cover was given to dire warnings over what might happen to the unauthorized reader. Alex quickly clicked past those details and was soon ensnared in the official summary of an operation that had begun in 1983 with a chance encounter between a CIA operative, called only "Tito," traveling under diplomatic cover in Buenos Aires and, the other key player, a Cuban government employee whom he had first run into at an airport in Argentina, after a trade show of home appliances.

The story was riveting. Tito was the leading player in the drama, with an undercover source in Havana named Gemini as the supporting player. Or maybe, Alex decided as she got deeper into the file, it was the other way around.

In any case, the file sought to recount the facts as recounted by the deputy director of the CIA himself. The D/CIA's signature was embedded on page 2. Rick had scored some high-altitude stuff, indeed.

Tito, the file stated, was a Cuban exile who had come to the United States as a child. His father was Cuban, but his mother was Costa Rican, with legal residency in Mexico. The files contained only the thinnest account of Tito's parents managing to get into the United States in the early sixties. That or the official events were too untidy and not suitable to be included in this file, Tito being a leading player and on the side of godliness and righteousness.

Suffice it to say that Tito had managed to go through high school in the US, then to Florida State University. He went into banking security after he graduated, Alex noted with a laugh since she had done the same. Then he had gone into private business and took a few freelance assignments for the CIA in Florida.

His assignments were nothing special, but he'd obviously been cleared for access due to family connections. Tito listened in on telephone conversations, gave running bilingual translations, and interpreted documents.

Again, this was all standard fare for a young man in his twenties with a penchant for making official mischief. But Tito got off on it and felt he was accomplishing two missions. First, he was lashing back at Fidel Castro, whom he loathed, by working for Castro's enemy. And second, he was building a small career for himself. The documents in front of Alex referenced letters of high praise from Tito's superiors, though the letters were not embedded in what Alex had accessed.

Despite Tito's lack of pedigree — the agency at that time was run by windy, frequently incompetent Ivy leaguers; it was no accident that George H. W. Bush was head of the whole operation — Tito did have his growing groups of friends in high places. These were people who believed in him and appreciated his own down and dirty style, which was a contrast to the silk-shirt agents who were still in positions of command.

He fell under the aegis of a regional commander for Latin America named Bill "Cap" Anson, who believed in him. "Give Tito enough plate appearances in a favorable ballpark, and he will put up a sound batting average," Anson wrote. Thus, seeking green playing fields for his protégé, Anson got Tito a small budget to work with, gave him some special phone numbers, and packed Tito off to the southern hemisphere.

At first Tito labored out of embassies. He had the cover of a representative of a big American manufacturing company at the time, one that primarily made kitchen appliances and air conditioners. He could travel without raising much suspicion since he always had commercial accounts to call upon. Peddling new cooking equipment and air-conditioning with a missionary zeal, Tito brought hot stoves and cool interiors to Peru, Colombia, Bolivia, and Venezuela, then stretched his webs farther south to Chile and Argentina.

He made himself a name as a businessman, and a pretty good one. Economies were cooking along nicely, and his appliances were finding customers. At the same time, the report continued, Tito was putting together a string of agents all over South America, men and occasionally women, who had insights into what was going on in the corridors of power as well as on the streets.

Local governments, which back then meant mostly military strongmen, not knowing exactly who he was but admiring his work, were often aware of his presence and used their own security people — who were none too subtle — to cut paths for Tito. In turn, Tito used part of his operating budget and business profits to grease the proper palms. Reading between the lines, Alex could see how Tito's influence grew, and she wondered whether he was empowered to murder anyone. On the surface, she doubted it, but he certainly wasn't contributing to his opponents' safety or longevity. He demonstrated a gift for infiltrating the local opposition and undermining their operations to bolster the prevailing right-wing governments.

Tito struck Alex as a bit of a Sam Deal on steroids, yet born to foreign parents and gifted with perfect Caribbean Spanish. He helped prop up governments from the generals in Argentina to Pinochet in Chile, from Somoza in Nicaragua to Valdez in Honduras. According to fourteen meticulous pages in the document, Tito had spent time in the field in eastern Honduras as the United States established and outfitted an entire pro-American army that existed to this day — with air-conditioned trailers for the commanders in the jungles, of course.

Over the first three years, Tito's fingerprints could be seen from Guatemala to Tierra del Fuego. He even picked up some accolades from CIA headquarters in Langley at the time, the Merit of Freedom for his work suppressing democracy in Chile, the Palm of Bogotá for work that resulted in the fiery accidental death of a major Calista cocaine baron, and the Order of Liberty for some dicey operation in Paraguay, which was too confidential to be contained in this report.

In Langley, the hard right loved him. How could they not?

Yet in the world of espionage, this was all middle- to lower-high-level stuff. The big enemy remained the Soviet Union, and that's where the major battles were being fought. Operations in Central and South America were seen as backroom activities — important, but not prime time.

In his fourth year Tito acquired the title of Operational Director for Covert Operations in South America. He banked a good check in the Cayman Islands every month. Alex noted that some of the checks were detailed during the years 1985 and 1986. This went on smoothly for a long while, with ample help from the CIA, who provided him with two escape passports, one Canadian and one Costa Rican, in case he ever needed to get out of someplace in a hurry.

According to the file, however, Tito was the original smooth operator. He never used the ersatz passports, never even seemed to leave a country in a rush. Tito, it could be said, was doing great work.

Yet overall, the CIA was in the doldrums. Tito was igniting a reverse Robin Hood feeling of good news through South America, catering to the rich and keeping the seething leftist poor in their place. Yet he was now stuck at high-middle level — too good to go down, not quite running high enough quality operations to go farther up. Still, these were the Reagan years, so when the Iran-Contra scandal hit the fan, some at Langley were having a huge belly laugh as Ollie North took the heat. Meanwhile, Tito's imprint was all over several operations, but no one ever nailed him.

"Breakfast? Coffee?" asked a flight attendant, jouncing Alex out of the world of espionage. The attendant smiled and held a tray.

At least business class tended to have more edible fare than the twenty-nine rows of steerage behind her. So Alex accepted it and went back to Tito.

His career might have remained stuck had it not been for a day early in 1989 when he turned up in Washington with a sample of some sterling new products.

The centerpiece was a seventeen-page Cuban naval document that inventoried every bit of post-Soviet-era naval hardware left behind in Cuba after the Soviet empire had collapsed. Included were the number of warships, advisors, and Russian sailors assigned to the Cuban fleet, as well as the number of MiG jets turned over to the Castro government, how many Cuban troops were equipped with Kalashnikov rifles, specifics on their shore-to-sea strike power, Cuba's various installations on the coast, and their enemy-alert procedures.

The document had remarkable relevance; the Pentagon had been screaming at the CIA for years for such material. Now, with Gorbachev alive and on the throne in Russia, the socialist Cubans left to fend for themselves, and ex-CIA Director George H. W. Bush in the White House, there were enough nasty, gnarled old hawks in the military in the US who still wanted to go in and forcibly remove Castro. Just as there was always room for Jell-O in the CIA cafeteria, there was always room for payback when it came to Cuba.

At first the CIA analysts took the material to be standard stuff, glitter on the outside but suspect in the details. It was typical end-of-the-Cold-War garbage — or perhaps a deliberate plant. Conventional wisdom had Tito's star on the down slope.

But as Langley began to reexamine the document, unravel it piece by piece, and pick through its details, it gained some glitter. Eventually, it glowed. Far from Tito being washed up, sunlight was now breaking from behind his noble crown.

It was the real thing, the pros decided, the best composite piece on Cuban armaments that had been gleaned from the Castro government in decades, perhaps ever. Tito was flown from Mexico City, where he was headquartered at the time, to Washington. He was wined and dined, and the senior inquisitors cornered him after the *foie gras* and asked where he had come by his documents.

He told the story of having befriended a member of the civil guard, whom he passed in the airport in Buenos Aires many years before and then reconnected with—by chance, he said—in an airport in Belize. They had developed a new working relationship.

The individual, an old pal from the world of washing machines, wished to do business with Washington and eventually get out of Cuba. He felt bitterly betrayed by the Castro government both personally and professionally. He had more axes to grind than he could find whetstones. So the individual was anxious to deal and squeal.

Tito refused to identify him—assuming it *was* a him—but he said that "the individual" had a treasure trove to sell, had eyes close to the heart of the Communist government in Havana, and would continue the flow of product if certain demands were met.

Tito christened his source "Gemini" for reasons known only to him. And he said that he vouched for Gemini's street cred one hundred percent. Most of Gemini's demands were financial, but there was a retirement plan of sorts, other perks, and an array of security arrangements to be put into place.

"I've been in this business long enough to know a rat when I smell one," Tito wrote in a covering correspondence. "This is top-drawer stuff. A-1, sky-high, top of the heap. I've developed a fine personal relationship with Gemini. We should be excited, celebrating instead of questioning it too closely. Let me run with this Gemini, and no one will look back."

Tito made the sale in Langley. He was taken off his existing South American contacts, and other case officers were assigned, some of whom brought agents along nicely, others who failed.

Tito was given the cryptic title of "Operational Manager of Gemini" and assigned to Cuba. Solo Cuba.

There he would remain.

The file was unclear as to whether Tito shared the actual identity of his source with anyone higher up but again the thumbprint of the D/CIA appeared. So Tito had obviously sold the bona fides of his sources to all the big shots.

The ongoing file scrupulously offered no hints to the real-world identity of Gemini. And the agency, sensing a coup against a pesky and hated adversary, was ready to let Tito rumble. Thus he received the most unusual permission to fly solo on the operation. It was unorthodox by anyone's standards: Tito had hooked a big fish and insisted on playing it all by his lonesome self. The file hinted strongly that if anything happened to Tito, Gemini's identity would die with him. Looked at from a different angle, Alex realized, Gemini was Tito's life insurance policy within the American intelligence community. And Tito was Gemini's.

Months slipped by. The late 1980s oozed into the 1990s.

The flow of covert information continued, sometimes with a rush, sometimes with an ebb. As two or three years passed, there was also a strange duality to the harvest of information. Some of it was mundane, routine, not much above what a day-to-day observer might be able to report from Havana. These results were tolerated because they tended to support what other sources related. But then there was the other half, which was highly valued because it cut so closely to the highest levels of the Cuban government, both professionally and personally.

At this point Alex, drawing upon her knowledge of mythology, thought that Gemini, the mole in Cuba, seemed more like Janus, the Roman god depicted with two faces, looking in two directions. Janus, she recalled, was the god of beginnings and endings, and therefore the deity of gates, doors, entrances, and transitions. Such an image could not have been more appropriate to what Alex was digesting.

Gemini had some sharp sights on Castro, public and private. Gemini was the first, for example, to report that an illegitimate Castro daughter named Alina Fernández-Revuelta had fled Cuba in 1993, disguised as a Spanish tourist; hence when she sought asylum in the United States, US intelligence already knew who she was and stood ready to grant asylum to her. Later, after settling in Florida, Fernández-Revuelta would develop and host a popular and fervently anti-Castro radio show called *Simplemente Alina* on WQBA in Miami.

Many other small details littered the intelligence haul over this period. There was a nasty spat about money, a high-tech camera, and a miniaturized recording device in 1993. Gemini insisted on a particular Japanese brand that needed to be smuggled into Cuba. The CIA said they had no problem with that but maintained that the cost for the equipment — about $2,500 — be taken out of the future proceeds to Gemini that were being stashed monthly in foreign bank accounts.

But overall a trend emerged. Gemini asked for more money since the product was so good and dependable. Yet the CIA's budget had been cut that year, and the spy's request was turned down flat.

Gemini threw a raging tantrum and made noises about jumping over to the opposition, which nearly torpedoed the whole operation. It took Tito's best efforts to smooth things out, but smooth them out he did. The requested equipment was sent to Cuba via a Canadian diplomatic pouch. A Canadian diplomat hauled it one evening in a duffle bag to a café in old Havana where Tito picked it up and passed it along, a rare personal appearance in the Cuban capital for Tito, who probably would have been executed if he had been caught.

As for the money, some true believers in Gemini rallied and managed to misdirect some other agency funds into a pair of bank accounts that Gemini held, one in Switzerland, one in the Cayman Islands. Crisis averted. Tito had interceded and again beaten the Langley overlords.

The flight attendant reappeared in Alex's row and cleared her finished breakfast. Alex was barely aware of the intrusion.

But now, at this point in the file, there appeared a new but important bit player, named Adolf J. Frelinghuysen, who was apparently a senior evaluator of CIA material in the Caribbean.

With a name like Frelinghuysen, a Smucker of a name, Alex assumed this fellow better be good. He was. Frelinghuysen was in the habit of overseeing operations at random, just dropping in on the paperwork, acquainting himself with what was transpiring, making waves, and moving on.

Looking at the documents with fresh eyes, reading them perhaps from back to front rather than the normal way around, A. J. had spotted a few questionable areas. The pressure points were not so much in content but in the magical and near-impossible nature with which they had appeared.

"I draw your attention to some questions, inconsistencies mostly involving dates," Frelinghuysen wrote in one of three highly articulate memos.

Gemini cites a meeting (Gemini No. 62-a) in Caracas on January 18, 1990, from which information is gleaned on ten years of oil sales by Venezuela to the Soviet Union. Yet Gemini No. 54-c dated January 19, 1990, submitted earlier, suggests that the inestimable "Gemini" was in Havana within an audience of Raul Castro at the Palacio de Justicia. Seven other documents (see list 2, attached) arriving at the agency in various orders, have similar time spans that shake the imagination in even the jet age. (Am I the only one who has noticed this?) One even suggests that Gemini was in Havana on the morning of August 7, 1990 and in Veracruz, Mexico that same afternoon: possible, yet highly unlikely. We all agree that Gemini is a nimble fellow, but this again shakes the imagination as well as the laws of physics.

Conversely, however, the entire product seems valid and free from contradiction. Could someone explain or is the answer obvious? I honestly don't know whether to laugh or cry over these "quirks."

Frelinghuysen was abruptly cut off from access to the file by Tito and rudely told to go jump in a lake or stick his pointy nose somewhere else. He could pose his queries to a less belligerent audience, but not here, Tito raged.

Frelinghuysen vanished. But the damage was done, temporarily at least. Frelinghuysen had posed questions no one else had dared to ask. Suddenly, inquiries were all over the place, pro-Tito officers had switched sides, and an insurrection was brewing. Similar questions were put to Tito by agency overseers who had never noticed the enigmatic dates before but who were anxious to cover their backsides in case the house of cards came tumbling down.

At the same time, eyebrows were raised for the first time by the overwhelming amount of cogent material that had been turned in by Gemini. Since the Agency had a success on their hands, no one had wanted to ask questions as impertinent as Frelinghuysen's.

Inquisitors made their way to Cuba — to Camagüey — by midnight motorboat to address their concerns to Gemini in person. Tito was told — not requested, but told — to be present as well.

Here was a detail of the episode that Alex, in attempting to understand it more than twenty years later, felt as if she were juggling chain saws.

The two CIA visitors to Camagüey traveled by boat from Jamaica and entered the island illegally, brought ashore in a skiff by CIA contacts on the island. Alex, of course, recalled her own recent similar escapade. Tito, however, traveled by air from Mexico City on July 17, 1994.

In a small paper notebook, Alex noted the date. She knew she would want it later.

She also confirmed what she had long suspected but had not seen spelled out in the documents. Tito was able to travel without an American passport, as such a flight from Mexico would have been somewhere between impossible and highly imprudent. Backtracking, she noted again Tito's parentage and residency: Cuban and Costa Rican on the parents' side, Mexican on the residency side. Chances were that Tito held one of those three passports, maybe two, unless he had used one of his dummy imprints, and yet another section of the same report said he hadn't.

No matter. Her hunch told her that his travel papers might be Mexican since that would cause little commotion anywhere in the southern hemisphere.

Picking up the story in the file again, she read that three visitors made their rendezvous with Gemini at an isolated factory on Cuba's south shore. Thereupon, Tito was forced into a startling admission to save his operation. Thanks to the blur involving the dates, and the overwhelming amount of material that had been sent north, it was no longer possible to extend the longevity of the primary falsehood of the entire operation. Much like the namesake of the operation, in a nod to astrology, Gemini turned out to be more than one person. Gemini was a twin source, a modern and nefarious Castor and Pollux.

Tito personally introduced the two halves of his team to the handlers who had flown in. The handlers spent Sunday individually quizzing both halves of Gemini. They came away convinced that the persons involved were real and did, in fact, have the access they claimed.

Yet unlike the two astrological stick figures in the sky, joined hand in hand, one — Castor — flew at low range and did the dirty work. The other — Pollux — soared at much higher altitudes and grasped higher-value information. Hence the disparity of some of the work.

Impressed, celebrating with bottles of Caribbean Club rum and contraband Coca-Cola, they pinned another medal on Tito. Everyone broke late on Sunday afternoon to be at work on Monday, vowing to keep their mouths shut on the details.

Alex read this and sat up straight.

So Gemini was a pair, as she had begun to suspect. A tag team. Mutt and Jeff. Yin and Yang. Bob and Ray. Sonny and Cher.

But could Gemini have been *more* than two people? A team of five, for instance? Suddenly the possibilities exploded on her. The possibilities for Gemini were as unmeasured as Gemini's place in the sky.

Mystified over the thrust of all of this, and still only three quarters of the way through the document, Alex reread this important section three times. Had anyone been watching her, she probably would have struck the same pose and depth of mental intensity as she had a decade earlier while studying Russian in Moscow.

Then a sudden thought hit her, a potential interpretation that she was not yet ready to give to anyone. So far away were her thoughts that the flight attendant had to reach over to her, gently touch her shoulder, and ask her to close down the laptop and move her seat to the upright position.

The three-hour flight was nearly over. The aircraft had begun its decent into scenic Newark, New Jersey, while Alex attempted to emerge from the fog of the past

FORTY-THREE

Alex was back at her office by 2:30 p.m. Her first two hours were spent on administrative detail. As much as she had tried to keep up with the Dosi operation while away, there was a volume of emails and files from her European contacts. She would have to catch up with all of them. Eventually. She hadn't even had time to finish the file McCarron had swiped for her, and its thrust was still difficult to gauge.

She sat before her computer monitors and jumped back and forth between her contacts in North Africa and Europe, as well as some of her Fin Cen contacts with the much-beloved Internal Revenue Service.

From North Africa, she was hearing ominous rumblings. The Dosis had just returned to their lair outside Casablanca and seemed to be comfortably ensconced there. Her sources in Rome confirmed that the Dosis were in fact the couple that the Italian police had just missed at the Excelsior. Alex still smoldered with anger over the breach of security that could have cost her the end of that operation. But she persisted. Her surveillance units on the ground told her that there had been much coming and going from the complex from which the Dosis held court and the security ring had been bolstered. There now seemed to be at least a dozen heavily armed young men at any given time.

Rizzo checked in from Rome. He would be flying to New York the following Tuesday as planned, with his girlfriend, Mimi, the twentysomething punk manga-loving computer geek in tow. He had some business to transact with the security company run by a former mayor of New York, so his cover was perfect. If Alex needed him to travel to Miami just to watch her back, he would be able to, he said.

She wrote back, getting the details of Rizzo's arrival — he

would be arriving at JFK late in the afternoon. They scheduled a late supper. As befit a man of his tastes and expenses, Rizzo had arranged a suite for himself and Mimi at the San Remo, a smart European-style boutique hotel on Lexington in the Gramercy Park area. The choice suited Alex as it was not inconvenient to where she lived. Not perfect, but not inconvenient either. It would also be Mimi's first trip to New York, so the frisky couple would want to have their fun.

Late in the afternoon, Alex got back to her IRS contacts and exchanged a series of emails. Working the proposed Social Security number of Jonas Frederickson into a batch of legitimate suspects from another Fin Cen fraud inquiry, she sent out the number to IRS Enforcement to see what might turn up. She later phoned Rick McCarron in Miami to confirm that she was on the case for him and had made inquiries.

He thanked her profusely. They chatted. Apparently Laura was on her way to visit that weekend. He sounded upbeat. And why not?

All of this, and an avalanche of other small bits of bookkeeping and administration took her well into the late afternoon. Then, thinking ahead to her own weekend, she decided to open some web sources for a casual inquiry of her own.

Eric Robertson.

She was allowed a few guilty pleasures, or at the very least, to run a public-record background check on someone who asked her to brunch. Right? A few clicks and keystrokes took her to an entry on a reputable professional site for actors.

Robertson was born in Owensboro, Tennessee, just west of Knoxville, in 1977, making him thirty-five years old. He was the son of a teacher and a book editor, a former scholar who had once taught Italian, Alex learned. Eric had one younger brother, Matthew, who was now his personal manager, and a sister, Sarah, who was a physician.

Alex skipped past the childhood stuff, feeling a little like a spy, then realizing again that's exactly what she was.

She focused on Robertson's professional path. How did one

come out of an ordinary middle-class American background to become an actor recognized worldwide? Well, being talented and stunningly handsome helped, a voice inside her reminded her. Aside from that, such social mobility happened all the time.

Eric Robertson was best known for his roles in American films, the account read. He had starred in both big-budget Hollywood films and the smaller projects from independent producers and art houses. Robertson had first caught the public eye at the age of sixteen, when he was cast in a major supporting role in one of Martin Scorsese's movies. Later, he portrayed a sociopathic bank robber in a gritty crime drama filmed in San Francisco, a romantic lead in a pair of light comedies, a Santa Monica, California, cop in a spiritual ghost story titled *Cemetery of Angels*, and did a highly memorable tour as a troubled American soldier returning home after two tours in Iraq in a powerful 2009 hit in which he was nominated for, but didn't win, an Oscar.

Robertson's first foray into acting was a commercial for a candy bar in 1985, when he was eight years old. A year later, he appeared in a toy commercial playing a child rock star riffing on an electric guitar. In 1988, he made his stage debut in a Kennedy Center production *Nicholas Nickleby*, in Washington, DC, playing a destitute street urchin. Other roles followed, as did his education. As a child, he also trained in music and drama. Robertson's father was very supportive of his son's acting, resigning from his underpaid and underappreciated editing job to travel and manage Robertson's burgeoning career. The elder Robertson passed away at age sixty-two, on April 20, 2007 from brain lymphoma.

Then, in 2010, Robertson sang the role of Curley McLain in the musical *Oklahoma* on Broadway. He won the Tony Award and the Drama Desk Award for Outstanding Actor in a Musical cementing his reputation as an A-List American talent, a man who could move from stage to screen and back again, barely taking a moment to catch his own breath while leaving the audience — particularly female members — breathless.

Alex skipped to the end. She was on her employers' dime, after all.

A summation on the site suggested that Robertson's success stemmed from a confluence of talents. He was said to possess Johnny Depp's quirkiness, Christian Bale's smoldering intensity, and Hugh Jackman's good looks.

"Well, okay," she smiled, "that's a good straight-male trifecta." She was still musing on the quixotic nature of actually having a meal with such a man, so well out of her territory, when the Instant Message sign on her computer flashed. Her boss was calling.

It was now 6:00 p.m., and she still hadn't had the opportunity to bring her boss up to speed on the Miami trip. They made a decision. They would have dinner together. This would allow some decompression for both and save office time on Monday.

"I'm sympathetic to these trips to Miami," De Salvo said over their dinner at Faunces Tavern, "but are you sure you're not going to get your head blown off, if not by the opposition then by some eager beaver supposedly on our side?"

"I'm not sure of anything," she said, "but where's the choice? I'm either locked in combat against the Dosi organization or I'm not. We've got at least three recent murders to lay at their feet in Miami, maybe more. Either we get them, or they get us."

"Have a drink," he said.

"No thanks. I'm working."

"Have two drinks."

"I've been that route, Andy. I prefer not to get started again."

"Point taken. Apologies."

"Accepted," she said.

"I'm looking after you," he said. "You sort of remind me of a daughter or a niece I never had."

"I'm flattered."

"I flatter myself," he said. "Well, what the heck? Where are we on all this?"

Alex alluded to a file she had come into possession of from Rick McCarron, the one she was still reading.

"Should I ask how you obtained that?" he asked.

"You'd be happier not knowing," she said.

"Thought so," he said. "A little light-fingered professional give-and-take as you develop your own networks?"

"You could describe it that way," she said. "With no cyber fingerprints either, I hope."

"Good. We'll leave it at that. The less I know the better," De Salvo said.

Beyond that, Alex brought him up to speed on everything that had happened in Florida, including the twenty minutes of terror she had spent in Ramona's bedroom closet. He seemed pleased, but wary.

FORTY-FOUR

Returning that evening to her unfinished reading of the Gemini file, Alex felt all the more perplexed about its direction and the purported plurality of the Gemini persona.

With two, three, or more agents to keep track of, the possible paths of where this led increased geometrically. But still she persisted. She followed the final twenty-eight pages of the stolen file as best she could, reading slowly. She also read keenly enough to notice a change of tone after the admission that Gemini was more than one individual.

Yet something else struck Alex. In 1993, the quality of the yield hit a depression of sorts. Or maybe it was a speed bump, because it definitely slowed down. Not the quantity, though that diminished also, but the quality.

Something was off, and Langley, who was still signing off on wire transfers of funds to various banks around the world, started to complain.

Again Tito was quick to ride to Gemini's rescue. Alex used her notebook to note the date at the enigmatic nature of the entry.

"I think I have made it clear that Gemini suffers from a temporary medical condition that precludes complete immersion in intelligence gathering at this time," wrote Tito in June of 1993. "The condition is highly personal and equally transitory. Allow twelve to fourteen months, and all systems will again be go." This was followed by the contact and date: *Langley Inquiry confirmed: J. Montefiore, MD, August 17, 1997.*

A hiatus followed. Then, like clockwork, the product picked up again during the final years of the twentieth century, the mundane stuff and the more refined stuff.

The thefts of intelligence from various Cuban high commands

then took on a more regular pattern, much as if Gemini, or perhaps Tito, knew how often he needed to turn in product and how good it had to be. But the product became less audacious, as if the operation had fallen into a comfortable middle age and was not looking to rock many boats.

Similarly, Tito's tone took a wicked new spin, alternating between defensiveness and aggressiveness. There was a backhanded allusion to Gemini — meaning at least one of the individuals who comprised the entity — visiting Florida in 2005 for medical treatment of an undisclosed sort and a reference to a Dr. Sanchez in Miami.

Thereafter, for about a year, the entries became shockingly consistent: something every eighteen to twenty-one days, usually having to do with the naval ministry or civil guard.

Again Alex noted that much of this was run-of-the-mill stuff, which could have been inventoried earlier for rainy days. Some of the previous inquisitors had come to the identical conclusion. But then after a year, the electricity of thefts began to amp up again, and there were more pearls from Fidel and Raúl Castro's inner circle. Never mind Castor and Pollux, Gemini had taken on a Jekyll-and-Hyde quality. Jekyll seemed to have been home minding the store while Hyde was out and about and absent. Now that Jekyll was back, he or she seemed on the razzle again, turning over top product. Alex wished she could see some of the product and made a note to inquire of McCarron.

But Alex noticed something else here in these years, which began around 2006. Tito had become almost obsessive in his protective approach to Gemini.

"I repeat again," Tito wrote in one report that covered a posting from 2007,

```
that this entire operation is extremely secret
and highly personal. The more circulation
these reports get, even at the highest level,
the greater the danger increases for those
```

involved, as well as innocents who might be attached in a familial way. Do I have to be graphic about what happens to apprehended agents in Russia or Cuba? Do I need to make reminders about the firing squads that followed Fidel Castro's ascent to power? A bullet to the back of the neck in a prison basement, Lubyanka style, would be considered merciful by many.

Alex was again perplexed. Tito was writing passionately now, almost pleadingly. What personal connection had kicked in? A romantic interest? Stockholm syndrome? An overall weariness of having been in the field too long? Career fatigue or galloping paranoia? The files posed questions but no answers.

Then there was a final entry, or at least the final one that Alex had before her. Tito wrote:

Gemini has been at the service of the United States for a considerable time now, much of an adult life. As the influence of Fidel Castro declines, it is time to reward those who have served the anti-Castro opposition: withdrawal from Cuba and a permanent vacation abroad would be fitting. Fidel and Raúl have made Cuba an enormous prison surrounded by water. The people are nailed to a cruel cross of torment imposed by the godlessness of international Communism. Gemini has lived two lifetimes in this prison and does not deserve to die in it also. It is time to start an operation to remove Gemini from this hell in the Caribbean. Saludos y Vamos.

Alex blinked as the tale smashed to an abrupt ending, at least the part she was able to see.

She started to put together a list of things she wanted to know. She wondered what else Rick could snag for her. She also noted Tito's remark: "two lifetimes in this prison."

Alex sighed. Were those words an oblique confirmation that Gemini was two people at most, as its sign in the Zodiac suggested? She wondered.

Alone in her apartment, she stared at the screen for several minutes, flitted back and forth in the file to try to master some dates, and move them to the small notebook where she had already filled two dozen pages. Then she shut down the file and the laptop.

She was exhausted, physically and spiritually, and, if quizzed on what she had read, she would not have been able to provide concise answers. Only one conclusion flitted into view, and it had done so slowly and inexorably over the course of the evening as the backstory of the case sunk in.

Somewhere over the course of the next sixteen years, the sobriquet *Gemini* had fallen away. What Alex had been reading, she knew, was the operation that had centered on the spy known later as *Figaro*. Figaro was Gemini. Or Gemini was Figaro. Or half of Gemini was Figaro who, in turn, was the late Major Mejías, the man she had ushered out of Cuba several weeks earlier.

What that had to do with Tito, Mejías's murder, or the content of the final message the late Major Mejías had had for Alex, was something that she had not yet deciphered. Who had been the other part of Gemini? That posed another question. Was the other twin dead maybe? Or still alive under deep cover? Or had the other Gemini long ago saved himself and fled to another nation, living quietly with the loot gained from the CIA?

And for that matter, who was Tito? And where?

Alex looked up from her laptop screen and noted with horror that it was now 1:30 a.m. Fatigue was settling in and putting her in a stranglehold.

As she got into bed, she knew all of those questions probably locked together and remained for her to answer. Mercifully, she was asleep within minutes.

FORTY-FIVE

On Saturday morning, Alex dressed casually, a denim skirt, a heavy T-shirt, and a jacket. She packed her gun in a shoulder bag and hung the bag over her shoulder, looping it across her opposite shoulder so it would be harder for someone to steal. Simple urban precaution. She shuddered at the thought of ever losing her weapon to a smash-and-grab artist.

She walked from Chelsea up Eighth Avenue to the theater district. The morning was bright and Manhattan looked its best. September had faded into October now, but it was a bright day, sunny and crisp. World Series weather, New Yorkers liked to say, and sure enough, the Yankees, whom Alex had started to follow, remained in the thick of things.

The walk was quietly exhilarating. She walked purposefully, enjoying the anonymity of the city. And this brunch with a professional actor would be interesting at the very least, she had decided, a one-time thing to amuse her friends with as time went by. My "date with Eric Robertson," she mused mischievously. The unlikely nature of it made it all the more entertaining.

Alex found her way to Giacomini's Trattoria a little before eleven and gave her current cover name to the hostess at the door. The hostess cheerfully led Alex through the first room of tables to a more private section in the back. She seated Alex at a corner table, spacious and comfortable, private enough to see the room and be seen by the room, yet not heavily on display. She liked the positioning. Alex ordered coffee and enjoyed watching the room come to life around her. The restaurant was between breakfast and lunch and starting to bustle. The theater district was waking up.

Alex waited, sipping coffee, as the room steadily filled. She spotted another actor with his family. More than once, she looked to the passageway from the main dining room, anticipating Eric's arrival. She glanced at her watch: 11:00 a.m. and counting. Then it was five after, then ten, and, against her better judgment, she began to entertain the notion of being stood up. And why not?

She was here against her better judgment, after all, and if the famous Eric Robertson had really wanted to take her to brunch, there were plenty of places closer to home. Actors! Actors and their degenerate lifestyles! Men who have so many female contacts that they don't care about any of them. How could she have been so dumb as to get suckered into this, she wondered.

Eric was probably nursing a hangover in the apartment of some casual liaison, she decided as her watch showed twelve after. And he probably did things like this for sport, making ten brunch dates, then selecting one to show up for, if any, at the final moment. It was then quarter after and of all the stupid ideas she had ever entertained, why had she fallen for an obviously self-centered egotistical, pompous —

Then she spotted him. He was making his way through a crowd between tables in the next room, stopping as a hefty woman with big hair handed him a *Playbill* to autograph. He did so patiently, removing his dark glasses and folding them into the pocket of a navy sports jacket, then moving away quickly toward the back room. He gave a tap and quick hello to the waiter and waitress working the room, both of whom greeted him with a smile. He turned toward Alex, found her quickly, and gave her a wave. With the grace of an athlete, he moved to her table and slid into the empty chair.

"Apologies, apologies, Susanna," he said. "My meeting ran late, then I couldn't find a cab. I gave my driver the weekend off so he could watch his son play football." He rolled his eyes, amused. "Maurice. I think you saw him one night when I was arriving home."

"Ah. I did," she said. "Big guy."

"That's him. Used to be a police officer in LA. Haitian by

birth. Wonderful fellow. He's also my bodyguard. He's armed, by the way."

"You need a bodyguard?"

He shrugged. "There are some crazy people out there."

"No doubt about that."

"Anyway, today ... I ended up walking from midtown. Well, the exercise won't hurt. I hope."

He drew her close and wrapped her in a quick hug, then released her. She went with it, and for several seconds watched him in disbelief. The famous face, the famous smile, and there they were having a midday meal together. In the back of her mind she was again noting how good-looking he was and that he sure knew how to sweep a woman off her feet. Yet how many women would have killed to be sitting right where she was if only for a few minutes. A million?

"All is forgiven," she said.

"Thank you," he answered. "What a pleasure this is."

For some reason, she was almost tongue-tied.

She felt a sudden compulsion to impress him and wondered why. She quickly searched her psyche and found the answers in the Saturday nights of her girlhood in Southern California. Little Alex, the girl who was too smart, who no one wanted to date, was sitting here in New York with a star of stage and films. Oh, if her tenth grade class could see her now, the geeky too-smart girl the cool kids snickered at!

And yet, she had dealt one-to-one with an American president. Why should fame or celebrity impress her one bit?

But of course, it still did.

Some small talk ensued: the weather, the neighborhood, the national news. Eric gave Alex a moment to glance at the menu. A pretty waitress appeared. Eric knew her first name, Maggie, and used it. But she addressed him as "Mr. Robertson."

Alex ordered a salad.

"Care for a drink?" Eric asked.

"No, I'm fine with coffee," she said, "but feel free."

"I have a performance in three hours," he said with a half smile. "I must be one of the few actors who rarely touch booze. My mother was a card-carrying Tennessee Methodist, and my grandmother was WCTU — Women's Christian Temperance Union," he grinned. "So maybe an antialcohol gene got passed down. Who knows? But again, don't let me stop you."

"You're not, thank you," she said, starting to feel surprisingly at ease with him.

"John Barrymore used to perform Hamlet drunk as a sailor," Eric continued. "'The Profile.' He got away with it, Barrymore did. It's not something I want to try. Or would dare."

Eric collected the menus without looking at them and with one of his multikilowatt smiles handed them back to the waitress.

Then he turned to Alex. "So," he said with self-deprecation, "you know who I am and what I do for a living. You probably know too much if the complete truth were known. Internet, newspapers, and all that. But I don't know anything about you other than we live in the same building and stumble across each other now and then. That's not fair, is it?"

"I suppose not," she said.

"Then, what do you do for a living, may I ask? Something to do with finance is what I hear."

"And where do you hear that?"

"The busybody gossips in our building," he said. "I overhear all sorts of things."

"I might have known."

"So are they right?" he asked as his iced tea arrived.

Alex drew a breath and tried to keep it as close to the truth as the situation would allow. "I work for a firm involved in financial security, yes," she said. "There's a close relationship with the US government and so for that reason, I can't say too much about the exact nature of what I do. At least not right now."

"Ah. Secretive stuff."

"You could say that."

"But not secretive to you because you know what you're doing."

"You could say that too," she said.

Her mind raced furiously. Less than two years ago, Alex herself had been in so many major newspapers following the tumultuous events in Kiev that had left her fiancé dead. Then just as quickly, she had dropped out of the news. Obviously, Eric wasn't connecting her with the news stories, for which she was glad. Then again, he was an actor, maybe excellent at pretending not to know.

"But you work in Manhattan?" he asked. "I see you setting out in the morning sometimes, if I'm awake early. All dolled up in Wharton-style 'monkey clothes': my term for conservative business attire. Not that there's anything wrong with that. I'm a benign capitalist at heart. You look like you're on your way to work in some place that smells of money."

"I have an office down in the financial district," she said, amused by his terminology and his flow with words. "I take the subway." She paused. "I deal with people who misuse money, more than earn it, if you catch my drift."

"I catch it. Good for you."

"Nothing glamorous," she said with a wry smile. "Not like what you do."

"Ah, well," he said. "It's not all glamour, but I'd be lying if I didn't admit that I'm a very lucky man. I get to do what I like and get well compensated for it. I work with some outstanding creative people, and we enjoy what we do. Granted, I've worked hard, paid my dues. But I've been richly blessed, let's say. That's not too corny a way to look at it, is it?"

"Not to me," she said. "I think it's a great way to look at it."

"I'm glad," he answered. "Look, I've learned to not let anything go to my head. At any given time I could show you a sheaf of reviews attesting to how bad I am. You need to develop a thick hide if you want to survive in this business. And if the public doesn't come to see my show or my films, I'm out of business very quickly. There are some wonderful actors out there on the street, driving cabs and waiting tables. Some are better than I am. I'm lucky."

"And maybe too modest," she said, going with it.

"Ha! No such thing. I learned that long ago," he said. He paused. "There are always people out to get you, the critics and naysayers, and some day some of them will."

"I can relate to that," she said.

"That's life," he said. "It is what it is."

An awkward pause followed. She was inclined to break it and was opening her mouth to speak when a female figure arrived at the side of their table. Eric turned in that direction and smiled. Alex turned with him. There was a girl of about twelve holding a restaurant menu and looking at Eric in thinly veiled adoration, not knowing what to say.

Eric helped her. "Well, hello," he said. "Who are you?"

She still didn't speak.

"Let me guess," he said pleasantly, reaching for the menu in her hand. "You'd either like me to help you order, or you'd like me to sign this menu."

"Yes," she said, flustered. "Please?"

"Well, I don't know what you'd want to eat, so I'll just sign your menu for you," he said.

Still flustered, she said, "Okay."

Alex watched as Eric's dark eyes glanced over the girl's shoulder to find an adult couple sitting at a table about thirty feet away, parents obviously astonished, watching their daughter encounter the actor. Eric gave them a slight nod and a wink to indicate everything was okay.

"First you have to tell me who you are. What's your name, dear?" he asked.

"Kimberly."

"Just Kimberly?" he asked. "Like Madonna or Fabio, no last name?"

"Kimberly Ann Cody," she said.

"Ah! Lady Kimberly. Where are you from?"

"Smithtown, Iowa."

"You're a long way from home. Did you walk here?"

She giggled. "I'm with my parents. We flew."

"Ah. That must be them over there. Your parents."

Kimberly laughed. "Uh-huh," she said.

Eric reached into his sports jacket and pulled out his own writing instrument. It was a blue Sharpie with a medium point, his own just for autographs, Alex guessed, for occasions such as this.

He autographed the menu, big bold handwriting in royal blue, bold and assertive, making sure he had her name perfectly. She reached to take the menu back, but he held it.

"Are you coming to see *South Pacific*?" he asked.

"My mommy and daddy tried to get tickets, but they were sold out of the seats we could afford," she said.

"Were they? That wasn't very nice of them, was it? Do you think you and your family would still like to see the show?" he asked.

Kimberly looked for a trick in the question, didn't find one, shrugged and answered. "I guess."

"How many in your family?"

"Three."

"How long are you in New York?"

"Until Thursday."

"Well, that's good. You look like nice people. So I have something else for you," Eric said. He found his wallet and removed a small ticket form. He filled it out and handed it to the girl. Alex watched him write a big 3 in the space after "How Many Tickets?"

"Tell your parents to take this to the box office today or tomorrow," he said. "Your family can go as my guests. How's that?"

"Wow!" she said.

He laughed. "Enjoy," he said.

The girl turned excitedly and scampered back to her parents' table. She showed off the signed menu, and her parents looked at the guest passes with absolute shock, then looked at Eric, who gave them a half smile, a shrug, and a slight wave.

"That was amazing of you," Alex said.

He shrugged. "Like I said, I've been blessed. Everything I have is because of the grace of God." With a wink, he added, "So far be it from me to be anything but a blessing to the people around me."

Intrigued, "How many free passes do you get?" she asked.

"None. Those are house seats. I pay full price for them."

She laughed. "You just gave away a few hundred dollars' worth of house seats to strangers?"

"I guess I did, didn't I? That was careless of me," he added, making a joke of it.

"It wasn't careless at all," she said. "You knew what you were doing."

"Bless to be a blessing."

"How often do you do stuff like that?" she asked.

"More often than my accountant says I should, Susanna," he said. "Some people in my line of work blow their good fortune up their nose, but I like to give stuff away. So shoot me."

"I wouldn't think of it," she said.

"That's a relief."

"Are you always so quick with a witty response?"

"When I'm in the right company," he said. "Like now."

"Can I ask you something?" she said.

"Of course."

"How do you keep so balanced?"

"Ha!" he laughed. "I didn't know I was balanced."

"Don't be modest," she said, starting to greatly enjoy the give-and-take.

"You're asking an actor not to be modest? That must be some sort of historical first. Ah," he then said, looking at Maggie, the waitress, who was arriving with a tray. "Just in the nick of time. Lunch."

Small talk followed. It was a Midwestern touring company of *South Pacific*, it turns out, that had been his first exposure to live musical theater. His parents had taken him to see a production in Chicago, and the theater and the story had hooked him.

"James Michener was writing about racial tolerance seventy years ago," Eric said in admiration. "That wasn't the easiest message to sell in postwar America. In fact, it was a tough one. I always loved the show. So when the production here moved from Lincoln Center to Broadway and the role of Joe Cable opened, I jumped at it, had my agent and business manager call the producers, and attempted to convince them they couldn't do it without me. Which is false, of course, but they bought the notion."

"The show has done well," Alex said, launching the day's best understatement.

"It's done okay," he said, outunderstating her understatement.

They shared some common bonds, she discovered. Both had done well academically and had excelled at sports. His rugged body had come to maturity early, and after taking a postgraduate year at a prep school in New Hampshire, he had been offered scholarships to play football at some well-regarded universities.

"Really, though, I wanted to go for the education," he said. "Nor did I have any interest in being walloped by three-hundred-pound free safeties for fourteen Saturdays a year. So a recruiter talked to me from one of the better eastern schools, and I went there."

"Which one?" she asked.

"Don't hate me for this, okay?"

"Tell me."

"Princeton," he said.

She laughed. "Yeah, that's a good one," she said. "Did you play football too?"

"For three years," he said. "Got beaten up by some of the finest minds of my generation when we played Harvard, Yale, and Penn. Hey, Princeton used to turn out diplomats. Woodrow Wilson. George Shultz. And writers. John McPhee. Scott Fitzgerald. Now it's Brooke Shields, Dean Cain, me, and a couple of major league baseball players." He laughed. "Then I went to NYU Film School. If you're going to make money acting these days, you need to do some of it in front of a camera."

He paused, as if tired of speaking about himself. "What about you? College?" he asked.

"I went to UCLA," she said.

"Party school," he teased.

"Not for me. I did a course of studies that gave me a master's in international finance in five years. It was mostly comparative economic structures, a lot of nuts-and-bolts stuff involving money, plus languages."

"How many do you speak?" he asked, intrigued.

"Five or six."

His fork stopped in mid-path between plate and mouth. "Wow? Which ones?"

"English, French, Spanish, Italian, and Russian," she said. "I'm fluent in those. I can get along in Ukrainian."

"Where did Ukrainian come in? How'd you get into that?"

"That's a story for another day," she said.

"I'm sure it is. Probably a long story."

"You pick up on things quickly."

"I like to think so," he said.

The rest of the meal, they chatted over topics of general interest. She spoke of the places she had traveled to, without telling exactly why, only "for work" or "on an assignment," as she recounted it.

He told amusing anecdotes of plays and films he had been in, television he had done, recounting small stories about famous people he knew in the entertainment industry that most people only read about in newspapers. Eric was a fine storyteller, an easy raconteur with distinctive gifts of voice and speech. Alex always appreciated a good storyteller, and today she was a particularly entranced listener. So lunch was congenial.

Time flew.

Before she knew it, it was 1:00, an hour before curtain time, and Eric had to rush to the theater.

No formal bill arrived. Eric had a private account. He initialed a tab and slipped a twenty-dollar tip to Maggie on what was probably a fifty-dollar tab. Then they were out on the street, Alex thanking him for the experience.

"I'm sure we'll pass in the mail room again," she said.

"Oh, I'm quite sure of that," he said. "But I'm not sure I've given away my quota of passes today. When would you like to come see *South Pacific*?"

Surprised, "Oh, I — ," she began.

"Please don't protest. I insist," he said. "Have you ever seen a production of *South Pacific*?"

"I've seen the movie."

"The movie is for museums. This is one of the great pieces of the American musical theater. You owe it to yourself to see a live performance."

For a reason that she couldn't explain, Alex found herself fleeing from the invitation.

"Really, I'm horribly tied up at work and — "

Eric was in no mood to accept a "no."

"Give me a date on the calendar; come with a friend," he said. "The seats are in the seventh row in the center. I'll give you a wink after 'There Is Nothing like a Dame,' and one for your friend too. How's that?"

For a moment, Alex stood poised between two worlds. Eric was in the magical world of show business and was as ebullient as the day was clear. He was like the good angel sitting on her shoulder. Meanwhile, there was a darker presence on her other shoulder and visions of Miami and all its evil were doing pirouettes in her head.

"Eric, I'm, uh ..."

"What could be wrong with that?" he asked. "What about you and that lovely lady I saw you with the other night? Who was that?"

"That was my friend, Laura. She's visiting from out of town, staying with me."

"Is she still here?"

"No. She's back in Washington by now."

"Well, you must know someone," he said. "And by the way, I'm not leaving here till you agree. The show will go on late, and it will be entirely your fault."

"What if it were a male friend who accompanied me?" Alex asked.

"Ah, ha! So there is a boyfriend-in-waiting. Well, I won't hide my disappointment, but I'm a good sport. That would be okay, I guess."

"He's not a boyfriend-in-waiting," Alex said. "He's a friend-friend who's working for a law degree. A buddy. I helped him through some rough times, and he helped me. An army vet. We used to play basketball when I lived in Washington."

"What's his name?"

"Ben."

"I know him!" Eric said.

"What?"

"Just kidding. Come on. Invite him. Then come backstage and say hello. Both of you."

"For real?"

"No, I'm making this all up. I'm not even really an actor. Come on, Susanna. Of course, for real."

Alex drew a breath and tried to find a reasonable course.

"Wait," he then said. "Here's another suggestion. Toward the end of next week, or maybe the week after, my sister and her husband are hoping to come to town. They want to see the show. Then they'll come backstage so I can introduce them to the cast. We go out to dinner afterward. Please join them for the show, then all of us for dinner. What do you say?"

"Eric, listen," she said, still fumbling, still resisting. "Let's do it like this. I think I have a business trip next week. Miami. Some nasty unsettled stuff. It keeps taking me out of town, and I never know exactly when or for how long."

"Ten years? Twelve? The show is doing well but we might not be there that long."

"When I get back, I'll take you up on your offer. If it stands."

"It will stand," he said. "And how will I get in touch with you? To remind you once you're back? Pound on the ceiling, see who answers? Or should I use the phone number that I already have for you?"

"You can use that number," she said. "Or, there's another one. Business." She thought for a moment. She knew she was at a small crossroads right here: she could go forward in life, take a chance, or cling to the past. She knew someday there would be a life beyond Fin Cen. Should she trust God, she wondered, to move her in the right direction, or should she hide from life and all its decisions, large and small?

"You okay?" he asked, picking up on her silence. "You're rather young for a senior moment."

"I'm fine," she said. "I'm going to take a chance on something. It's between you and me, all right? What I do, where I work, okay? Absolutely no one else in the building, for example. No one at all. I have your word?"

"Absolutely. I'm good at keeping secrets," he said, suddenly quite earnest. "You have my word."

She reached into her purse. She found one of her business cards. She handed the card to him. He looked down at it. She watched the surprise register on his face as he read,

Alejandra LaDuca
United States Department of Treasury
Financial Crimes Enforcement Network
414 Wall Street
New York, New York 10001

"That's me. That's what I do. I investigate financial fraud for the government. And that's my real name. I have some personal security issues from some unpleasant cases in the past. Hence the Susanna."

He was still looking at the card. Then he looked up.

"If that's something you find difficult to handle, what I do, I don't blame you," Alex said. "But if we do see each other again, please call me Alex, except in the building, where I'm Susanna. Okay? I'm sorry I deceived you. Wrong name and all."

"Beautiful," he said.

"What is?"

"Your real name. Alejandra. I love the way it rolls off the tongue." He chuckled. "Alex? Is that what I should really call you?"

"Yes. Please do."

He studied the card for several seconds more, going silent again. Then he looked up.

"Bummer?" she asked. "I'm on a different day-to-day planet than you. I'm a straight-up law-enforcement type, maybe a little to the right of center on some things, maybe a little left of center on others. I'm a churchgoer, and a proud American. Why didn't I tell you earlier, huh?"

"You're telling me now." He sighed.

"Deal breaker?" she asked.

"Not in the slightest. It's refreshing. I respect what you do and how you think."

"People don't say that to me very often," Alex said.

"How wicked. I deal in make-believe; you deal with the real world, maybe the worst aspects of it. Correct?"

"Exactly. Yes. So?" she asked.

"I think it's awesome," he said. "People like you deserve medals. You should be proud of what you do."

"I am," she said.

"Right," he said. "So, look, Alex. I have something that I don't give to everyone either." He took out a small piece of paper from his wallet. She watched as he wrote down a ten digit number.

"It's my personal cell phone," he said. "The other number you have is an answering service. Let me know when you're back in town. It would be fun if you could see the show with my sister and her husband. They're both doctors. They do stuff that's important. I work in the candy store. Okay?"

"Okay. Thank you," she said, accepting it.

By then a small crowd was gathering. "I must be on my way," he said. "I need to keep moving."

"Of course," she said. "How do you get to the theater?" she asked.

"Like any other human being. It's only four blocks from here. I walk."

"You don't have trouble with fans?"

"I talk to everyone. The key is to be polite and keep moving."

"Have a great performance," she said.

"I'm sure I will. I feel good today," he said. "Very good, in fact."

Then, to her surprise, he leaned forward quickly and embraced her again. It was a firm hug. In surprise, she turned a cheek to him. He kissed her there.

"Travel safe," he said. "Wherever you're going."

"You too," she offered weakly.

He then gave her a wink, turned, and disappeared down West 44th Street, recognized by several people passing. She watched him go until he disappeared into the crowd. Then, almost reluctantly, she turned and went in the other direction, trying to suppress the knowledge that she remained a little celebrity-struck as well as completely smitten. That ... and the fact that she knew that their two worlds had collided.

FORTY-SIX

On Monday afternoon, Alex's inquiry at the Internal Revenue Service about Jonas and Jenny Frederickson bounced back to her. The numbers that Rick McCarron had provided her and which she had provided to the IRS — birth date and Social Security — had made a clean contact. Her contact at the IRS sent her scans of the Frederickson's tax returns for the previous three years.

Alex glanced at them in passing, long enough to see that the Fredericksons were currently residents of Glendale, Arizona, and had deducted huge amounts of legal bills as personal and professional expenses. Looking at the documents, Alex could not discern why the Fredericksons had drawn McCarron's attention. But one often couldn't.

She held on to the information for the moment. She wanted her boss's approval, or at least his collusion, before she made a move with IRS material.

Rizzo and Mimi were arriving tomorrow, Tuesday. Alex had agreed to meet them at their hotel later in the evening. She tried to concentrate on that and, as she had since Robert's death, push all personal stuff into a mental chamber that she chose not to visit with any regularity.

Then her eyes drifted to the bottom corner of one of her computer screens.

"Alex," wrote her boss across the wireless network. "Can you come in here right away?"

"Problem?" she wrote back.

The response came back with the speed and inevitability of a yo-yo.

"Feds," he answered. "More interference, more stupid questions, more bloodshed."

"Uh-oh," she muttered.

She stopped what she was doing, cleared her screen, and headed for her boss's office.

De Salvo sat at his desk and hardly moved when Alex walked in. The chair to his right was empty; in the chair to his left sat a dark lanky woman with straight hair and an ill-fitting black suit. Alex had never seen her before.

"Have a seat," De Salvo finally said. "Any seat." The big leather one was the only one available. Alex sat. "This is Ms. Anila Vinjay," he continued. "Ms. Vinjay works for the Justice Department."

Politely, each of the two women rose, met halfway, and shook hands. They seated themselves.

"Ms. Vinjay, why don't you bring everyone in the room up to speed on why you're here," De Salvo growled, barely suppressing an evident anger. This was Alex's cue that trouble was brewing: there were only three people in the room. "Then we'll all be on a level playing field."

"Alex," Anila Vinjay began, "I'm sure you recall Special Agents Foreman and Wei who came by to talk to you about a congressional hearing on certain aspects of organized crime in the United States. They were here two weeks ago."

"Twelve days ago, actually," Alex said, thinking back quickly. She remembered the date because it was the day she had returned to New York—and the day after Mejías's funeral. "It's not exactly the type of thing I'd forget."

"Why don't I cut to the chase here?" De Salvo interrupted. "Our noble Senate subcommittee looking into criminal activity in the United States by émigrés has developed an insatiable interest in one Yuri Federov," he said. "And our distinguished elected representatives hypothesize that you probably know more about him than anyone."

"I'm not so sure. There were prosecutors who put him in

jail," Alex said. "They added investigators after my involvement ended. They might easily have known more than I did."

"But that was several years ago," Ms. Vinjay segued smoothly. "You saw him toward the very end. Final two years. In fact, if I recall what I've learned about your involvement, you saw him the day before he died."

"That's correct," Alex said.

"We're appreciative of your cooperation in answering questions," Vinjay said.

"Don't mention it," Alex said, hoping her sarcasm wasn't too evident.

"We'd like to ask you some more. Under oath."

"Ms. Vinjay here is a process server," De Salvo said. "For the United States Department of Justice. She's not here so much to ask for your cooperation, Alex, as to demand it. Some of our brothers-in-arms at the Justice Department don't understand the professional niceties of making a request, which would have been graciously granted, rather than a demand, which would be grudgingly obliged. There's a summons on my desk. You will see it in front of me. Alex, why don't you pick it up and place it in your possession. Then Ms. Vinjay can be on her way, back to her bosses, to whom I've asked her to extend my ill tidings and sense of deeply burning resentment."

Vinjay turned toward Alex. "You'll be under oath and before the committee for forty-five minutes," she explained. "Seven senators will be asking you questions, four Democrats, three Republicans. You will have two minutes to make an opening statement and two to make a closing statement, if you wish. You're entitled to legal counsel, and counsel can accompany you to the hearing."

Alex exchanged a glance with her boss as Vinjay spoke.

"Any questions?" Vinjay asked

"None right now," Alex said.

"Apologies, but I need to see you accept the subpoena," Vinjay said.

In a flash of anger, De Salvo picked up the document and

tossed it to Alex, softly but like an old-fashioned newsboy chucking an afternoon tabloid onto a doorstep. Alex caught it cleanly, like a first baseman, with her left hand in midair. Otherwise it would have sailed past her.

"There. It's accepted," said De Salvo. He looked back to the visitor. "You may be on your way now, Ms. Vinjay. The ensuing festivities that will take place in this office are not for you."

De Salvo and Alex held a silence as the process server rose quickly and left. The door closed slowly, and De Salvo followed it, and his guest, with a long, low profanity, then, "And *hare rama* to you too," he snarled, following her with his furious gaze.

Alex looked at the date on the subpoena. She was due in Washington a week from Wednesday. When she looked back up, her boss's eyes were on her.

"I don't know what they're rooting around for," De Salvo muttered, "unless they're trying to create their own headlines and make something out of nothing. God knows, you're clean as an unused white whistle in a nun's bedroom as far as I know, isn't that the case?"

"That's the case," Alex said.

"Maybe they've all gone bonkers down in DC, have you thought of that?" he asked. "Did I ever tell you about my batty Aunt Jessica, the Pancake lady? She'd ask you to come over for pancakes. It seemed fine, so did she. Then you'd go over, and she'd take you to her cellar. Her cellar was full of pancakes. Pancakes and mice. That's what our government is like these days. Everyone's batty and obsessive."

Alex managed a weak smile. A subpoena. Middle of next week — this was the last thing she needed, not that it would have been any more welcome at the beginning of the week.

"We'll hook you up with legal counsel," De Salvo said, intruding on her thoughts. "You'll need to confer with an attorney. Do you have anyone?"

"No. Not for something like this," she said. "Can you assign someone?"

"I'll make some calls over the weekend," he said. "I think I know the right attorney. Young woman named Judy Rosenberg. No relation to Ethel or Julius. Bryn Mawr and Yale Law. Sharp as a scalpel, which is not a complete coincidence because her dad was a classmate of mine at Princeton and is now the head of Orthopedic Surgery at Duke."

"Thanks," she said.

"Whatever you do, when you get in front of these senators, tell them the truth. Our legal person will intervene if there's anything involving security. But don't get caught with anything 'off' in the slightest. They're looking for something wrong more than they're looking for the truth, don't give them anything. They're like the FBI, except even more annoying and disreputable. Downright venal, if you ask me."

She nodded. "If you say so, Andy," she said.

"Don't you say so too?"

"Not as often as you do."

"Ah, well, I do. And more, I say much more, off forty years of firsthand experience with these rats."

She laughed again, knowing never to take him too seriously on his verbal riffs. "Thanks, Andy," she said, standing.

She caught him assessing her, head to toe. The up-and-down glance was unusual.

"What?" she asked.

"How's your wardrobe?" he asked.

"You tell me," Alex answered. "I think it's okay. Why? Are my skirts too short?"

"No, never. But you might want to check your wardrobe carefully. Prepare for your Wednesday in the spotlight."

"Why?"

"The aforesaid hearings will be on television," he said. "You'll want to look sharp as a tack."

FORTY-SEVEN

Alex sat in the lounge of the Gramercy Park Hotel that next evening at a few minutes past 8:00. From her vantage point, she could see the two elevators that served the lobby. She spotted Rizzo and Mimi when they stepped from the elevator. She smiled as the happy couple came through the door to the lounge.

Rizzo was looking dapper as ever, a dove-gray Hugo Boss suit and a light blue shirt open at the neck. He looked tanned and fit. Mimi was in a typical Mimi outfit, sweater, blue-denim mini, and brown boots. They walked hand in hand. Sometimes Alex wondered what men saw in certain women: this was not one of those moments.

Alex stood. Rizzo opened his arms and embraced her. The European double-cheek kiss ensued. Alex repeated a social smooch with Mimi, and they all sat. They spoke Italian, except to a waiter who was quickly at their table.

Refreshments arrived. Small talk followed. Rizzo and Mimi planned to stay in New York or follow Alex to Miami if she needed their assistance. Some extra eyes to cover her back, she knew, would be a good idea. So she encouraged the idea.

"When we're finished here," Rizzo said, "or finished in America, we're on our way to Brazil."

"To do what?" Alex asked.

Rizzo nodded approvingly in Mimi's direction. "Mimi has some computer-tech projects underway," he said. He gave her a visual handoff.

"A month ago I was thinking," Mimi said, switching to English. "People were trying to develop a hundred-dollar laptop to give to the Third World, you know, to bring them into up-to-date technology. It occurred to me that the cell phone *is* the hundred-dollar laptop. At university in Rome I studied art and graphic arts as well as interface design," she said. "So I invented a way to embed invisible-to-the-eye bar codes on even the smallest scraps of paper used for financial transactions at coffee plantations. Ninety percent of the working population of Brazil has access to a cell phone. So I created an application on a chip that retrofits used cell phones. So now the old phones on remote plantations will read the bar codes and then issue voice prompts to input the financial numbers. At one and the same time planters can accurately keep their records and shop for the best prices for their crops. Similar, there are public health applications that will allow the same phones to be used to treat and diagnose illnesses, so I think it's a viable business."

"Mimi's been running around Rome like a drunk squirrel gathering used cell phones," Rizzo said.

"We shipped more than two thousand on ahead of us," Mimi said proudly.

"And we've had some contacts in Brazil who can collect another two thousand," Rizzo said. "So Mimi's going to stay for a month and set up a small company." He paused. "I financed it for twenty thousand dollars."

Alex blinked. "Fascinating. And after a month?"

"I return to Rome, I think," Mimi said.

"Who runs your company then?" Alex asked. "You can't leave it behind to run itself."

"Ah. Grand question, this one. This here is why we choose Brazil," Mimi said. "My brother is in business in Rio."

"And he knows how to run a business, I'm sure," Alex said.

"Yes. Very much," Mimi said. "He went to business school at Dartmouth. Then after, he travel to Brazil and fell in love on the beach and married a Brazilian girl. They get married and make two babies, so now he runs his family and four companies."

"Well, at least he didn't do it in the opposite order," said Alex, enjoying Mimi's story and violence upon English syntax almost as much as Rizzo admired her spunkiness.

"No, no, he's a very strict Catholic," Mimi insisted. "But he will run the day-to-day business along with his others. We will visit every two to three months to study expansion."

"We're doing the applications in Spanish too," Rizzo said. "There's a big need in all the coffee producing countries: Colombia, Costa Rica, Honduras, Guatemala . . ."

"Well, I'm pleased for you," Alex said. "I admire your creativity and entrepreneurship. Good luck."

"Thank you," Mimi said. As conversation drifted in a different direction, Mimi abandoned the dialogue to Rizzo and Alex and withdrew into an e-tablet, where she got hooked into either a game or correspondence. Alex couldn't see the screen so she couldn't tell which.

"*Allora!* What's new with you, Alex?" Rizzo asked, jumping back into Italian. "Regale me with anecdotes. I know tragedy still lurks in your memory, as always it will, but perhaps does a glimmer of love threaten to sneak back into your life? Break my heart, but allow my spirits to soar at the same time. What transpires for you socially?"

She laughed. "Nothing much," she said.

"I don't believe you."

Alex sighed. "Okay. I had lunch with an interesting man this past weekend," she allowed.

"Ah, ha! And he treats you well, I hope? If not, I'll find out and there will be trouble."

Mimi looked up and smirked, wide eyes visible over the tablet.

"I don't think anything will come of it," Alex said. "He's quite handsome, quite charming, but he's in a completely different line of work."

"Why is that a bad thing?" Rizzo asked. "I say that's a good thing. See who has the better world, then you both move to that one."

"I think it was more a friendly occasion than a potentially romantic one," she said.

"And why do you think that?"

"I just do," Alex said, now wishing the subject would go away.

"If you will pardon my inquiry," Rizzo pressed, "would you like it to be a romantic one? Are you ready to allow this to happen for you?"

She was starting to feel uneasy with Rizzo's line of inquiry, despite his gentleness and sincerity. He was, she suddenly realized, asking questions that she was afraid to ask herself. Probing emotions that were too delicate and painful for her to examine. She wondered how he had focused in on them so quickly.

"Heaven knows that a man or a woman needs sunshine in life," he said, tapping Mimi gently on the bare knee. "I've found mine even at my advanced age. You deserve to find yours."

"Thank you for your concern, Gian Antonio."

"It's more than concern," he said. "It's a worry. On your behalf, of course. Perhaps more than anyone, I've seen up close what you have been through, how you have suffered and wept. So I ask as a brother might, or a benign uncle, but most of all as a friend who would do anything for your well-being."

"Thank you," she said. Impetuously, she leaned to him and kissed him on the cheek.

"Thank you," he said. "I like to think I earned that."

"You did," Alex said, settling back.

"I would not want to see you emulate those old Italian ladies from the last world war," he said. "They lost their husbands young, wore black the rest of their lives, and sat in second-story windows watching the street. Bah! That was no way to live. I mean no disrespect for your lost love, of course."

"I know," she said.

Rizzo paused thoughtfully. "This 'different world' you talk of. What world is this man in?"

There were not too many trusted friends with whom Alex would have continued such a highly personal discussion. "Entertainment," she said.

"Entertainment?" Rizzo echoed.

Mimi's gaze rejoined them.

"He juggles fiery torches in the circus?" Rizzo asked.

She laughed. "He's an actor, Gian Antonio."

Rizzo's eyebrows shot toward the ceiling. "Cinema? Television? Theater?"

"All three," Alex said.

"Successfully?"

"Very."

Mimi, suddenly captivated, switched into English. "Is he famous?" she asked Alex.

"He's very well known," she said. "Please don't press me for a name. I'm not going to tell you."

"Is he *hot*?" Mimi blurted in English. "Is that how you say it?"

Almost blushing, Alex laughed and answered. "A lot of women would say so, yes. He's hot."

"Then you should jump him before he gets away!" Mimi insisted.

"Mimi!" Rizzo scolded. He put his hand to her mouth as they both laughed. A mock struggle ensued. "The poor girl has a one-track mind these days," he said. "Romance. Carnality. I don't know why. Surely I don't encourage it."

Mimi coughed.

"Of course not, Gian Antonio," Alex said.

The struggle over, ending with something akin to a bear hug, Rizzo switched the conversation back into Italian.

"Basta!" he said. "Enough of this!"

But now it was Alex who felt compelled to clarify and add more, perhaps in touch with her feelings better than in most recent times. "Yes, I guess I would say I'm interested. How could I not be? But I barely know him, and, let's face it, he travels in a world of fame, celebrity, and wealth. Why would he be interested in me for anything other than a short time? I offer none of those things."

"But those are the things he has, those things you named," Rizzo said. "Is there a woman in his life?"

"I don't know. Maybe many. He'd certainly have the opportunity."

"I hesitate to ask ... is he married?" Rizzo asked.

"No! He's not."

"Then potentially you offer him something that perhaps he wants. Is he intelligent? Educated?"

"By what I could see, yes. Highly."

"Then you offer something that perhaps he does not have: a bright, caring woman as a companion, highly exciting in your own private way."

"You flatter me, as usual."

"I am your friend, but I have cold, steely eyes," Rizzo said. "I act as your *consigliere* and offer advice that is yours to take or reject. And I have your back, as always."

Alex sighed. "Maybe he's the right man at the wrong time," she said, now trying to get off topic. "We'll see if I ever hear from him again."

"Right time, wrong time," Rizzo said. "We don't control the times in our lives. Death is inconvenient, life is opportunistic. God closes doors to us, God opens other doors if we allow him. We must be alert and navigate those passages, those corridors, when they are in front of us, the same as we negotiate the impediments. That is today's installment of free personal advice."

"Thank you," Alex said.

"So, now I suppose I should get right to the ugly matter at hand," Rizzo said, his tone changing. "Your Párajo. We've done some extensive security inquiries in Rome, you know. Following up on the people who slipped so quickly and efficiently out of the country. We have wiretap and listening facilities available for a policeman's signature. And sometimes we choose not to go through the red tape and interference as you have here in America. It's best to ignore it sometimes. That's what I plan to do in the future, and ..."

"Go ahead," she said. "I still have a rule book I need to worry about. Listen, I've already linked the Dosis to three murders in Miami. Anyone who they suspect of being an informer or in any way working against them can draw their wrath." She paused. "Your own Captain Cabrini provided that to me: three small-time wannabe hoods named James Kevork, Nicholas Skypios, and Thomas Vierra all had the misfortune to turn up in seriously terminal health in Miami within the last month. Coincidence? I think not."

"Animals!" Rizzo cursed. "And often they make a point of their assassinations, the Dosis. As a lesson to others. Often an extra element of brutality or the macabre. Murder someone with his own weapon, for example. To hoist a man with his own petard. They do these things to demonstrate how powerful they are, that they can get away not just with murder, but with murder plus!"

"One of the victims in Miami was pulled out of his car and shot. Then they hung him over a causeway bridge in the rain."

"As I said, animals," Rizzo muttered. "And so where does that leave us, morally and logistically? The more we pursue them, the more we endanger innocent people. What is our solution?"

"I don't know yet," she said.

"We should send in a special team," he argued, now on a vengeful roll. "Your government could do it, the same way they did to Bin Laden. Laws are nothing to these people. The only law is execution. Why do we let them live when they will kill us?"

Exasperated, not wishing to follow this line of discussion, she opened her hands in frustration. "Again, I don't know."

"Well, that is my solution," he said. "I would organize a team. Strike them first. Cut the heads off the two lead snakes, and the other little serpents will slither off into the high grass and get lost."

"I understand your point," Alex said, "but it's not something I can authorize."

"Would you if you could?" He sounded as if he were fishing for specifics.

She thought long. She sighed even longer. "I don't know that answer either. I pray that I won't ever have to make such a decision."

"Could your boss authorize it?"

"I doubt it," she said.

"All right, all right, listen," he said, shifting gears, seeming to put a lid on an ample amount of frustration. "The larger things, let's move to them, the immediate ones we are here to discuss. In my youth, and I suspect you do not know this, Alex, I was a fine player of football. Soccer to you, European football. I played with teams in my university days, and we had road trips against some foreign opponents." Rizzo sat up a little taller. "I think anyone who knew me could attest to the inadvisability of allowing me an open shot within twenty meters of the goal from my striker's position."

"I'm sure," Alex said.

"Too old for it now, of course," he said. "So I content myself with the games that I can still play vigorously." He looked at Mimi and winked.

"Like Angry Birds," Mimi said with a schoolgirl grin.

Rizzo continued, "Even as a young man I knew which way my career was headed. So I made it a point to network early, much as you have in these last few years. I would always be cordial to the other players, visit their locker rooms and club houses, and learn who they were. Over the course of many years, faces would reappear, either in person or in the newspapers, in the smart Sunday magazines or in the news. One such, whom I will refer to here only by his first name of Mario, became a nodding acquaintance of mine over several years as we played against each other in Rome. I assessed him as a man with a laudable future at that time, and I did him favors. Mostly, in terms of women. He was a bold man in sports and business but lacked confidence with beautiful females. So I would arrange introductions for him. He eventually found his stride and poise as a gentleman, and at that time I did him an ultimate favor. I introduced him to a spectacular young Athenian girl from a wealthy shipping family. They wed. I was the best man at their wedding. They prospered. His wife made a second fortune in wallpaper design and home furnishings while he accrued personal power within the government. They had five children, two of whom have moved to America, one of whom lives here in New York with her American husband."

He paused to sip water. Mimi made herself busy now with a Blackberry, seeming to not pay attention, but Alex knew she was tuned in.

"I would see Mario from time to time in Rome," Rizzo continued. "He had a high title and position in the Italian Foreign Office, but I did some digging a few years back. People know people in significant places, you know. Foreign Office people chat and snoop, and pretty soon it becomes an open but unacknowledged secret as to what a chap is really up to."

Alex grinned. "Well done, Gian Antonio," she said.

"Grazie mille," he answered with a polite but small bow. "But do not jump ahead. My *amico,* Mario, was assigned to the antiterror brigades, the gentlemen who fought the Marxist Leninist street scum, the *Brigate Rosse* — the Red Brigades — in the eighties and Baader-Meinhof in the seventies. They now concern themselves mostly with this plague of trash and sedition that darkens Italian shores from North Africa. So I figured that this would be the perfect time for Mario and me to share a glass of wine one evening at a bar overlooking the Tiber. So there we were last week, two dignified older gentlemen in dark suits chatting over Strega. Have you ever had Strega, Alex?"

"Yes. And we have something in America that tastes like it too. Called Pine Sol."

With mock affront, he answered, "I take it that you don't like it."

"You take it correctly. Galliano I'm fine with. Even Sambuca is okay. Strega ..." She stuck out her tongue with amused distaste.

"Ah, well. In any case, Mario and I, we were talking about Berlusconi, Juventus, Marine Le Pen, Lionel Messi, and Zucchero. So there was finally a pause, and Mario looked at me and said, 'Gian Antonio, *dimmelo,* why are you here? I suspect you have an agenda.' And I said, 'Yes, I do. Many years ago, I did you a favor with a woman, Mario. Today, I come to you to ask you a favor on behalf of another woman, as spectacular and wonderful as the one to whom I introduced you and whom you married. This is a woman named Alejandra, who is among my dearest and most cherished friends, who works for the US government and whom I would marry in an instant myself if only she would have me, which she will not because she is too smart and sophisticated for a filthy, lecherous, toothless, disagreeable old dog such as myself.' And he said, 'But how could I help you, you toothless, disagreeable old dog?' And I said, 'Old boy, there are no secrets at this table. I know what section you work with, and I know what information is at your disposal.'"

"And how did he answer?" Alex asked.

"By pouring another drink," Rizzo said. "More Strega. Then he said that he also knew what I did, both for the police in Rome and for my American employer. And he further asked if this was an official inquiry that had brought us together this evening. I said no, it was too important to be official, and there had been breaches in security already in the matter in which I was interested. And then I explained what had happened in Rome and about those people who are being monitored in Morocco, and what the highest levels of our government might have on these despicable Dosi criminals and who their contacts are. He listened, and we sipped more Strega, and we looked out upon the river and the lights of Rome beyond. You see, three or four drinks and anyone's tongue will wag with too much enthusiasm. So I was creating this as a factor too."

"Capisco," Alex said, understanding.

"So 'These Dosi people, they are after your friend, Alejandra?' he asked. And I said yes. And I said they had made an attempt on her life, had missed, and needed to be stopped before they succeeded with another try. They needed to be imprisoned at the very least, but I had already established, and I shared this with him, that they had also already had some very dirty dealings in Italy, perhaps involved in an unsolved case in Brindisi where two policemen were murdered. So these were people, the Dosi couple, with whom he might definitely have a file and see some ongoing surveillance. And I added, hoping this is all right with you, Alejandra, that if Mario could do us a favor of significance, your agency in New York might be able to do some back-channel favors in the future."

"Absolutely," Alex said.

"That's good. For that is the arrangement I made."

"Fine," Alex said.

"Two days later," Rizzo continued in Italian, dropping down a few more decibels, "Mario and I meet again. Same hour, same place, but the mood is more somber. He tells me more about the policemen in Brindisi who were murdered. They had interfered with a smuggling case that touched upon this Dosi operation. One man got into his family car one morning to come to work, and it was rigged with a bomb. It blows up, kills him and his five-year-old daughter, whom he was taking to school. The other man, the very same morning, he comes out of his apartment building and a stolen van, it explodes, killing him and a bystander."

There was a long pause as Alex stared across the table at Rizzo.

"There are three other cases across Europe," he said. "Car bombs, all of them. One in Bremen, one in Italy, and one in Marseilles. All involved Dosi cases; all were involved in smuggling and export. This is one of their most frequently chosen ways to strike, Alex."

"Well, I don't own a car," Alex said. "Not right now. And I don't think they know where I am."

"Never be too sure about their not knowing where you live," Rizzo responded. "As for the car, it doesn't matter. You walk by cars every day." He paused. "The car bomb is their usual signature. The gunshot through your window was an aberration." He assessed Alex coldly. "Something extreme will have to be done to eradicate these people," he continued. "Mr. and Mrs. Dosi. The world would be a better place if they were dead. If they were sitting at that table over there," he said, indicating a couple seated several feet away, "I should walk over there and shoot them. Your country should give me a medal for doing so. I make no apologies for saying this."

Alex thought about it.

"Obviously, they don't plant their own bombs," she said. "Who does it for them? Do they hire people or have their own roster of specialists?"

"Our intelligence says they have their own teams," he said somberly. "That's what our intelligence reports told us they were doing in Rome. They dispatched a new man — to the United States, Alex. A Panamanian, working alone. Our sources say this man met the Dosis at the hotel in Rome and they paid him his opening stipend. Then he flew to America. He is already in your country. He may have more than one assignment. But it would appear that you are one of them."

There was a long pause. Then a sinking feeling came upon Alex, much as if a doctor had told her she had a terminal disease. She stared at her friend from Rome whose eyes had become dark pools of sympathy and sorrow.

"I am truly regretful over bringing you this news," he said. "But better you should know now than too late."

"Of course," she said.

"Alex," he said, placing a hand on hers. "You must not drop your guard for a moment. You must be excessively careful. And someone must constantly cover your back until the danger passes." He paused. "Oh, and one other thing," he said.

He reached into his pocket and withdrew the silver pen with Alex's name engraved on it. He handed it back to her.

"Yardena Dosi left this behind in Rome," he said. "In the future, take better care of it."

FORTY-EIGHT

Shortly after midnight, Alex's cell phone rang, rousing Alex from sleep. She reached to the bedside table and answered.

"Alejandra?" The caller was a young woman.

"Yes? *Si?*"

It was Sister Ramona from Miami, babbling in Spanish in a low lilting voice. She was back from some sort of family convocation and was working again at the botánica, she said. She was ready to talk. Even better, even more miraculously, she said she was ready to convey a message from the dead, though she was vague about whether she had received the message before or after the deceased was deceased. All this was in the way of small miracles, she said, and there would be even more miracles if Alex could return to Miami.

"I've been to Miami twice in the last month, Ramona," Alex said, irked and sitting up. "Talking my boss into paying for a third trip would be a real miracle. So why don't we talk right now?"

"Now is not the proper time, Señorita Alejandra," Ramona said, continuing in Spanish. "And the phone is not the proper way. Not conducive to the spirits."

Alex blinked awake, not completely pleased with the manner of the intrusion, pleased even less by the cat-and-mouse game. "Both would work for me, Ramona," Alex said. "Why don't you have a quick meeting with your spirits and talk them into coming on the phone. Now."

"These details do not work for me. I am so sorry."

Alex tried to suppress her anger. "Why don't they work for you?"

"It isn't proper," Ramona said in a small, cryptic voice. "We need to have the right time and setting."

"I thought the setting was fine the other night at the restaurant," Alex said. "You followed me, then you bugged out. Now you want to meet. Which is it, Ramona? I don't have time or patience for your sort of nonsense."

"Apologies," Ramona said. "It will all be worth your while."

"Then why'd you run out last time."

"The man you were with."

"He was fine. A friend."

"Bad vibrations. I didn't like. He looked like a policeman."

"He wasn't."

"Still. Bad vibrations."

"And who was your wheelman?" Alex asked. "I don't have a chauffeur around Miami, so I'm impressed that you do. Who's your driver."

"We need to have a *mediación*," Ramona said, ignoring Alex's question.

"A what?"

"A *mediación* — a meeting between spirits in this world and spirits that have moved on to the next."

"A spirit like that of Yvar Mejías?"

"Yes."

"And where would this unique and highly desirable event take place, Ramona?"

"*Mi casa.* My home," she said.

"When?"

"Late this week. Friday? Saturday?"

"And, uh, the spirits will feel obliged to make my third trip to Miami worthwhile?"

"*Creo que si, Señorita Alejandra,*" she said. "I think so. And we must convene in *la madrugada*, the early morning hours."

"I don't suppose the spirits are interested in money, are they?"

"That would not be a bad thing," Ramona said.

"It never is, is it? I mean, sometimes it's amazing what the US Treasury will pay for as long as you hide it deep enough and the taxpayers never find out."

After a moment, Ramona offered a polite laugh. Or maybe it was a nervous laugh. Alex couldn't tell.

Alex looked at the bedside clock radio and its printout: 12:34 a.m. She liked the orderly flow of the numbers but didn't like the hour of the phone call, much less the recalcitrant spirits for hire.

"Please give me a number where I can reach you tomorrow," Alex said. "I'll have to get my boss's approval. Then I'll confirm the meeting, if I can."

Ramona gave the cell phone number again, the one she was calling from, the one Alex had called several times in the days that the elusive, self-proclaimed priestess had been unreachable. She then struggled to get back to sleep, her fatigue mixed with annoyance.

But when Alex called back the next day, she reached Ramona again, and some dark shadow seemed to have lifted. Ramona was in good spirits — or maybe surrounded by them. She was cheerful and talkative. Questions would be entertained and questions would be answered if they could meet at Ramona's home, the one that Alex had already visited.

Alex ran it by Andrew De Salvo. Even if Ramona blew off the meeting, they decided, one could have a final look around Miami before washing one's hands of the possibility of finding anything there. So De Salvo approved the new travel expenses. The only caveat was that Alex needed to be in Washington by the following Wednesday to talk to the Senate subcommittee. And an hour or two of preparation and consultation with attorney Judy Rosenberg, her assigned attorney, before the questioning would be a good thing also.

"I think Ramona's looking for a little payout too," said Alex. "How are we on doing such things?"

"There's a healthy domestic rodent fund," De Salvo said. "Invoice a thousand dollars. I'll sign it. See if you can hold her to five hundred."

"Okay," said Alex. "One other thing. What's our policy on swapping files with other agencies?"

De Salvo rolled his eyes. "You're certainly getting down and dirty in this job," he said. "What's up your sleeve?"

"My CIA contact in Miami," Alex said. "He asked if I can pinch an IRS file for him. He did me some favors in advance and is in a position to do more."

"Good favors?" he asked. "Not chicken feed, but solid stuff?"

"It would appear that way."

"Ha! It always does. Well, file swapping. It's like wife swapping and heavy drinking in the various departments. Everyone does it but nobody talks about it — and you sure don't want to get caught. Does that answer your question?"

"Yes, it does."

"So, are you going to do this deplorable trade-off in the near future? Or have you already done it?"

"No, I haven't done it yet. I waited to ask," she said.

"Nice of you. But next time, don't bother. Just do it. You know what you're doing."

She stood, thanked her boss, and left his office.

Next Alex phoned Rizzo. He and Mimi could be in Miami on the weekend, Rizzo promised. Alex planned to fly late the next day, Thursday, and suggested, as a precaution, that Rizzo and Mimi fly separately the same day. Then they could rendezvous at the Park Central in Miami on Friday. Rizzo was fine with that.

Working quickly from her desk, Alex also called Rick McCarron to let him know she would be returning to Miami the next day. She also told him that she had printouts of the IRS information to hand over. She didn't want to leave a cyber trail if it could be avoided and didn't want to meet in person in case either she or McCarron had watchers on them. So she asked if she could FedEx them overnight to his home and if Rick could wait another twenty-four hours. He thanked her and said he could. She would send them under a dummy account later that day, paying cash.

Getting back to Rizzo late in the afternoon, Alex confirmed everything for the end of the week and weekend. A subsequent call to Ramona set up a meeting at Ramona's home for late Saturday evening. Alex said she was bringing a friend, maybe two, both from Italy and both of whom were interested in Santería, which was not untrue.

"Are they police?" Ramona asked.

"They belong to no state or federal police agency in America," Alex said. "They are friends visiting here on business. And there's a small amount of cash in it for you if things are productive."

Under the circumstances, Ramona promised that things would be productive. She was even more specific. The meeting at her home would be, as promised, an intervention between her and the departed spirits. A séance, of sorts.

"And you think that's a good thing, do you?" Alex asked.

"A very good thing," Ramona said. "Come to my place shortly before midnight."

Through it all, as Thursday approached, Alex continued to work with her internet contacts on the Dosi operation. At the same time, she kept her eyes carefully honed on the street and watched for any unusual vans or cars on her street. Heeding Rizzo's warning, anything on four wheels was a potential threat. But yet over all, the Dosi threat did not seem imminent. And after the first few hours of her fearfulness, the threat seemed to recede. She tried to remain vigilant, however, knowing that there was nothing so fatal as a false sense of security.

As for Eric Robertson, that threat, or promise, seemed to recede also, or at least fade into the many background themes of Alex's life. She ran into him late Wednesday evening in the building lobby, and he was gracious and polite, but something didn't seem quite right.

"Oh, yes, I do indeed need to connect with you again," he said. "Susanna. Sorry I mean, Alex. So hard to focus on anything when I'm in a show. Hope you understand."

"I do. I've been slammed at work, myself."

"I like you," he said. "You're a trooper too."

He seemed, in fact, a little tipsy. Almost as if he was on something.

She should have known better. She gave him a second glance, and he was downright unsteady on his feet. He was on too much of something.

Then he swooned. He looked to be in danger of falling. She held out both arms and steadied him. He pedaled backwards unsteadily and leaned against the wall.

"Are you all right?" she asked. He was breathing hard, then a silly grin crossed his face. Her hands were still upon him, keeping him upright.

He laughed. "Can't you tell?" he asked. "I'm flying high!"

She drew a breath. Slowly, she released him.

"Ever take anything that flew you to outer space?" he asked.

"Drugs, you mean?" she asked.

"Yeah."

"No," she said. "Not my thing. And I'm disappointed if they're yours."

"I had a filthy performance," he said. "I'm so not in the mood for a lecture."

"Don't worry. I'm not in the mood to give one."

She released him. His eyes locked on hers.

"You are very beautiful," he said with all the acuity and logic of the truly intoxicated. "May I kiss you?"

She stepped back and let him slide down to the floor. He struggled back to his feet without her help.

"Good night, Eric," she said.

"Good night, dear lady," she heard him say as she left him

So much for beautiful dreams and beautiful dreamers. Dreams and dreamers, in more ways than one, Alex thought as she disappeared to her proper floor. She wondered if her business card, what she did for a living, had been a giant turnoff after all. He was an actor, after all. If he could fool two thousand people in a cavernous theater into thinking he was Lt. Joe Cable in the South Pacific in 1945, well, fooling a gullible working woman on a New York cross street wasn't such a challenge.

She wondered why she had even been foolish enough to think

he was doing anything more than taking a neighbor to lunch. She felt blown off. Insulted.

She replayed his line in her head. Oh, yes, I do need to connect with you again.

He was the smoothest guy she had ever met at blowing a girl off, as it turned out. Actors. They had women throwing themselves at them every day. Typical. Connect. Sure! There, she concluded. Just as well. Not putting my heart and soul at risk again, maybe not ever. I am not going to love and lose twice in a lifetime. I'm too smart for that. Too smart or too vulnerable.

But there was one bizarre footnote.

Early Thursday morning, Alex's phone rang in her office. It was Rizzo. Mimi wanted to see a show on Broadway and there was a good chance Mimi would be going on to Brazil after Miami.

Rizzo had promised a top show. Rizzo had a scalper on the other phone line and could obtain tickets, he said, that evening to *South Pacific*. Would Alex be interested in joining them, he asked. If so, they could all change their flight reservations to Friday.

"I'll pass on that, okay?" Alex answered.

"You're sure? I understand it's quite good," Rizzo pressed.

"I'm sure it is," Alex replied smoothly. "Just not in the mood for it this evening."

"Final answer?"

"Final answer," Alex said. "Enjoy. I'll see you at the Park Central in Miami on Friday."

"You will indeed."

"My contact wants to do a séance to communicate with insightful spirits," Alex said. "You okay with that?"

"Whatever works," Rizzo said.

"Glad you feel that way," Alex said.

There was a pause. Rizzo spoke to his scalper. Then he came back on the line to Alex. "Listen," he said, "I can get three seats in the fifth row for $600. My treat. Come with us."

"I'm sorry, Gian Antonio. The answer is no."

"But it's *South Pacific*. It's the hottest show in New York."

She snapped. "I don't want to see it! I don't have time! I'm not in the mood! Okay?"

"What's bothering you, Alex?"

"Nothing!"

"Va bene," he replied evenly. "And when the 'nothing' stops bothering you, we'll meet in Miami. I'm here for you."

Rizzo rang off. Alex set down the phone and stared at it for a moment, exhaling long and hard. The small conversation, touching upon Eric Robertson even in absentia, pressed her into a snarly mood that she didn't understand until she admitted to herself that she was more attracted to Eric than she had thought. Now he was history, at least in light of his miserable wobbly performance in the building lobby that week. She already felt contrite but resisted the impulse to call back and apologize. She needed more cooldown time. Then she would call. Her mind needed to unscramble.

So, as was her habit in such cases, as had been her habit for several months, Alex returned to her work with a surly vengeance. Due to thunderstorms in New York, flight schedules were scrambled on Thursday, and she nudged back her return to Miami till Friday, using the extra day at her desk in lower Manhattan to decompress and pull together as many details as possible on the case before her. And she did everything she could to push away any outside distracting thoughts except for one: at the end of this — if she survived — the Dosis were going to pay one hell of a price.

FORTY-NINE

In the quiet hours of that same evening, Luis was hard at work in his garage. Señor Ortega would return the next morning, and Luis was putting the finishing touches on an explosive device for him, one which, as ordered, would ride innocently in the storage space of a motor vehicle until detonated.

Luis turned his attention to his explosives. He had enough dynamite to damage a quarter of a city block. He needed to pack the explosives into a series of steel pipes along with a grab bag of nails and ball bearings. "Belfast confetti" this stuff used to be called. The provisional IRA had used such scraps to make Improvised Explosive Devices against British troops in Northern Ireland. The technique had been refined horribly over the years, but the primitive devices still left people just as dead. And that's what Ortega had asked for. Stuff that was so low tech that it couldn't be traced.

Luis blocked all the window shades in his garage and carefully threw the extra bolt on his door. He loaded a Colt .38, just in case he was disturbed, and laid it at the right side of his work space. He pulled on surgical gloves and then went to his supply closet, found the bag he had buried, and withdrew one stick of dynamite.

Intent on his assignment, he constructed his bomb. He placed six sticks of dynamite in steel canisters, two in each can. Then he found three smaller glass vials with screw tops in his workshop and loaded each with a supply of liquid chlorine. These he sealed tightly and packed each into one of the canisters. Then he filled the empty area in each device with his "Belfast confetti." The process was painstaking and continued for two hours.

Then, tired but still working carefully, he prepared his detonators and his initiation systems, the mechanism that would provide the electrical charge to ignite the device. Ortega had asked for a device that could be detonated from a remote location. Luis rigged the devices with detonators linked together and keyed into a cell phone that he had purchased from an electronics store.

By 2:00 a.m. he stepped back from his project. The device was complete. Ortega himself would have to do the final stages of implementation and work the device as close to the target as possible.

Luis didn't care to consider exactly who the target was. It was a rough world out there, he reasoned. People fought with the weapons they had available, and even those on the side of the so-called law were sometimes not the most moral of souls. So it was with a clear conscience that Luis packed away his work in the early morning hours of the day and then slept.

The sleep was fitful. He had worked for Dosi associates before. From time to time, police had made inquiries of him. He had never squealed in any way, but who could prove that to an angry madwoman in North Africa?

The pistol was near his bed as he dozed. The sooner Ortega was out of New York, the better Luis would feel. It was one of those occupational hazards, but a hazard nonetheless.

FIFTY

Late Thursday evening, Alex's flight from New York touched down with two friendly bounces and a fun skid. Then it taxied. Business as usual.

Alex traveled with a single overnight bag and a carry-on that included a small but powerful netbook. No need to stop at baggage pickup or wait for the aircraft to unload. So the voyage was smooth and the arrival pleasant until she was halfway through the concourse of Miami International Airport, when, from behind, a man hooked his arm through hers. A second man fell into stride on her other side.

"Just keep walking," a male voice said.

Reacting instinctively, her hand started for the weapon under her jacket. But a firm strong hand landed on her wrist and held it like a vise. She was about to drop her bag and start throwing elbows and knees when a third man stepped directly in her path and blocked her. He was a nasty looking sort in a suit with a vest. He stood about six four. He had the build of a grizzly bear with an IQ to match.

"Ease up, Alex," the man said, holding aloft a badge and tacking a profanity onto his greeting. "Give it a rest. Miami Police Department."

In return, Alex gave him a colorful greeting of her own.

"You gonna act like a lady or you gonna be trouble?" he asked.

"I'll act like a lady when I'm dealing with gentlemen," she said.

"Right," said the man in front of her. "And when you stop giving us problems, we'll stop giving them to you."

One of them held her left arm. The other one held her right

wrist. A strong hand from the man in front searched the inside of her jacket and swiftly took away her weapon. She made token resistance, but her arms were yanked sharply behind her. Another probe of her pockets found her cell phone, which was also seized.

"Just keep quiet if you know what's good for you," one of them said.

"I have a federal permit for the weapon," she said.

"Makes no difference."

"You arresting me?" she asked, incredulous.

"Nope. Worse than that. So shut up."

Instinctively she wondered if they were really cops. They pulled her away from the crowd and closed in tightly around her, escorting her at a quick pace down a corridor and, swiping an entry card, through a door marked No ADMITTANCE.

Then they marched her down another short corridor, which led to a small chamber. She knew this was an interrogation room. A steel table was bolted to the floor, and the chairs were linked to each other. They pushed her in, tossing her bags onto the floor against the wall.

"You got any other weapons?" one of them asked.

"You guys are detectives," she said. "Why don't you figure it out?"

They didn't bother. Two of them left. The last man stopped for a moment and looked at her. "Sit and wait," he said. "This shouldn't take long." Then he too left.

Alex sat. She waited. It did take long.

She suppressed her anger as well as she could. She remained at the table and stared at the door. Assuming there were surveillance cameras, she scanned the edge of the ceiling and found a device in one corner. The devil in her suggested that she flip it off, New York style, but she decided it was better to keep her awareness of the camera to herself.

A half hour crept by. She made mental notes of the time, details of the room, where in the airport she probably was. Then she heard footsteps coming in her direction. "Something wicked this way comes," she growled to herself. Beyond the door was a rattle of keys and the lifting of the lock before the door blew open.

Lt. Clarence Woodbine hulked through.

"Well!" he said as his three bulls followed him into the room and set up an impromptu backfield behind him. "Back in Miami, I see."

"It's legal."

"So it is. It's also irritating."

"Why is that, Lieutenant? I get the idea that if I didn't visit, you wouldn't know what to do with yourself."

While his acolytes remained standing, Woodbine turned a chair around and sat down on it backward, facing Alex. "Where is she?" Woodbine asked.

"Who?"

"You know who."

"Sorry," she said, selecting a facetious tone, "but until you tell me who you're talking about, no, I don't know."

"The one your CIA is hiding from me."

"Well, it's not *my* CIA," Alex snapped back. "I don't work for them."

"How do I know that?"

"How do you know anything?" she answered angrily. "I work for an agency called Fin Cen in New York. We work financial crimes, and I was straight up with you about all that. So get off my back, why don't you? And when you're finally off and get your balance a little, why don't we get back to the question you asked me. We can help each other, in case you haven't noticed yet? So who? *What* woman? Who are you looking for?"

After a grudging moment, "The one who murdered her husband," Woodbine said.

"What are you talking about, Woodbine? Give me a name."

"Don't play games. Forensics scoured the murder scene. They put everything together. DNA under Mejías's fingernails. Only fingerprints in the room. Jealousy, he was seeing younger women in Miami. It all fits together."

"Maybe for you. Not yet for me."

"You're here to see her," Woodbine insisted. "Why else would you be here?"

"Sun and fun on the playa. The Cuban food. Really, it's a vacation paradise for a working girl from New York, as long as you can avoid running afoul of the local cops."

"Don't be a smart-ass."

"Then don't treat me like a criminal."

"Take me to her," he insisted.

"Even if I knew where she was, Lieutenant, I wouldn't take you. That's not my job."

His voice was a low growl. "I have a warrant for her arrest," he said.

"If I happen to see her, I'll mention it," Alex said. "After all that's happened, I'm sure she'll be thrilled."

Many things went through Alex's mind as she heard herself dish it back and forth with Woodbine. That he must have had a contact in the airlines and had asked to be notified if Alex was coming back to Miami. How else would he have known? He also must have been at wit's end on the high-profile Mejías case, was flummoxed and publically embarrassed and thoroughly frustrated. Then again, she thought, when a wit was so dim, the end was always in sight.

Why else would he have pulled such a crude assertion of power in the airport?

"Don't be difficult, LaDuca," Woodbine tried next. "The Mejíases hated each other. CIA mined Mejías for all the information he was worth, then put his wife up to killing him after they had set him up with young women in Miami. Hot-blooded Latina, you know that? Now they're trying to get her out of the country before she can talk, and I've got a major case to close with a mayor and a press in two languages kicking my butt for a resolution. So there's the overview, and I want the Cuban woman."

"And where did you get all this?"

"I have my sources on the street."

"What if your information is wrong?"

"It's not."

"I'm still not buying it. No sale."

He leaned back, folded his arms, and fell belligerently silent.

His assistant, the big bear in the suit, better spoken, stepped into the void.

"Sorry about all this, Alex," the man said. "But we've got a hot case to work. Got to knock heads. You should see how the Spanish-language press is ripping us. Have you seen any of those obnoxious little rags?"

"I only look at the sports," she answered facetiously. "My favorite team is whoever is playing the Dolphins."

"Love your New York attitude, woman," Woodbine returned.

"Yeah, well what do you expect?" she answered, her voice rising. "How 'bout if I tell you that after I'm back in New York, I file a complaint with the Justice Department over how I've been treated here, and see if I can get your badges and pensions lifted?"

"Stifle it, Alex," Woodbine said, "if you know what's good for you."

But the bear, smarter and more articulate than his trainer, was still talking. "Well, listen, New York lady," he said. "If I told you that our sources also have indicated that Señora Mejías is ready to leave the country within a few hours — with passports for a party of four — you'd share our astonishment?"

She looked up. "I would, yes. And I still don't know where she is."

Woodbine had developed an unpleasant mannerism, Alex noticed now as her gaze jumped back to him, one which he probably retreated into when he was angry and frustrated and didn't even know his next move. He was holding his lower lip between his thumb and the knuckle of his forefinger, pulling the lip out as if it were deformed.

Sensing his befuddlement, that he'd fired his best shots and now had nothing, Alex went for the kill, or at least an exit.

"While you're all thinking things through," Alex said, "I'd like my weapon back and my telephone. Then I'd appreciate hearing your apology, opening the door, and letting me out of here. I'm willing to not mention what's happened here today to any of my superiors or make calls to my buddies at Justice as long as all that is done now. That offer stands for the next sixty seconds, so don't brood about it too long, Lieutenant."

Mystification, frustration, resentment, confusion. Woodbine wore elements of all four. Then he turned to his top thug. "Okay. Let her have all her crap back," he said.

One of the big dumb boys near the door fished into his pants for the telephone. The second one came forth with Alex's Glock. They laid both on the table with loud clatters.

"You can go," Woodbine said, turning back to her. "But if you catch a glimpse of that woman, you contact me. You're dealing with US law, not UN law, and not CIA bull-slinging law, all right?"

"Sure thing," she snapped, not meaning it. "I'll send you a postcard from Little Havana."

"There are more moving parts in this case than you'd ever understand from behind a desk in New York City, you hear me?"

"Sure thing, Lieutenant," she said, checking the clip and the chamber of the Glock, holstering the weapon, and putting the cell phone in her jacket pocket. She grabbed her bags.

"And stay out of my way in Miami if you're not going to cooperate. Next time we meet it'll be worse."

But it became an admonition for Alex's personal rearview mirror. One of Woodbine's gorillas, perhaps sensing who had emerged victorious from the tête-à-tête, held the steel door open for Alex, and she marched through.

"Have a nice life," she said. "All of you."

Woodbine was still rambling angrily as his words disappeared into the din of the airport and Alex returned to the busy concourse and freedom.

Alex went to the Park Central and checked in. She worked off her netbook that evening, took dinner in her room and exercised in the gym. As Friday midnight approached, she was still buried in office work.

Alex's mind was distant, still trying to sort through everything that had happened. Her reverie was so complete that she was jolted when her phone rang. She grabbed it on the third ring. She read the time, 11:47 p.m., and the caller ID in the same glance. Rick McCarron.

"Hi," she said, using no names.

"Me," he said, using the same exchange. "Not too late, is it?"

"Never."

"I got a few tidbits for you," he said. "How about a crash meeting? Tomorrow lunch maybe? It'll have to be late, maybe 2:30. A neutral place. Neutral and secure."

Listening between the lines, she knew he didn't want her coming near his office or his home, even on a weekend.

"Sure," she said.

"Your place. The deck," he said, meaning the rooftop restaurant at the Park Central.

"That would work," she said. "My relatives from Italy will be here. You get to meet them."

"All the better," he said. He understood. He rang off.

She closed down her internet access and prepared to call it a night. In her mind, she kept replaying the incident at the airport. The more she thought about it, the more one detail, almost buried at the time, stood out.

Four passports? Leaving immediately. For Spain?

What was that all about?

FIFTY-ONE

Alex met Rick the next afternoon, Saturday. They made their rendezvous at the newly built rooftop sundeck at the hotel. McCarron was dressed casually, athletic shorts and a light sweatshirt, a baseball cap, shades, and sneakers. The outfit needed no explanation. Alex figured he went out ostensibly on a jog by the beachfront in case anyone was following him. Then he ducked into the Park Central to meet up with her after he had cleared his back.

Rizzo and Mimi were there too, having arrived from New York an hour earlier. The four ordered a light lunch under the umbrella of an open-air table. Rick knew who Rizzo was and vice versa. Mimi was introduced as a friend.

"Okay, look," Rick said. "I've got my butt on the line with what I'm involved with here, so, with all due respect," he said looking at Rizzo, "I can only speak directly to Alex on this subject. You understand, I hope?"

"Of course," Rizzo said. Indicating Mimi, he asked, "Shall we withdraw?"

"What I'd really appreciate is for you to watch our back," he said. "I'd like to go for a walk." He nodded toward the beach. The ocean, with its surf that would cover conversation, was about fifty yards away.

Rizzo eyed the water and the beach. He smiled, gave a thumbs-up and an aggressive nod.

"Very good idea. Miami reminds me of Sicily," he said. Alex wasn't sure the remark was a compliment.

McCarron dropped two fifty-dollar bills on the table, weighted them down with a glass, and they rose to head for the beach.

Alex and Rick easily fell into stride at water's edge. Alex was wearing a skirt above the knee and espadrilles, so walking at the water's edge was easy and refreshing. She pulled off her footwear. Rick removed his sneakers and walked barefoot. Rizzo and Mimi followed from a promenade above the beach.

"So," Rick began, "you bring along your own godfather these days?"

"I do," she said. "And he'd be flattered to hear you call him that."

McCarron laughed.

"What's on your mind, Rick?" Alex asked. "That IRS file I got for you, you received it? Was it helpful?"

"It was," he said, "very much so. That's a big part of why we're here. There was nothing in it actually incriminating. But it did help paint a more accurate picture of Mr. and Mrs. Frederickson. Plus their location."

"Good," Alex asked.

"Why is that good?"

"Because I wouldn't want to ask you for another favor unless the first one I'd done had panned out," she said.

"You're a persistent woman, aren't you?"

"I take that as a compliment."

"It was meant as one," he said. "Yeah, I owe you another favor or two, but I might be asking you for one or two again down the road. So let me bring you up-to-date on what you got for me, okay?"

"That would be fine," she said. A small wave broke on the shore and rose up beyond their ankles. Then it withdrew. She liked the feel of it.

"Ever been to the Bahamas?" Rick asked.

"Once, for a week. Vacation. I was in graduate school at the time," Alex replied. "I went with a friend."

Rick said, "A cozy little place, the Bahamas. British Crown Colony. Prosperous. Very pro-American. And corrupt as hell. This couple I had you run up for me, Frederickson and his wife, or one or the other, committed a murder there and walked. Got out of the country scot-free. Happened about a year ago."

"American, right? I saw the IRS files but don't remember the nationality."

"Ugly American," said McCarron. "They were well known in the Bahamas. Had a big yacht moored in Freeport Harbour, right near the cruise ships. *Well known* doesn't translate to *well liked*. They were notorious for hard drinking, public brawls, and spendthrift ways. A boat-taxi driver disappeared a year ago. February fifth. A young guy in his twenties named Lonnie Sharp. Mr. Sharp's body turned up down-current from the Frederickson yacht with a bullet hole through the head. He was last seen giving Jonas and Jennifer a ride back to their yacht at 1:00 a.m. that morning. The Fredericksons were charged with homicide. First-degree-murder convictions carry a mandatory death sentence in the Bahamas. By hanging. The Fredericksons claimed they were innocent, of course, sang the usual song: claimed they were the victims of corrupt officials who wanted to extort money from wealthy Americans." Rick shrugged. "Most Bahamians sided with the Sharp family, which claimed the killing was racially motivated. Jenny had said she wanted to kill a black man to some of her social contacts. Claimed she told them she wanted vengeance because a black man had raped her in Barbados."

"Any truth to that?" Alex asked.

"None that we've ever come up with," Rick said. "In fact, passport registry told me that Jenny Frederickson had only spent a week in Barbados. We looked into that, anyway. The Fredericksons were there on a snorkeling trip in 1995. The allegation didn't hold up. No police report at the time. That should tell you something." He paused again. "Frankly, Frederickson and his wife were trouble everywhere they went. Fights. Unpaid bills. Incidents with police. Fights with local courts. Wealthy trash. Just a matter of time before they killed someone, in my humble opinion. Jonas was arrested twice in the eighties for conspiracy to traffic in cocaine in West Virginia and Pennsylvania, but there was never any conviction."

"Flimsy evidence?"

"Family pull. He's an heir to a coal-mining operation. They owned mines and mining equipment. He ran the company himself until a few years ago when he met Jenny. Then he sold it, pocketed millions, and decided to sail around the world. Slowly, and with incident. You know how these things play out."

"All too well," Alex said, adjusting her sunglasses.

"Anyway, none of the bullets found in Lonnie Sharp's motorboat or in his body matched those found in a box on the Frederickson vessel. But they were of the same .38 caliber as a gun the Fredericksons had declared to Bahamian customs. Frederickson was known to carry it with him. Claimed people were after him. Know what? Some people probably were since he'd made so many enemies over the years. Oh, and he was well known to be a race-baiter. Anyway, the gun went missing after the incident. Probably got dropped in some pretty deep shoals, if you ask me. The Fredericksons said the island's government didn't want to look for local suspects. Tourists might be scared away. So the Fredericksons went looking for help in Washington. White House. Congress. The Frederickson lawyers bombarded Congress members with material about the case. The material included a statement from a Puerto Rican lawyer saying he was negotiating to pay up to $250,000 to buy the Fredericksons' freedom. He said negotiations stopped when newspapers began publishing charges from a South African yachtsman that he paid a $50,000 bribe to get off the hook as a suspect in the fatal stabbing death of his wife. Anyway, the Frederickson case finally went to trial. It took eight months, and the Fredericksons were in jail in Freeport the whole time. The locals wanted to lynch them, save the government some expenses. Jonas must have had some great sleepless nights, wondering how this would end: walking free or swinging from the gallows. It was either one or the other. How do you think it turned out?" Rick asked.

"Not too well for the forces of truth and justice," Alex said.

"Why do you say that?" he grinned. "Because it never does?"

"That's one reason. Plus they had a history of buying their way out of trouble. But really I say it because you asked for IRS information. I looked at it before I passed it on. The Fredericksons live in Arizona."

"Right," said Rick. "They beat the charges and then flew out of the country to Florida an hour later. Had a plane waiting. Optimistic? Or was the fix in? There was a fistful of incriminating evidence that was never introduced. Again, fix? You decide."

"From the way you tell it, I already have," Alex said. "So have you."

"Anyway, they'll be useful for inventory," Rick said. "The Bahamians are the worst wheeler-dealers in the Caribbean. Baghdad on the Antilles. That makes them useful, doesn't it?" He rambled thoughtfully. "Lonnie Sharp had some friends. They don't like what happened. Frankly, I don't either. There's going to be a payback day for the Fredericksons, mark me. Unofficial, probably, but nasty payback. There's all this banking information in the Bahamas. Any middle-level manager can see accounts and numbers. Things I can use. So let's hypothesize: someone wants to visit the Fredericksons in Arizona, and I need to know where some sheiks have stashed some money. Do I really care if Jonas Frederickson or his wife pull up their garage door some morning and are welcomed into the new day by a barrage of bullets if I've scored one for Uncle Sam and sniffed out a ring of Islamic fascists?" He gave it a long pause. "I don't think so," he said.

"Sadly, that's how the world works," she said. "Hardball."

"Hardball," he agreed. "And don't forget I can probably do some Dosi snooping for you in the Bahamas. Baghdad on the Antilles, as I said. And that's being kind. Corruption is an art form on those islands."

Rick fell silent. The beach landscape suddenly seemed very inviting to Alex, very inviting and very innocent. It was like a great landscape portrait upon which nothing bad had ever been painted. It made her think of the similar seascapes she had seen in Cuba, coming ashore amidst a volley of bullets, leaving airborne much the same way, with Mejías and a very quiet wife in tow. The Cuban universe seemed to be another reality, and yet without that one she wouldn't be here dealing with another.

"So. Now that I've told you what's on my mind," Rick said, "tell me what's on yours."

"Quite a bit."

"Feel free to unload," he said.

"The file you provided for me," she said, "the one on Gemini. Figaro. Still fresh in your memory?"

"Reasonably," he said.

"There was a section in which an overseer of information reviewed the work of a case officer in the field and began asking questions. Adolf J. Frelinghuysen. Name mean anything?"

"Not noteworthy, except it might be the longest name in the whole agency."

"Frelinghuysen reviewed the work of an agent in the field. Or at least he attempted to. The agent, a guy named Tito, didn't care for being reviewed and essentially told him to go jump in the lake. Isn't that a bit of the tail wagging the dog?" she asked. "So how could that happen?"

"The guy in the field, this Tito, is pulling reverse rank," Rick said. "He's got some big-time juice coming from somewhere. He's linked in to power, maybe through a personal contact. Or a very important case."

"Or both?" Alex asked.

"Or both," McCarron answered. "That would explain a lot. Is that what was going on?"

"Yes."

"Unusual, I'll grant you that," Rick said. "But it happens. Agency politics."

"Would it explain how someone involved in the Mejías case might suddenly have access to four European Union passports and be set to use them to hightail it out of the country?"

"Why, yes. It would," he said very deliberately. He rubbed his chin. "Where did you hear about that?"

"A lieutenant in the Miami police force. He's a fan of mine . . . but not very bright. He lets things drop."

McCarron chuckled. "I get it." A silence as the sun bathed them. "Four passports like that are akin to a retirement present," he said. "It would be odd that they'd be issued to four agents. Four in a row, four aces like that, usually that's for a family. That make any sense?"

"It's starting to," Alex said.

"Let me know when lightning strikes," he said.

Near them, a couple of teenage girls overturned a Sunfish. They crashed into the water amidst innocent laughter. Rick stepped out a few more feet into the tide, helped them steady the boat, and they turned it upright again. They waved and sailed off.

"I should have been Jimmy Buffet," Rick said.

Alex grinned. "I'm convinced more was going on than just an agent overseeing the case. I want to know *todo* about Señor Tito."

"That's going to be a tough one," Rick said. "You're going to get closer to *nada* on Tito." He paused. "I'll see what I can do, though. I have some friends, some pull here and there."

"Thanks," she said.

Rick leaned down and picked up a shell. "Nice, huh?" he said, showing it to her. "Every color of the rainbow, exquisite." He handed it to her. "Miguel Orestes Milanés," he said.

"What?" She looked at him.

"Tito's real name. You didn't hear it from me, okay?"

"Okay."

"Just examine the shell while I lean in close," he said. The surf rolled in on their feet and ankles with a nice rumble. Rick took a few minutes to talk about Tito, his real name, his background, his career. No notes. No questions. He pleaded with Alex to never write anything down. Alex slammed the information into her memory vault, memorizing the name and as much of the backstory as she could. She was good at retention.

Standing close, they continued to turn over the shell. "Like it?" he asked, dwelling on the ambiguity of the shell and the information.

"Exquisite," she agreed.

"A keeper?"

"Absolutely."

"A souvenir of Miami," he said. "Put it among your possessions and use it accordingly."

She slid the shell into a skirt pocket. "Thanks," she said.

"Any other names?" he asked. "While we're on a roll?"

"One, maybe. A doctor. J. Montefiore," she said.

"Where's this coming from?"

"The Gemini file," she said. "One facet of Gemini was under the care of an MD by that name. August of 1997."

"What do you want to know about the doctor?"

"Anything? Where the practice is. What field of medicine. What Gemini's medical problem was. If the name is in your files once it's probably there more than once. Correct?"

Rick nodded. "Correct," he said.

They walked onward. They reached a point along the shore where a flotilla of plastic rafts had been beached. A gaggle of kids and nannies splashed and played with them, ready to launch a small joyful armada.

"Let's turn back," Alex said. "This will only take a few minutes."

They turned and repeated their path back to the hotel. Rizzo, from about a hundred feet away, picked up the move and stayed in place, ready to turn. He and Mimi were holding hands. Alex gave a subtle gesture with her hand, indicating they were going back to the hotel.

"Here's the further favor I'm going to ask you, Rick," Alex said. "And I'm going to owe you big-time, even bigger time than already, if you can provide this for me. I need airline passenger manifests for any airline that was flying from Mexico City to Havana in July of 1997. Do you think such a thing exists in the CIA archives?"

He thought for a moment. "I suspect it does. Somewhere," he said.

"I also need passport lists. What do you think? I want to know who was on those flights. Can you get stuff like that for me?"

"I think it can be done," he said.

"I'd be forever in your debt."

He winked. "I know. That's why I'm getting things for you. So you'll be forever in my debt."

"That's all," she said.

"Let me see what I can do," he said. "Meanwhile, I think I earned some extra credit."

"In what way?"

"I kept my ear to the ground on all this, since your Mejías hit happened right under agency noses here. There was one other piece of office scuttlebutt." He paused. "Your pal Mejías wasn't the most pleasant fellow to live with."

"What's that mean?" Alex asked.

"Chronic wife abuser," he said. "I talked to people who'd seen the file. Just fishing for anything that might help you. Seems Mejías was in the habit of waling on the little lady pretty hard from time to time. More like all the time, really."

"What a pig," Alex said.

Rick paused. "You know, you might not realize it now, but Juanita was quite a pretty woman when she was young. I saw some pictures. Came from what we used to call a 'good Cuban family.' Banking class. Very white. But she threw in her lot with Mejías, who must have been a dashing young officer at the time. Who knows what she saw in him?"

They continued to walk, but Rick was talked out. He had nothing further to add. He glanced back over his shoulder. So did Alex. Rizzo was still back there; so was Mimi.

"So, this Rizzo guy," McCarron said. "You trust him?"

"He's got my back right now, doesn't he?"

"Yeah. How do you know him?"

Alex explained it briefly.

"He's in Rome, right?"

"Usually," Alex said.

"Isn't that where your Dosi project blew up?"

"It is."

"Any possible connection?" McCarron asked. "No offense. Surely you've considered it."

"Of course I have. Gian Antonio I trust. We've worked together."

"Part of your network," Rick said. It wasn't a question.

"It didn't start out that way, but it's developed that way," she said.

He grimaced. "Welcome to the field," he said. "Who's the cute girl with him? Daughter? Protégée?"

"Protégée and girlfriend from what I can tell," she said.

McCarron looked back and shook his head in admiration. "He's got to be about sixty, your pal. Granted, he's in good shape. But the girl's what? Twenty-five?"

"Rick, it's none of our business," she said.

"No. But it could be."

She laughed.

FIFTY-TWO

Late that same evening, Alex's rental car pulled up in front of Ramona's home. It was past 11:30 p.m. already. Alex had reconfirmed the time and place with Sister Ramona earlier in the day, then had met Rizzo and Mimi in the lobby of the Park Central. From there they had driven to the address, Ramona's home, on the fringe of Little Havana. They had made only one stop: at a small bodega where Alex had purchased a half dozen eggs.

Ramona had insisted that Alex bring an egg. The spirits desired it.

They spoke English.

"Do you believe in any of this Santería stuff?" Mimi asked.

"Not for an instant," Alex said, parking.

"That makes two of us," Rizzo said.

"Three," added Mimi.

"But I did throw some salt over my shoulder for good luck," Rizzo said. "One can never be too careful."

"I'm convinced she has something to say," Alex said in a distinctly not-amused voice. "And that she'll put on a good show."

Ramona was dressed in a black gown when she met her guests at the door. There were fantasy appliqués in gold and silver on the gown. A strong whiff of incense followed her as the door opened.

"Please," she said. "Enter."

Alex did the introductions in Spanish.

Ramona eyed her guests. "Do we speak English or Spanish this evening?" she asked, speaking English for the first time in front of Alex. She spoke it fluently and natively. No trace of an accent.

"Either," Rizzo answered.

They went to the living room. There was a heavy ceiling fan rumbling. It broke up the stuffiness of the chamber. Ramona had prepared a small buffet of food, mostly cheeses and vegetables and a bizarre dip of which Alex was afraid to ask too many questions involving the ingredients. There was also an iced wine drink, Chilean red with cut fruit, a Sangria of sorts, that was better than it had any right to be. The late supper proceeded at a leisurely pace.

When the meal was finished, Ramona began to seal off the living room from the rest of the house. A sliding door closed to the entrance alcove. Ramona positioned her guests back in the living room.

"It's *madrugada* now," she said, referring to the early morning hours past midnight. "We can proceed."

On the old clock on the living room wall, a few minutes had ticked off past 1:00 a.m. Ramona drew a card table into the center of the chamber. Alex looked around. Ramona, or someone, had hung heavy draperies over the windows. Ramona methodically closed the two exterior doors. She made a production of latching them from within. She turned to her guests.

"Please sit," she said.

Aside from the table, the remaining furniture had been moved to the sides of the room. A worn carpet covered the floor. Alex tried to assess the logistics of the room before the lights inevitably went down. She looked for accesses and escape routes in case either became necessary.

By 1:20 a.m. the room had been "dressed" for the ceremony. Alex stood, watching as Ramona steadied the table. Four unmatching wooden chairs around the table.

"Where do you want to sit?" Rizzo asked Alex.

"Nearest the door," she answered, only partially in jest. She was the first to sit.

Rizzo drew a breath and sat down next, facing the door that led to the rear of the building. Alex's hands were already on the bare metal table. She wasn't quite sure what to expect. Gian

Antonio sat beside her to the left. Mimi seated herself next to Rizzo.

"Will the room be completely dark?" Alex asked.

"Yes. But your eyes will adapt," Ramona said. "When the spirits rise, they take their own light. It's God's wish."

"Yeah," said Alex.

Rizzo winked. "If it's God's wish, it's fine by me," he said.

Mimi looked both skeptical and fascinated.

Ramona covered the table with an ornate tablecloth, linen, mostly white, but bearing embroidered text in Spanish. Alex recognized the text: translations or permutations of Christian psalms. At least she found one she liked — the Twenty-third — and recognized: *"El Señor es mi pastor, nada me faltará ..."*

Next, Ramona produced a candle that Alex recalled from the botánica. It was a candle in the image of the deity Olodumare. It was about a foot tall in garish red, purple, and gold. Alex felt something within her telling her that she was in over her head, that she was treading on dangerous territory. But that was not her purpose here. She almost wondered if this was a provocation of sorts — so again she kept quiet.

Ramona set the candle down at the center of the table.

"We begin with a devotion to Olodumare," Ramona said. "And we will see what happens."

Ramona snipped most of the wick off the candle. She lit it. The flame blazed, then burnt very low. She turned off the room lights from a single switch on the wall. The shadows from the small candle threw an array of shadows across the room.

Ramona returned and sat down at the table. Suddenly visible, a large ornate cross hung on a chain at her neck. It swung loose, emerging from the open neck of Ramona's blouse and reflected the flame. It reminded Alex of the smaller, more dignified gold cross she wore. Alex fingered her own pendant, for courage, faith, and a reminder that God was with her.

"Please, now, everyone," Ramona said, "we hold hands."

Ramona led them through a brief prayer in Spanish, then went back to English.

"Now," Ramona finally said. "Everyone try to settle yourself. Close your eyes if you can. Put yourself in a receptive frame of mind."

Several seconds passed.

"Oh, yes," Ramona said. "And now we rest our hands on the table. Allow yourself to drift. Think about heaven if you wish. Heaven as you might want it to be."

Alex did as instructed. She tried to imagine the presence of God, of Heaven, of Jesus, and she knew what she was envisioning was probably different from everyone else in the room. But so be it. This, to Alex, wasn't a church, it was a show, a performance, a crude transmutation of what to her was a true faith. But again, she went with it. This was work, not genuine prayer. Well, okay, she thought further to herself, almost bemused. It was work with some of her own prayer mixed in.

"Now we all open our eyes," Ramona intoned, back in Spanish. "We will begin our *mediación* with the spirits."

From a small bag at her side, Ramona withdrew a small blue plate and a slate writing tablet, accompanied by a piece of green chalk. Ramona showed the writing surface of the slate. Alex looked at the slate, front and back. The writing surface was blank. She set them down on the table. "Who has the egg?" Ramona finally asked, remaining in Spanish.

Mimi withdrew the egg from the small carton and passed it to Ramona. Ramona refused to take it until everyone had touched it. She held her own hands open to demonstrate that there was nothing in them. Then she pushed back her sleeves in a quick motion and took the egg from Alex who was now holding it.

"*Gracias, Alejandra,*" Ramona said.

"*De nada,*" Alex answered.

Sharply, Ramona rapped the edge of the egg on the side of the saucer. She broke the egg shell and, with another quick flourish, dropped the yolk and egg white onto the saucer.

Sitting on top of the yolk was a small ceramic skull, about the size of a penny, hollow eyes, staring upward. The skull was black and wore a grotesque grin. Even Rizzo reacted with a chill. They all blinked at the swiftness and professionalism of the production. Mimi stared at the skull.

Predictably, Ramona said nothing, trying to play her audience. Alex played her in return several seconds, maintaining her own silence, waiting for the self-proclaimed priestess to speak.

Ramona wouldn't. Finally Rizzo spoke.

"I assume that's not a good sign," he said. "A skull in an egg shell. If I were making breakfast I would take that as a bad omen for the day. "

"No," said Ramona ponderously, not acknowledging Rizzo's snarky attitude. "It's not. You're bewitched."

"How horrible," Rizzo said without a suggestion of the sarcasm that lurked beneath his words. "We Romans, we hate omens like that."

Alex held her own silence, marveling how quickly Ramona had pulled the skull out of her sleeve after showing her empty palms. After several more seconds, Ramona turned to business.

"We will need to converse with the dead," she said, as if this was late-breaking news. "But we have need in our mediation," Ramona said. "Who will come forth with an offertory for Olodumare?"

The old cross-the-palm-with-silver game. Or cross it with green, Alex assumed. Alex had been waiting for it. She reached into a side pocket and withdrew one of her hundred dollar bills and laid it flat on the table.

"How's this?" Alex asked. "Would this put Olodumare in a talkative mood?"

Ramona looked at it and didn't touch it. Slowly, she began to shake her head.

"The knowledge that we request from the spirits is formidable," she said. "A hundred dollars is insufficient."

"It is, is it?" Alex asked.

Ramona nodded.

"Well, Ramona," Alex said soothingly, "let me tell you a little about the gods I have to deal with in New York, the gods of the

Financial Crimes Enforcement Center. A hundred dollars is all you're getting out of your mediation here tonight. If Olodumare comes up with something good for us, we'll be back and I'll have more cash. But in the meantime, I think we should proceed."

Ramona lowered her eyes again.

Smiles appeared on the faces of Mimi and Alex, then eased.

"Let me communicate with the other side," Ramona said. "Hands?"

She signaled that they were to join hands again. A strange silence fell on the room. "Please close your eyes," Ramona said. "And for good measure ..."

She produced a handful of blindfolds, straight from a drug store, meant for sleeping. She passed them around. Alex and Rizzo exchanged a glance, then put on their masks. Mimi went along with it also. Alex kept her mask adjusted so she could see peripherally. She had a hunch Rizzo was cheating also.

Several seconds passed. Alex became aware of noise beyond the house. The sounds of traffic. Very distantly there were voices of two people walking by. There were a few nearby creaks from floorboards beyond the room. Once there was a small lonely air-craft overhead. Nothing else.

Then Ramona blew out the candle. The room was dark. Ramona began to hum. Interspersed with her humming, she spoke, or chanted, aloud. Alex cocked her ears. Ramona was attempting to cover the sound of movement in the room.

Alex thought she heard something very faint, some move-ment in the room, a light footfall, the slightest sound of contact upon an old floorboard. Simultaneously, Alex thought she felt contact with the table. She knew how vulnerable she was. Some-one could come up to her under these circumstances, shoot her in the back of the head, cut her throat, or stab her in the back. She wondered how she could have been so stupid as to indulge Ramona in this way. She broke hands with Rizzo for a moment and lifted her own blindfold to her forehead. She glanced at Rizzo. In the dim light she could see that he had done the same thing. Oblivious to this, Ramona appeared to have kept her own mask in place.

Then the moment passed. Ramona stopped humming.

Hands rejoined, came down, and settled onto the table.

"We have received a visitor," Ramona said. "Please remove your masks."

All three were happy to. Hands disconnected. Masks came off.

There was a flash in the room as Ramona lit a match and relit the candle. The hundred dollar bill was gone. The blue saucer had been replaced by an identical saucer with the same skull in it, but the egg had vanished. And the slate tablet had moved.

Or *a* slate tablet had moved. Alex's eyes readjusted to the candlelight. Upon the tablet before her was handwriting. As if the chalk had moved. Alex eyed it. It faced away from her.

"Is this a message?" Alex asked.

"If the gods will it," Ramona said.

"May I?" Alex asked, reaching for the tablet.

"The spirits desire it," said Ramona.

"I'm so glad," Alex said. Alex reached to the tablet and pulled it to her.

The writing was very clear and bold in green chalk. An address was apparent: "2011 South Marina Drive, Miami."

"So? This is where I should go?" Alex asked.

"That's what the spirits wish," Ramona said.

Alex took out a pen and notepad and wrote down the address.

"The mediation is over," Ramona said. She made the first move to get up and stand.

"That's all?" Alex asked.

"That is all for today," Ramona answered.

"Doesn't seem like much."

"When the spirits leave something small, it is often of great value," Ramona said. "Don't jump to conclusions."

Alex looked at her, then at her allies at the table.

"All right," Alex said. "I'll see where this goes."

"May *todos los santos* guide you," Ramona said.

Rizzo made an initial hand motion to object, but Alex silenced him with a gesture.

"Thank you, Ramona," Alex said. "Come on," she said to Rizzo, switching to Italian. "Let's go for a drive."

FIFTY-THREE

Afterward, in the car, as Rizzo drove and Alex navigated, Mimi revealed from her place in the backseat that she had nailed the final quirk of the mediation. Her eyes had adjusted quickly to the darkness, more quickly than Alex and Rizzo, and had also run a fingernail through her eye mask so she could see, doing this even before Alex and Rizzo had fiddled with their own masks. She had seen the visitor, the so-called spirit that had come to their table.

"There was a panel in the wall," Mimi said in English. "Over by the bureau to my left. The panel swung open like a small door and a figure about a meter tall emerged. Maybe about four feet tall in American measurement."

"So what are we talking about, Mimi?" Alex asked.

"It was a small person," she said. "A female, I think. Thin and lithe, dressed all in black to make it difficult to see, moving very fast, but she knew exactly what to do."

"A child?" Alex asked.

"I child, I think, which is obvious," Mimi said. "But I couldn't see the face, and I couldn't tell the age."

"A child," Alex repeated. "Four feet tall. Maybe nine years old then.'

Rizzo pursed his lips as he continued to drive. How a child worked into the equation was not anything anyone of them could guess, least of all Alex.

They continued to 2011 South Marina Drive and found themselves at yet another deco-streamlined house in South Beach, ominously lurking beneath a streetlamp. It had the usual pastel paint job, pink and blue on white stucco. Two stories on a neat quiet street, all windows shuttered. Alex eyeballed it from the car. She glanced at her watch. It was just past 1:30 a.m. — not the greatest time to drop in on anyone, but not the middle of a Miami night either.

"Give it a drive-by, okay?" Alex said.

"Sure," Rizzo said.

In a strange confluence of thought, Alex fingered the cross at her neck and the Glock that rode in its holster.

They drove past the address. There were no lights at the address in question, aside from a single muted bulb on the front porch. As they passed, Alex looked around, wondering where any surveillance cameras were.

A less keen eye might have missed them. There was a miniature security setup on a light post twenty feet to the right side of the door.

"Slow down for a second," she said to Rizzo.

He did. Alex stuck her head out the window and looked in the opposite direction. Scanning diligently, she found the first security unit's companion piece, a similar small black box halfway up a tree near the sidewalk.

They circled the block, came back, and parked a hundred feet away from the address. "Now what?" Rizzo asked.

"I don't know," Alex said. "Go to the door? Have a look. If so, who?"

"I'll go," Mimi said

Alex thought about it. Mimi looked the most innocent. But she was also the most vulnerable.

"Whoever goes should be armed," Alex said. "Just in case."

Rizzo agreed. Mimi sulked for a moment.

"Let's give it a few minutes," Alex said. "See if anyone turns up."

They waited a quarter hour. No one did. The house was still, quiet as a tomb. They were all exhausted, but working on adrenalin and nervous energy. Nothing moved on the street, other than a cat that skulked quickly between parked cars close to the target address. Soon it was 3:20.

"Okay," Alex said. "I'm going to have a look. Drive closer and cover me."

"If there's surveillance, are you going to want to go that close?" Rizzo asked.

"I'm going to risk it," Alex said. "Ramona sent us over. I'm guessing it's friendly."

"What if it's not?"

"That's why we're armed," Alex said.

Rizzo made a low whistling sound. "Sometimes you're crazy," he said. Rizzo moved the car up the block and parked again, sliding in parallel to the curb between two cars that were already parked. He cut his lights. He left the engine idling.

Alex stepped out. Miami was deeper into the *madrugada*: thick nasty air, humid and gritty, bugs buzzing around the vapor streetlamps. Rizzo stepped out and stood on the driver's side, his hand on his concealed gun, watching like a terrier.

Alex went to the door. No knocking, no calling. This was pure surveillance. The door had an all too familiar glow: Solid wood with metal reinforcements.

The house was completely dark within.

Everyone sleeping? Or no one home?

No way to know. She also didn't feel like getting shot.

Alex moved up close. The front porch creaked. She waited to hear a dog bark. No dog. No nothing. Alex peered at windows, half of her waiting for all hell to break loose at any moment. Her damp blouse was clinging to her ribs again. Beneath her skirt, she could feel the sweat on her legs.

Absolutely nothing from within emerged. Not even a nightlight. Then she realized, the windows had been reinforced too. Black curtains were drawn tightly. This joint had a professional feel. But why? For whom?

Safe house or crack house? Gangbangers or CIA? Good or evil?

The front yard was well manicured. There was a mailbox by the street. Alex retreated, backing up slowly so she could keep her eyes on all windows and doors, looking for a curtain to rustle or anything to indicate movement from within.

Nothing.

She exhaled deeply and backed away. She went back to the car and slid into the passenger side. Silence for a moment as they both tried to assess.

Finally, "I think you need to press your fortune-teller for a better explanation," Rizzo said. "She obviously knows much more."

"She knows much more, but she's ambivalent about sharing it, I can tell you that," Alex said. "I still can't figure out whether we're dealing with a head case or a con artist."

"Or both," Mimi said.

Or both, they all agreed.

Alex's mind was distant, still trying to sort through everything that had happened.

"We go now?" Rizzo asked.

"Yes." Then, as he reached for the switch to illuminate the car lights, she grabbed his hand. "Wait!" she said.

Down the block, facing them, a car — a big one — had turned up the street. It moved slowly. "Down!" Alex said as the bold headlights swept the area. They dropped to eye level and watched. The car slid into the empty spot in front of 2011 South Marina, facing the wrong way. Alex watched, her Glock in her wet hand.

In the car, they hardly drew breath as they maintained their vigil and the scene down the street unfurled.

The car was a big blue muscular Impala, at least ten years old. The front door on the passenger side swung open, and a woman stepped out. It took several seconds in the bad light and the partially obscured view for Alex to recognize the woman as Juanita Mejías.

By the time Alex recognized her, however, two other car doors had swung open and two more figure appeared. Both were bulky, but one towered over the other. As recognition slowly descended on the scene for Alex, she dismissed her disbelief and squinted to make sure she was seeing this correctly.

The driver of the car was Lionel Dickey, the CIA expert in personal charm and anti-Castro defections. Not shy about what he was doing, or maybe making up for some other personal inadequacy, Dickey brandished a monster of an automatic pistol in his right paw as he stepped from the car, a strong visual deterrent to any good citizen with an IQ above fifty.

The backseat passenger, the bigger of the two men, hulked into a position next to Señora Mejías, protectively shielding her with his mountainous frame, and taking her hand. She moved close to him. Alex could see that the man was holding something in his free hand. When they hit a better swatch of light, Alex could confirm that it too was a pistol.

Dickey raised his free hand. Alex knew the move. His consorts were to hold their position until the all clear was given.

Looking quickly in all directions, checking fences and rooftops, Dickey crossed the street. He went to the door of 2011, unlocked it with a key, and went in. A slow minute passed. Lights illuminated on each floor, little cracks of yellow peeking out from the sides of the black curtains.

Dickey reappeared on the front porch and then came halfway across the street, beckoning with his left hand as the right hand remained in charge of the artillery.

Juanita and her human shield crossed quickly and went into the house. Alex watched with astonishment. Dickey gave a final look around from the street, then backed into the house himself and closed the door.

"Let's give it five minutes," Alex whispered. "Stay low. Then let's get out of here."

"Anyone you know?" Rizzo asked after several seconds.

"All of them," Alex said.

"Do tell, my dear."

"The woman was the wife of the assassinated defector, Major Mejías," Alex said, low but succinct. "The lead guy with the gun is a CIA guy, a case officer. Nasty piece of work named Lionel Dickey. He was her husband's case officer."

"That's two of the three," Rizzo said.

"The second man is a nasty piece of work too," Alex said. She turned slightly toward her car mate. "Remember the story I told you about being trapped in a closet at Ramona's house. A big smelly thug came into the room, searched for some documents, found them, and took off."

"How could I forget a story like that?" Rizzo asked.

"That was him," Alex said. "The man shielding Juanita."

Rizzo raised a pair of eyebrows and pursed his lips.

"Makes no sense," he said. "Or no connection."

"No," Alex said. "It's starting to. It's starting to make both."

"Can we get out of here?" Rizzo asked.

"Yes," she said. Then, thinking further, Alex corrected herself. "No," she said.

"What?"

"Hit the horn."

"You crazy?"

"Maybe. Hit the horn."

"No!"

"Okay, then I will."

Alex reached in front of her friend and pushed the car horn. Three long blasts. Then a fourth. Rizzo gazed at her in horror. Ahead of them, the door to the house swung open, and a man lurched out, his arm hanging at his side, the pistol visible. He stared in their direction.

"Now see what!" Rizzo said.

"I know. That's what I want. Got your gun?"

"Of course!"

"Then cover me!"

Alex stepped out of the car. She held her hands aloft to show that they were empty. From the porch before the safe house, Lionel Dickey loomed.

Alex walked to the sidewalk. Humidity misted and gnats swarmed. Dickey took two steps down from the porch, silhouetted by the bad light.

"Hello, Lionel," Alex said aloud.

"What the—?" Dickey snapped.

"We need to talk."

"I ought to shoot you, you meddling idiot!" he yelled back. "Go back to New York, girl! Go back to your desk."

"My hands are up," she said. "You should listen. Unless you want trouble from both Langley and Washington. It's your choice."

Dickey let loose with an unimaginative chain of obscenities. But he moved to the sidewalk. Alex took two more steps in his direction and kept her hands up. The door opened behind Dickey. The other man loomed.

"Lionel?" the man asked.

"It's okay!" Dickey answered. "Go back inside. I'll handle it."

The door closed. Dickey moved to a spot on the sidewalk ten feet in front of Alex, then six.

"You're a nuisance. What do you want?" he asked.

His eyes flicked to the car. He spotted Rizzo and Mimi. His anger increased. Alex could almost touch it. His gaze came back to Alex. "This better be good," he said.

"It is."

"Then talk."

"I'm going to put a theory to you," Alex said, "based on my many questions."

He waited, unblinking.

"There's been a disconnect in this case," Alex said. "I couldn't figure out what it was. Now I have a theory. It's you. You and all that time you spent in Latin America, buying, selling, inventorying: everyone and everything. May I lower my hands?"

"Sure. Why not?"

She lowered them.

"Why don't you put your cannon away?" she said. "Someone might get the wrong idea."

"I like it where it is," he said. "I'm working right now."

"So am I," she said.

"Then talk."

"Seems to me the Mejías family wants to have a conversation with me," Alex said. "Why didn't you set up a meeting? Why didn't you see that whatever information they have, or the major had, got to me? Or how about the principal of Gemini, the main lady, *la señora*? Why didn't you see to it that I had an audience with her?" Dickey held his silence. "Why don't they even know you have passports for them?"

"I don't have to answer your questions."

"The answers suggest themselves, Lionel," Alex said. "They're scared of you. They don't trust you. They think you might be trying to pull something at their expense, and they may be right. So they're frightened. That's how my theory goes. Want more?"

"Suit yourself."

"They obviously want to get to Spain, or somewhere, because there are too many hostile Cubans in Miami of whatever extreme. If they stay, someone's going to kill them here. Pro-Castro people, anti-Castro people. The city seethes with both. But their biggest fear is you. They're afraid you could set them up, then sell them out to some organization more powerful than either them or us. Make sense?"

"No."

"Liar. Does the name Yardena Dosi mean anything to you?"

"I might have heard it somewhere."

"Heard it or negotiated a deal here or there? You had a free hand all over the southern hemisphere for decades. You know the name as well as I do. Maybe better. Ever met Señora Dosi? Wouldn't surprise me if you had, somewhere along the line."

Dickey wavered. "You're playing with fire, LaDuca," he said. "Little girls get their fingers burned that way."

"Maybe," she said. "But sometimes that's the only way to snuff a flame."

Alex feared she may have overplayed her hand. Being right wouldn't amount to much if she got killed. She sought to defuse the moment.

"So I'm just saying," she continued, "I don't have prosecutorial powers, but some people close to me do. I want some assurance these people will be able to safely leave the country. If they do, we don't have any further issues, you and me. If anything happens to them, expect me to hound you for the next fifty years if that's what it takes to send you to prison."

"Spend fifty years. See if I care."

"I suspect it would take closer to fifty days, Lionel," Alex said, "based on what I already have, what I already know. Want to take that chance that I can't find a federal prosecutor who dislikes you as much as I do?"

He glowered at her again.

"What is it you want?" he asked.

"Some access and some answers, and for their exit to go smoothly. Do we understand each other?"

"Maybe."

His gaze had not left her face for a full minute. He slowly raised his pistol, and for half a second, Alex thought he was going to shoot her. His emotions seemed locked in a furious silence, his body unable to go forward or retreat. Then the gun disappeared into a leather holster on his belt.

"You're on a long road, LaDuca," he said. "What happens if you get lost? Or never reach the other end?"

"It was a theory. But worth sharing, don't you think? I appreciate you listening."

"You're nuts. You're out of your mind," he said, turning in a lumbering fashion the way heavy-set men do. "Sooner or later someone's going to take a shot and find the target."

"It won't be the first time," Alex said.

Dickey's short forehead was soaked. He turned. She watched him walk away in his furious resentful silence and she realized she was soaked too. She hoped, like the rain that had just started, she had gotten through.

He lurched back up the porch steps and opened the door.

"So do I get to talk to her?" Alex asked.

"I'll see what she wants," he said "I'll check with the bosses. For now, go away. Hear me?" Then he closed the door with a slam, disappearing into a bold yellow light within.

Alex exhaled long and deep. She waved a persistent bug away from her eyes, turned, and went back to the car. She slid in.

"Success?" Rizzo asked.

"We'll see. Let's go," she said.

Rizzo eased from the parking place.

Then, quietly, gently, he backed down the block, did a three-point turn in a driveway, and left in the direction from which they had come, not passing 2011 South Marina Drive again at all.

FIFTY-FOUR

For several minutes the following afternoon, Alex loitered in the shopping area of the Park Central, watching the front entrance. She wore a loose shirt over her maillot and shorts, looking like any other woman on vacation. Added to this was a straw hat for the sun and round sunglasses.

Then she turned and went toward the pool. She left a guest pass for someone named Wilson, to join her there. She carried a small straw bag. Pool and swimming equipment, plus a camera and her Glock.

Toward 2:00 p.m., she walked to the well-guarded and closely enclosed swimming pool area behind the hotel. She took off her blouse and shorts, put on a pair of goggles, and entered the water at the shallow end and began doing laps. At least today she could combine some exercise with business. She completed a brisk ten laps, watching the other visitors to the pool as she swam.

She saw Rick McCarron enter the hotel's pool area, using the guest pass that she had left for him. She continued her laps as McCarron, in dress pants, a pale shirt and tie, spotted her bag and walked to it. He pulled a beach chair next to the chair where she had left her things. She finished her laps, waved to him from the water, then pulled herself up onto the concrete area that surrounded the pool. She walked to him, dripping and pulling off her goggles.

"Some job you have," he said. He picked up the towel on her chair and tossed it to her. She caught it and toweled her hair and shoulders.

"What are you complaining about? You're my guest."

"As if I have time to enjoy it," he said.

314

"There's a gift shop in the lobby that sells trunks. I have lotion. Live a little. Enjoy yourself."

"Right," he said, conscious of her irony.

She settled onto her chair, enjoying the feel of the sun. She pulled on her blouse, donned the dark glasses, and plopped the hat onto her head. The towel remained around her shoulders.

"You do have a point, though," Rick said. "At least no one's shooting at us here."

"Not yet anyway," she answered. Then, "What have you got?" she asked in a low voice.

"Answers," he said in lowered tones that matched her. "Or facts. Responses to my morning queries that mean nothing for me but may be answers for you."

"Like . . . ?" she asked.

"Your physician. The one you asked me about. J. Montefiore, M.D. That's actually a Dr. Julia Montefiore," he said.

"Ob-Gyn?" Alex asked.

"Yes," he said, surprised. "How did you know?"

"Educated guess," she said.

"Pregnancy and childbirth," McCarron said.

"Two fields of medicine," said Alex. "And also two reasons why one half of Gemini was out of commission for a year. I'm also guessing that Dr. Montefiore is in Miami but is retired now. I checked the local listings. No such doctor in practice now. But I assume there was in 1987."

"Wow," Rick said. "You should be over in the big gray skyscraper working for us."

"So you can reconfirm everything I guessed," Alex said.

"Yes, I can."

They both fell silent as a pool attendant passed, a teenage girl in short shorts and a hotel T-shirt. She carried chilled containers of purified water. They each grabbed one. Alex tipped the girl with a wet five-dollar bill. They each opened containers of water and drank liberally. The sun blazed down.

"Rather seductive here, isn't it?" he asked, looking at the girl, the sky, and the distant beach. "A little part of Miami that I never get to. I should make a point more often."

"Don't say I didn't invite you," Alex said. "Why don't you and Laura stay here next time she flies down. She'd love it."

"You're onto something," he said.

"Maybe in more ways than one," Alex answered. Alex turned back to McCarron. A welcome breeze swept over the pool.

"Another tidbit I can give you is that obviously the powers that be are planning to move Señora Mejías to Spain very soon. Very quickly. There is an odd wrinkle to that, however. You were right. There are four new passports assigned to the case."

"And what kind of sense does that make?"

"Not an awful lot, tied in with what we know," McCarron said. "Family sense, as I suggested before. This sounds more like a tidal wave of immigration than repatriation. Unless someone is planning to sell a pair of passports."

Furiously, Alex was trying to make sense of it. Originally there were two parties being returned to Spain under the post-Franco laws of return. Now one of them was dead — Alex had seen the body in the coffin, she was sure of it — and that absence had been made up for by three more travelers.

"What are we talking about, Rick? US passports?" Alex asked. "Or something more seditious?"

"Spanish passports," he said. "And real ones. Not dummies knocked off by the CIA."

"What do you make of that?"

"Either there are more people of anti-Franco Spanish lineage than we imagined, or someone is owed some very big-time favors," Alex said. "Or both. That would seal the deal, wouldn't it, if someone was owed both?"

"But Mejías was the major player," McCarron said. "That's what we're supposed to think, anyway. Did you ever look at it in reverse?" he asked. "Maybe Mejías was lured to the US just so he could be assassinated. Payback time. Then there's a whole new group of four making a break for Spain."

Alex let the question hang in the air for several seconds. Then Alex turned back to McCarron.

"Rick," she asked. "I don't suppose you could angle to get a look at these passports, could you?"

"Not possible, Alex. They're locked up in a safe."

"Recently issued?"

"It would appear so," he said.

"Waiting for local delivery, I assume."

"One would think so. And delivery wouldn't be until the voyagers were on the way to the airport to leave the US. No point to take chances, you know."

"Obviously," she said, thinking. "Drawn up here or in Madrid? Would you happen to know?"

"I know they arrived from Spain."

"And they're here now, if what you hear can be believed?"

"Yes. They arrived about a week ago. I double-checked an inventory manifest. They were identified specifically on the list, but they're the only new ones to arrive."

"How did they arrive?"

"Secured diplomatic courier," McCarron said. "Madrid to Washington, Washington to Langley, Langley to here."

"So we could conjecture that the passports were created when Mejías was murdered. But why send them through from Madrid to Washington after he's dead, assuming Madrid knew he was dead? And again, why *four* passports?"

"Are you asking me or thinking out loud?" he asked.

"Both. Just in case."

A loud couple on vacation passed them, a conversation in motion with Bronx intonations.

"Rick?" she said. "May I ask you: do you have European Union passports in the bag of tricks at your office?"

"Downstairs and down the hall," he said. "They have blanks."

"Any chance to borrow some blanks for a few overnights?"

"What?"

"You heard me."

He sighed. "How many?"

"Four would be a cozy number," she said.

"For how long?"

"A day, maybe."

"It could be done. I'd have to go into the office and get them today. Much easier to 'borrow' something on a Sunday. They'll be people around, but not as many."

"Does it raise eyebrows, you going in on a weekend?"

"No. I'll just warn you, there will be hell to pay if they don't get replaced within seventy-two hours."

"I understand," she said. "So we'd need to work quickly. So maybe early this evening? We could meet somewhere between here and your place and pick them up?"

"It would work," he said. "But I am so not happy about it."

"So, what else do you have?" Alex asked.

"You'll find this interesting too," he said. He pulled a small black memory stick out of the breast pocket of his shirt. He dropped it into her pool bag. "A lot of details, a bit of cross-referencing. Names and dates and all. But it may sew some of your theories together."

"Thanks," she said.

"Any time," he answered. "I'll keep you updated on the Fredericksons. And get you some Dosi payoff in the mix."

"That sounds good," she said.

McCarron rose, swigged some water and departed.

Alex tossed the towel back onto her lounge deck chair. She flipped her sunglasses on top of the towel. As events, past and future, Miami and Cuba and continuous points in between over the years swirled in her head, she wore off her nervous energy with another ten laps. Then, after drying off and taking five more minutes of sunshine, she went back upstairs to her room, inserted the memory stick into her computer.

There before her were several airline passenger manifests for the late 1990s and early 2000s. As she examined them, and worked names and dates forward and back through the final years of the previous century, she found a suggested corroboration of a theory that had been emerging: that between Tito and one half of the Gemini connection, there was a deeper relationship than could ever have been imagined when Tito first walked into the initial Gemini partner in Buenos Aires and later in Belize. But it was there all right. Miguel Orestes Milanés had zipped about so arrogantly under his actual name and passport that the truth bubbled quickly to the surface for anyone who knew where to look for it.

Toward 6:00 p.m., Alex phoned Sister Ramona.

She needed one more *mediación*, Alex said. And in this one she wanted to contact *todos los espiritos*, as Sister Ramona would put it. Midnight that evening would suit her fine, she said. All the spirits: everyone involved needed to be present, dead, alive or somewhere in between.

Alex was prepared, she said, to empty her wallet accordingly and empower all the spirits to a happy trip to a new life. To that end, she made a rendezvous with Rick at a Cuban coffee shop two miles from his home. From him, she picked up in a plain envelope four blank European Union passports of Spanish design that he had temporarily filched from the CIA's company store.

FIFTY-FIVE

On the night of the second *mediación*, Ramona again pushed the extraneous furniture out of the way, and set up the card table in the middle of her living room. She arranged the chairs and invited Alex, Rizzo, and Mimi to join her.

Ramona drew the shades and covered them with the blankets. She lit a candle — one with a tangerine scent — in a pewter candlestick and set it in the center of the table. All other lights were extinguished. Then they sat down, the four of them, joined hands on the edge of the table and waited. The ceremony commenced a few minutes past Sunday midnight, a few minutes into Monday morning.

Their eight hands remained in position. Many minutes passed. Ramona kept her eyes closed. Alex remained alert, her eyes open much of the time, waiting, watching the flickering of the candle as it cast strange images, fluttery shadows upon the living room wall.

There was a creak to the floor in the kitchen, but nothing more. Several minutes passed. "Where are the 'spirits'?" Alex finally asked.

"They need time. And the right mood," Ramona said.

"Maybe traffic is heavy between here and 2011 South Marina," Rizzo said to Alex in Italian.

Alex allowed a few more minutes for the right mood to settle in and for the right spirits to come forth. When they didn't, she finally grew impatient.

"Okay," Alex said at length in Spanish. "Here's what's going to happen, Ramona. I'm not waiting for spirits tonight. I'm in Miami because a defector from Cuba named Ivar Mejías had a message for me. You know that. You also probably know the implications of the message and the complications that it causes. You know that too, don't you?"

Ramona sat impassively.

"You don't have to say anything, Ramona. Just blink if the answer is yes."

Ramona turned her dark gaze to Alex. She blinked once, very deliberately. A blink that lasted a full second.

"Muy bien," Alex said. "Now. I want to speak with your mother."

Ramona's gaze remained steady, right on Alex, never wavering to Rizzo or Mimi. She blinked again.

"I know she's here," Alex said. "And I know you can communicate with other rooms in this house. That's not so difficult after communicating with the spirit world, is it?"

Ramona shook her head, almost imperceptibly.

"That's who the extra chair is for, isn't it?"

Ramona blinked again.

"Then call her," Alex said.

The table gave a slight tremble. Ramona couldn't help but put on her usual show.

"You just did," Ramona said, continuing in Spanish.

Several seconds passed. Alex was aware of movement in the next room. Then to Alex's left, the door opened. The recent widow, Juanita Mejías walked into the room. She came to the chair.

"Buenas noches, Juanita," Alex said.

Juanita nodded. *"Buenas noches,"* she intoned in return.

"You've heard everything I've had to say, I assume," Alex said. "You also know this is my associate, Señor Rizzo, and his associate, Señorita Mimi."

She nodded.

"Then we're ready to talk?" Señora Mejías said anxiously.

"I don't think so," said Alex. "Not quite. There's still someone very important missing. At least one person. Maybe two. We all know that. So let's make proper use of our time before we no longer have time."

Alex rose from the table and crossed the room, her shadow tossed across the walls by the candlelight. She found an extra chair and moved it to the table and slid it into a spot next to Juanita.

"I don't believe for a moment that we're alone in this house," Alex said.

"There are no other spirits present," Ramona said.

Alex opened her folio. "Okay, we'll do it this way," she said. She pulled out a small packet: four red European Union passports, the word *España* boldly across the upper portion. They were bound together by a rubber band. Alex plopped them down on the table beside the candle.

"Look at this," she said. "Four fresh passports from the European Union. Just what one would need for a voyage to Spain, I would guess. In fact, these would allow the bearers to reside legally in Spain under a new identity if they were made out properly. Valuable commodities, I would say."

"Where did you get those?" Juanita asked.

"From a contact in the CIA," Alex said. "I have friends there. I tell them secrets and they tell me secrets. That's how it works. One could play poker on a table like this. High stakes. Four passports that will get four people out of the United States to start a new life in Spain. High stakes, no?"

Juanita stared at the passports with wide eyes. So did Ramona.

"Then again, there's an issue with the Miami police, isn't there? Who knows what trumps what these days, *¿Verdad?*" Alex asked. "The passports get a family of four out of the country, but it doesn't work and the family doesn't leave if there's an arrest for homicide, right?" She paused. "So I think a concerned spirit needs to come forth. Maybe even two of them."

Ramona reached for the passports. Alex reached forward at the same moment and scooped them up. She repositioned them in front of her, beyond Ramona's reach.

"I get cooperation, and you get a pass out of the country," she said. "That's how it works. Now I want to hear from the absent spirit."

Ramona opened her mouth to speak. Then everyone in the room fell silent. There were footsteps from the floor above, as if a heavy man had just gotten to his feet. The sound of a man upstairs walking continued.

"Much better," Alex said. "I like what I'm hearing. *Muy bien.*"

The footsteps crossed the floor above them, then gradually moved to the stairs. Slowly, ominously, the individual above them found the top step and descended. The séance room remained in silence.

The footsteps hit the ground floor. Ramona's eyes darted nervously around. Then she licked her fingers and reached forward to the candle. *"¿Con permiso?"* she asked. With permission? She wanted to extinguish the lights.

"Go ahead," said Alex.

Ramona snuffed the small flame. The scent of the snuffed wick filled the room. In the abrupt darkness, Alex felt Rizzo move in his position next to her. She knew he had gone for his gun.

The footsteps came to the door of the salon and stopped. Alex sat in darkness. She moved the passports to her lap and placed one hand on her gun in case things went the wrong way. Deep inside her, she uttered a small prayer, hoping she had guessed right.

The door opened. A dim light shone from the room beyond. A husky male frame slid into the room, barely visible in the darkness. He seemed to know the room well. He left the door slightly ajar and moved to the free chair between Ramona and Juanita. He moved quietly in this room, perhaps because of the deep carpeting and the more solid floorboards.

Alex watched his silhouette. She thought she recognized him. There was the soft sound of his chair being withdrawn from the table, and then he sat directly across from Alex. Alex could sense his movements by the air pressure in the room and could feel a slight tremble on the tabletop as his powerful hands settled in.

She could also smell his sweat and cologne. Hence, she recognized him a second time.

"*Muchas gracias,*" Alex said.

There was a movement, then a flash. Ramona had lit another match. The room was illuminated as if by a strobe light; then the light dimmed. Alex stared straight ahead. The empty seat was occupied by a heavyset man of about fifty.

It was the face Alex expected. She had seen him before, up close, when he had come into Ramona's bedroom and looked for a set of papers. Alex knew that he had been functioning in some important capacity that night but now had come to guess that he was functioning in more than one important role in the lives of the women at this time, including Alex. And Alex had also seen him as one of Juanita's two male escorts outside of 2011 South Marina.

"*Bienvenido, Miguel,*" Alex said to him. "Or should I call you 'Tito'?"

"Either, Señorita LaDuca," he said.

"Ready to travel?" Alex asked.

"I'm hoping," he said. "Better sooner than later."

"It usually is," Alex answered. "And aren't we all? But I need some answers first."

The table was quiet.

"See," Alex said, "I have a problem. Moral, ethical, legal, call it what you want. Ivar Mejías is dead. I have a theory: the killer is in this room. I can let the killer move to Spain with his family. Or I can turn the suspect over to my good friend Lieutenant Woodbine."

She fingered the passports. Then she handed them to Rizzo. Rizzo had a gun out and held it tightly in his hand. He rested the pistol on the passports.

"Mr. Rizzo here is my associate, as you know," Alex said. "We've worked together before. Mostly in Europe. But Mr. Rizzo is also a *consigliere* of sorts. An advisor. He's quite familiar with the intelligence communities of several agencies. I posed a question to him. I asked, torn by my loyalty to my job and to various national intelligence services and against a local police department, which would I choose. Gian Antonio?"

"I advised Alex," Rizzo said, "that in the future, she will need friends and cohorts in the intelligence community far more than in the Miami Police Department."

"Exactly," Alex said. "Similarly, Señor Rizzo has some extensive background in the same line of work that has comprised your career, Tito. We understand how bad things happen. We commiserate. We're sympathetic. We had a source here and an investigation that began here. And I'm convinced that if anything major went down here, you would be able to help us. That's what I came down here to Miami thinking." She paused. "I'm also prepared to show my good faith."

She reached into her purse and pulled out her remaining stash of one hundred dollar bills. Nine of them. She laid them on the table and pulled her hands away. After a moment, Ramona picked them up and pocketed them.

"There. That should be a little lift when you get to Spain. The four of you," Alex said. "If you get to Spain."

"I do what I can," Tito said, leaning back. "You know that."

"Of course I do, Tito," Alex said, knowing no such thing. "Why it would be downright unpatriotic if you didn't, wouldn't it?"

"You could say that," Tito said. But he was on edge. In his eyes, there was surliness and distrust.

"I mean, as I said," Alex forged ahead, "we have a major case before us in Washington. It's terribly important that you'd be able to help us. And your future rests upon it also. So let me put a thesis before the three of you. I've looked at a lot of files, studied a lot of dates, personal travel, quick trips abroad, their dates held up against certain information at Langley. I pulled a lot of information and observations together and think I know what's gone down here. Can't do any harm to listen to me, can it?"

Her question was met by two shrugs and a hostile glare.

"We'll go back to the early 1960s. Bay of Pigs. One of the soldiers there was a man named Carlos Milanés, correct, Tito?"

"Correct," he said grudgingly but not without disinterest.

"Milanés was a good man. A Cuban-born expatriate, loyal to his homeland against Castro and a Communist takeover, active in CIA activities by 1961. He was taken prisoner and incarcered in Cuba for a while after his capture at Playa Girón."

"If Kennedy had given those men air cover," Tito said, "Castro could have been removed right then."

Alex ignored his take on history and continued. "Then there was a prisoner exchange. Carlos Milanés came back to the United States. He remained a CIA operative all his life, lived in Florida, had a business as a cover. He had a son who was born in 1962. The boy's mother was a Costa Rican woman, very pretty, a noble woman. Her son's name was Miguel Orestes Milanés. Carlos didn't meet his son until his release from a Cuban jail in 1965. That boy, Miguel Milanés is you, isn't it, Tito?"

Tito nodded. *"Soy yo,"* he said.

"Flash forward a bit. You worked hard, did your university, and followed in your father's footsteps. No one's blaming you. Bilingual, vicious hatred of Castro and the Cuban regime, which remains perfectly understandable, the convenience of a Costa Rican passport. You're doing odd jobs for the CIA as something of a stringer in the mid-1980s, thanks to your father's connections. You get your refrigerator-and-appliance cover, and you're all over South and Central America, making a name for yourself, blending in with the locals, plus bringing down some good money. Good times, right?"

"Good times," he said with a trace of a smile.

"As your work for the CIA continued, you took the code name Tito for yourself," she noted, going off on a short tangent. "I'm curious why."

"From Tito Puente, the musician," Tito said. "He was all over the continent at the time. Do you know his music?"

"My mother was Mexican," Alex said. "Of course I do."

"You like his music?"

"How could I not like it?" Alex asked.

Tito grinned, a little speck of rapport emerged. To Alex's side, Rizzo kept a nervous hand on the passports and the pistol.

"So then," Alex said, "we come to 1985. You're in Mexico City, looking to spot some talent, hanging out with Cubans who were buying appliances to be shipped back home. They loved to beat the embargo, didn't they? The power elite."

"Who wouldn't?" Tito asked, opening up. He grinned. "The people in power didn't pay much attention to Castro or his brother. Underground economy. That was the big joke at the time: thanks to the Soviet Union everyone had American dollars. Up until the Soviet Union collapsed, anyway. It was the easiest thing in the world, sell an appliance for ten dollars to a dummy corporation in Mexico or in the Dominican Republic, then resell to Cuban diplomats and security people when they were on the road."

"Makes perfect sense," Alex said. "That's when you met Major Mejías in Mexico," Alex said. "Selling dishwashers. That's where it started, where you started grooming him in the mid-1980s, nursing his possible-future-defector gene. Sometimes key events in world history turn upon acts as prosaic as washing dishes."

Tito gave a small grin and a little nod. "Mejías was traveling without Juanita. He wanted to send home something to make her happy, I think," he said.

"Amends?" Alex asked.

"Maybe."

"We're talking about the mid- to late-eighties," Alex resumed. "The Bay of Pigs fiasco was twenty-five years earlier. The CIA and various subcomponents had probably launched two hundred attempts to kill Castro, and the man was still happily blowing smoke from *puros* every evening. Worse, US intelligence wasn't able to pick up much on the ground against Fidel. Here was a hostile foreign capital ninety miles from Florida and penetrating its secrets was an insoluble problem. Then you spot Señor Mejías. He has a rank in the national militia, but in practice he's a higher-up in the Cuban Ministry of Information. You must have had a tip."

"I had a couple of tips. That's all I'll say."

"That's fine," Alex continued. "Mejías had access. He had so much juice in Havana that they even allowed his wife to travel with him. You get in touch with Langley and tell them you have a major Cuban source, but you'll only play it along if you can control it yourself."

Alex locked her eyes directly onto Tito's, coming to a key inquiry. "Now I need a straight answer from you: an admission. You *do* know a man named Lionel Dickey?"

A little frown, a large nod, a flinch in Tito's eyes. "Maybe," Tito said.

"Maybe? Let me help your memory. Most recently he came to the door with you a few nights ago at a CIA safe house. He's also been acting as Juanita's guardian ever since her husband was murdered." She paused. "Does that shake things loose a little?"

"Okay. Sure. I know Lionel," Tito said. "You too, huh?"

"Sure thing. We've met. We've spoken. As recently as a few days ago. Charming man," she said. Tito picked up on the mock enthusiasm and sarcasm. "Lionel is a no-nonsense sledgehammer sort of guy," Alex continued speaking to Juanita. "He was Miguel's, or Tito's, control officer during the Gemini years. But Tito was the insulation layer between you and your husband. Your husband reported to Tito. Tito reported to Lionel Dickey. Even now, or perhaps even more so now, in light of recent events, that remains the case. Doesn't it?"

"Yes," said Tito.

"And you know what?" Alex asked. "I pick up on spiritual vibrations sometimes even better than Sister Ramona. I sense Lionel's presence here tonight. You wouldn't be here without him. So let's invite him in."

Tito looked to Juanita and she looked to him. Then there was further movement at the door. Lionel Dickey loomed into view.

He then stepped in, folded his arms silently, and stood by the door.

"Thank you, Lionel," Alex said. "Nice to see you again."

At first, he said nothing aloud. His angry eyes spoke volumes. Then he growled. "You have fifteen minutes, LaDuca. After that, this voodoo claptrap is finished."

"So then, let's hurry along," Alex said, getting back to her narrative. "It's finally the late 1980s, the Soviet Union has collapsed and the CIA is clamoring for Cuban goods because they might finally have the window they wanted for getting rid of Fidel. They ask you, Tito, for a few samples, and Mejías gets them for you. Mostly Cuban Navy stuff with some fresh army and militia stuff sprinkled in for dessert. There's an overall picture of the Cuban naval forces after the Soviet withdrawal. Very up-to-date stuff, which was endlessly interesting for those creaking old hawks who still wanted to invade. Langley starts salivating. They ask you, Tito, where you're getting this great stuff, and you won't tell them. They ask if there's more, and you say there's a ton of it. You have a source, you say, emphasis on the singular. You've worked south and Central America for years, you remind them, so it's not surprising, you insist. But your source is your source. Either you play the big fish or you release it, you tell them. 'So? Sale or no sale?' You ask. Again, they're desperate for current Cuban product; they want to polish their own apples at Langley, and so they take the plunge. They take you off your other assignments, give you a budget and your own little fiefdom and set you up in business. You hung out a shingle and slapped the code name Gemini on your operation. To recap, Tito: Lionel was your control man, Gemini was your source in Havana, and your source was raiding the intelligence safe of the Castro brothers. How's my thesis so far?"

"Impressive," Tito said, folding his thick arms. "You're good."

"Gemini. The twins. Why did you take that name, Tito?"

"I think you know."

"Of course I do. But it ran some risks, didn't it, if Langley thought about it too hard?"

He shrugged and frowned a little, as if to say, maybe. Alex took the occasion to sip some water from a bottle in her bag.

"They never think too hard in Langley," he finally said. "Or if they do, they take it in the wrong direction."

"The files I saw were meager," Alex then continued. "Well, not the complete files, I never saw those. The ones I got my hands on and had a chance to read only gave me part of the picture. That's what was meager. But I've been able to fill in some blanks. This is a hypothesis, after all. But I noticed that Langley was all too anxious to harvest anything it could get from you. You were able to move in and out of Cuba thanks to the Costa Rican passport. But Gemini was also able to move in and out of Cuba. So the volume increased. Make hay while the sun shines, right? But that only amped up the difficulty of transferring the information. I noticed there was once a proposal from Langley for setting up a long-range radio operation in the Florida Keys just to service Gemini. You nixed it."

"I hated radio. Radio could be traced and triangulated," Tito said. "Same with internet eventually, but in a different way. There's a trail out there in the ether. The very brilliance of Gemini was the operation's mobility, the ability to appear in almost two places at once," Tito confirmed. "I always preferred to carry important correspondence right on me. I carried a gun. If someone tried to take it, I'd kill them. If they killed me first, it didn't matter anymore. That's how I looked at it."

"Sure," Alex said. "But the lack of radio led to a series of nearly arcane procedures. Special cameras, not the least of which was the one that caused that big flap over financing. Microdots inside paperback books, letters sent to postal drops in Mexico, Guatemala, and Honduras. There were even a few dead drops in Havana, fielded by members of the American Interests Section, though they were never allowed to open what they fielded. The bureau was technically part of the Swiss Embassy but American staffed and in the old US embassy. Those assigned to the case were supposed to seal whatever they pulled out of brick walls or storm drains into a larger bag and pack it off in a special diplomatic pouch. Then there were the occasional in-person meetings, weren't there? And that's where the complications began."

"Maybe," sniffed Tito, starting to look more than a little nervous.

Alex sought to calm him. "No need for anxiety here, Tito," she said. "In the end, all I want is the message that Major Mejías had for me. I want it because it may unlock and resolve the biggest case on my desk. In terms of homicides, I'm not a shoe-leather cop. I leave that to our nemesis Lieutenant Woodbine — who doesn't help me so I don't have any interest in helping him. *¿Entendido?*"

"Understood," Tito said.

Juanita Mejías said she understood too.

"Years began to pass. Gemini became a creature of habit, delivering goods from the Cuban vault. The value of the haul increases. Lionel Dickey gets taken off his regular assignments so he can handle Tito and Gemini, much the same way Tito was removed from his appliances to oversee Gemini. Then love and money entered in, spies being similar in nature to the rest of us. Tito had to protect his Gemini when Gemini wished to flee Cuba and retire. So additional requests for funding came. That led to the spat in 1999 where Tito had to reveal the dual nature of his source, that Gemini was more than one person. Two would be my guess. But who else was close enough to Mejías to work with him? A woman who was a typist in the defense ministry, as well as married to him. His wife, Juanita. The other half of Gemini. The good Señora Mejías."

"We happened across each other," Tito said. "She was pretty much at the end of her rope when we first met. She was a member of the Communist Party, cleared to see some high-caliber stuff but never allowed to participate in any of the top-table decisions. So at work she'd sit and work and wait, see everything, forget nothing. Thing was, life was miserable."

"My husband was a beast," she said. She made fists and

mimicked a beating motion. "He would drink, get frustrated with his own work, and take it out on me. Half my body would be black and blue, but never around the head or the face."

"Was that always the case?" Alex asked. "Or did it start after you had a daughter by Tito in 1987?"

A long pause. "Before," she said. "It was always his way."

"But I imagine it got worse afterward," Alex said. "And to your credit, you had the child. A daughter. And a charming woman in her way. A credit to both of you."

Alex glanced to Ramona. "It's all right, Ramona," Alex said. "You can acknowledge your parents. I'm here to seek truth, not to give away secrets or break up a family that's rarely been able to be together." She looked back to Tito and Juanita. "You even have a charming granddaughter. I believe she was the blithe spirit who visited during our first *mediación* the other night. I wish her well in Spain. I wish you all well in Spain."

"Thank you," Tito said. "The trips started out as his-and-hers events," Tito said. "Then they would send Juanita on the road by herself."

"And that's when your personal relationship blossomed, shall we say?" Alex asked.

"He was a brutal man," the widow said. "My husband . . ."

"I know. That's all documented. Which partially explains how and why you became involved romantically with Tito. On maybe one third of the occasions when in-person meetings were arranged, it was you, Juanita, not your husband, making the transfer of information. The irony, and dare I say, the beauty of the operation, was that as a typist in the interior ministry you had access to documents to which your late husband would never have had access. He photographed and handed over low-level stuff to the Americans while you slipstreamed right behind him with higher-yield material that he was probably unaware of. That would be my guess. And that would account for the disparity of the material yielded by Gemini. There was the *B* to *B*-plus stuff that your late husband was handing over. And then there was the top-quality stuff that you had access to. In its piggy-sexist way, the Cuban high command couldn't conceive of how dangerous female eyes could be on the wrong documents."

"They believe now," Tito sniffed.

"Of course they do," said Alex, "even though the damage is long since done. And yet at the same time, when the trail finally began to lead back to you last year, it was a given that the CIA was going to have to bring both of you out of Cuba for eventual relocation. Can't leave one Gemini behind and bring out the other. And I must admit there was some sympathy for you at Langley. You provided the top stuff, Juanita, not your husband. And you put up with an abusive brutal husband for twenty years, all the while in love with another man."

Tito placed a hand on Juanita's.

"It was time to leave," Tito said. "The vibrations in the air were bad, the rumors ominous. Meanwhile, after too many years, some of the top people in Cuban counterespionage were starting to smell a rat. Some of the security in Langley was shabby and had been penetrated by friendly services. There was a Venezuelan housekeeper, it was rumored, who was able to see top stuff in Spanish at night, photograph it, and pass it along to Caracas, and it started to make its way back to Havana. It was time to leave."

"So I'm getting the idea," Alex said, "that when I was run into Cuba with Paul Guarneri earlier this year to pick up a defector, that operation was secondary to the larger one: removing Gemini from Cuba. Both of the twins: Señor and Señora Mejías."

"If the shoe fits," Tito said, "feel free to wear it."

"Similarly, the romantic interest, the liaison which you, Tito, and Juanita had for years, was why you were so insistent at not naming who your contacts were to Lionel Dickey. If you were the only one who knew, they could never have been sold out or traded off 'for inventory' the way the CIA has been known to do. Much of your wealth had been safely stashed at banks in Europe and the

Bahamas. When the issue of Spanish passports arose, and Spanish citizenship, that's when you took your cue to leave. And why not? One Castro brother is already retired, the other can't have many years to go. A life's work is near its conclusion. Why not enjoy some peace and sunshine, particularly when the counter-revolutionary people were closing in? Why risk going to work in a gray windowless building and possibly being shot for a slight slip when you can live out your days in sunny Malaga?"

"Agreed," Juanita said and Tito nodded.

"Now let's clean up the details," Alex said. "Because it wasn't Ivar Mejías who had a final message for me. It was you, Juanita, because you were the source of all the important information. But when Ivar had his 'fatal accident' three weeks ago, it became impossible for you to speak through him anymore. So what is it, Juanita?" Alex asked. "What do you have for me that your husband was going to pass along?"

"I'm going to give you seventeen names," Juanita said. "Seventeen people who are dead. Murdered in the United States." She took a piece of paper and began writing names. Alex watched upside down as seven named appeared on the sheet of paper. Working from her extraordinary memory, one honed during a lifetime as a spy, Juanita added locations and dates, frequently accompanied by a small question mark. When she finished, she reread what she had written, then turned the paper around and handed it to Alex.

Alex read the names, places, and dates. Fifteen of the names were those of men, two were women. The places were along the east coast of the United States, the dates within the last few years.

She looked up. "So?" she asked.

"This is what I remember," she said. "These are homicides in the United States under American jurisdiction, all currently files that remain open."

"So?" Alex asked again.

"All of these were ordered by Yardena Dosi. Look into these cases, find the links. You will find extraditable crimes. Put these together, and you will have several solid cases to bring to court. Put all of these together and you will have your Dosis."

"With respect, Señora," Alex said, "how do you know these names? You were in a position to know about military and naval matters. Not criminal activity."

"My husband knew of your interest in the Dosi operation. Dosi ships came in and out of Havana countless times. Cuban security spoke with sailors. Files were accumulated for purposes to be determined later. Records may have been primitive, but they were kept on everything. Follow the leads. See where they take you. That's all I can do."

Alex nodded. Rizzo looked over her shoulder and nodded also.

"Thank you, Juanita," Alex said. She looked around. "I think we're finished, Ramona."

No one budged.

"The passports?" Tito asked.

"Oh, these?" Alex said, opening the blanks. "These are just for show. The CIA is still holding yours. You'll receive them at the airport. Mr. Dickey and his superiors will then see you safely aboard an Iberia flight to Madrid. Travel safe. Send me a postcard from time to time."

FIFTY-SIX

Lieutenant Woodbine never located his suspects, no help from Alex. Alex returned to New York two days later. Rizzo and Mimi continued on to Brazil the same day, each of them parting with an embrace from Alex at Miami International Airport. But they were not the only folks in transit. Late on Wednesday, her first full day back in New York, two bits of good news dropped on Alex, plus something unexpected that evening.

First, the Senate hearing over Fin Cen's activities was abruptly postponed. Political squabbling in Washington was the reason: a quorum of senators couldn't act enough like grown-ups to set the rules and boundaries of the inquiry. Alex wasn't off the hook and neither was Fin Cen. But the hearings were pushed back into the following year. Alex was relieved.

Then second, at the end of her afternoon back, Alex saw the internet message that she awaited. Juanita Mejías, Miguel Orestes Milanés, their daughter, Ramona, and their grandchild had arrived safely in Spain. Still, taking nothing for chance, Alex picked up her secure telephone and called them at a prearranged cell number.

Señora Mejías answered. They were in a small villa east of Malaga, they said, secure and happy under new names. A small detail of Spanish police had been assigned to keep watch on them for the first few weeks after their arrival.

They thanked Alex and signed off. In New York, Alex set down her phone. That part of Operation Párajo against the Dosis was at an end.

She was relieved to make her way home by 7:00 p.m. She kept her eyes on the street, on passing cars, nothing exploded, and nothing looked suspicious. Everything seemed copacetic.

Things were peaceful. Or, asked a little voice in the back of her mind, was this a lull before another great storm?

She had dinner at home alone. She was in bed by 11:30.

She was drifting off to sleep when her cell phone rang by her bed. A call this late was unusual. It usually meant trouble. The read-out read RESTRICTED. The caller had blocked his or her ID. She answered anyway.

"Hello?"

"It's late, but I know you're awake," said a male voice. The caller paused. "This is your second night back. I know these things."

She sat up. Instinctively her free hand went for her pistol. Her eyes went to her shades. They were drawn, and yes, her light was out.

"Do I know you?" she asked.

"I think you do," said the voice, toying with her. "But maybe you're not talking to me these days. Wouldn't blame you if you weren't. Here's a hint: I'm downstairs."

A bolt of fear shot through her. Then she recognized the voice. The caller identified himself simultaneously.

"Apologies," he said. "It's Eric. Your downstairs neighbor."

She relaxed. "Oh ... Eric. Hello."

"Sorry if I startled you," he said. "I know you've been away. I just got home myself, and as I came in I saw your lights on, then I saw them click off. Welcome back. I wanted to say hello. Am I calling too late? Did I catch you before you fell asleep."

"You're fine," she said. "A little nervy, but okay."

"Listen, first off, something's been bothering me. I owe you an apology."

"For what?"

He laughed. "Last time I saw you, I know I was acting a little spacey. Well, truth is, *very* spacey. At the show that evening, there's a scene at the beginning of the second act where I'm supposed to jump down from a ladder and take the hand of the actress who plays Nellie. Well, jump I did, I stumbled like the clumsy oaf that I am in real life and wrenched a knee. They gave me a Vicodin and a half to help me finish the show. It was that or call in the understudy. Then after the show they gave me another one and a half, put an Ace bandage on the knee, and poured me into the limo."

Lying comfortably in bed, she warmed to the conversation. It reminded her of times when Robert had called her while away with the president, and she would talk to him before going to sleep.

"So, three Vikes and the Ace was a size too small. My knee felt like King Kong in a size small jockstrap."

"Ouch!" she said, starting to smile and then laugh.

"Yes. A very loud 'ouch.' I confess that I might have used stronger language at the time, but I wouldn't repeat that to a lady."

"I know all the words. I've heard them before. I don't use them, myself," she said.

"Good for you. I respect that."

She wasn't sure where to take the conversation next.

"Am I boring you?" he asked to her silence. "Keeping you awake?"

"No. It's nice to hear from you," she said. "*Very* nice after what I went through on this past trip."

"Anyway, I finished the show that night when I saw you last, but Maurice, my driver, brought me home just as the pain killer was making me fly. The house doctor had also put a needle in my knee during intermission just so I could finish the show, then with the Vicodin and some ethyl chloride sprayed on my knee, plus the ache from the bandage, I probably seemed like a space cadet."

"Yeah," she said. "That about describes it, Eric."

"Did I give a bad impression?" he asked.

"Yes. Very. I drew the wrong conclusions."

"I know I saw you, but I don't even remember what I said. I'm sorry. Forgive me?"

It took less than a second. "I'm very strong on forgiveness," Alex said. "It's something important that I believe in. That's maybe the first thing you should know about me."

"Thank you."

"Let's forget it. How's your knee?"

"Fine. I've been using it for standing, walking, and kicking cans down the street for several days now."

"That's great. Didn't miss any performances?"

"Never missed one in my life. Don't plan to. But you've missed several."

"Hmmm?" Alex asked. She was lying back with her head on the pillow with her eyes closed. It occurred to her that she hadn't felt this tranquil for a long time.

"My sister wants to meet you," he said.

"What?" she asked, opening her eyes.

"My sister and her husband are arriving tomorrow. I can set aside three house seats for you for Saturday night. Please come and see us."

"Eric, I — "

"It's our one-hundredth performance. There's a little backstage party. You'll meet the cast, the producers, and the director. Get to flirt innocently with all the attractive gay men in the chorus. I think you'll like it."

Her instinct was to decline. "Oh, Eric — ," she began.

"Alex, please. The only thing I want to hear you say is 'yes,'" he said. "I will not accept no for an answer this evening. I'd be honored to have you as my guest."

Deep within her, some heavy emotional wall began to tumble. She resisted but then the wall crashed.

"Okay," she said. "Yes. I'll be there."

"And my apology is accepted? For the mail room miscommunication?"

"More than accepted. I owe you one too."

"Thank you. Good night," he said.

"Good night."

FIFTY-SEVEN

In the early morning hours of that following Saturday, Manuel Ortega was in the endgame stage of his strike on his two targets, the ones the Dosis had assigned.

In a private garage in Brooklyn, he packed four cylinders of explosives into the trunk of his Honda. He carefully rigged all four bombs to detonate at the same time. The command would be given by a cell phone impulse, set to a timer that would make a call. He carefully packed the fuses and relays and linked them to the incendiary device. He positioned them into the Honda's storage quarters so they would ride smoothly and not be sent off by road vibration. Then he covered the explosives with towels, keeping them out of view should the trunk be opened for any reason. Then he locked the storage area. At about 3:00 a.m., on a quiet street, he set the explosives in another place where they would do a job for him.

Now, on Saturday afternoon, from his home, he took a pistol. It was a snub-nosed Colt .38, a little antiquated but with enough firepower to win arguments or get him past a sudden run-in with the law.

He dressed in jeans and a black sweater, a Harley Helmet, and a leather motorcycle jacket. He wore boots. He tucked the pistol into a secure pocket of his jacket. And at 6:00 p.m., he set out from Brooklyn for Manhattan, taking the Williamsburg Bridge. He had been tipped that his target was on her way to the theater that night.

Ortega rode with confidence. He crossed the bridge by 6:20 and headed for Times Square and Broadway. The great thing about a motorcycle in Manhattan was that a man could park it almost anywhere, and no one would take much notice.

Manual Ortega was confident of success this evening. There was no reason not to be.

FIFTY-EIGHT

Saturday evening arrived. The theater was on West 46th Street just off Times Square. Alex arrived by taxi, but as was her precaution, she had the cab drop her two blocks from the theater. Then she walked down a street in which traffic went the other way. She scanned behind her. No one was following. The world being what it was, however, Alex carried her Glock.

She spotted the theater from a block away as she walked past Sixth Avenue. It was not as if she could miss it. *South Pacific* occupied the biggest and most prestigious theater on the block. It dominated the street even though other comedies and dramas crowded in nearby. As she neared it, she looked at the marquee.

There were three major stars in the show: one was a veteran Broadway actor who played Emile, the older Frenchman. The female lead was a woman best known for her work on television. She played Nellie Forbush, the Arkansas nurse. Eric, who played Lt. Joe Cable, was the third. All three names stood out boldly on the marquee. Alex shook her head in disbelief, socializing as she was with one of the stars, at least for this one evening. A sign on the theater doors proclaimed, "THIS PERFORMANCE SOLD OUT."

Alex entered the lobby. It was crowded. A line had formed for last-second cancellations. Another line jammed the will-call window. The whole place was packed, the atmosphere electric. The show was an enormous hit, but there was little doubt that Eric was the star, the person people were there to see. Alex smiled again. The audience seemed to be about two-thirds female. Mischievously, she wondered what the other women in the audience would have given to join Eric for dinner and the cast party afterward.

Alex enjoyed being out like this, lost in a crowd, finding safety and perhaps solace in a crowd of ordinary people. It was what she needed, she realized, after the tension and anxiety of the episode in Miami. She loved the eclectic nature of New York. Scanning the lobby, she could see the Manhattan professionals and the people who had come in from the outer boroughs, the tourists from America's great heartland, the visitors from Europe. Listening in, she heard British English, American English, New York English, and Spanish. There was a phrase or two in Italian, and she picked up some in French. She began to long again for a more tranquil life in which she could enjoy the arts and culture and wouldn't have to look over her shoulder.

The lobby was dominated by still photographs from the show. The tourists were having their pictures taken in front of some of them. Alex smiled. Then, Alex heard her name spoken by a female voice above the din. Simultaneously, she felt the polite touch of a hand on her arm.

"Alex?"

Alex turned quickly. She found herself looking into the face of a pleasant woman in her midthirties, smart blue eyes and sandy-blonde hair.

"Hi, I'm Sarah Myers," the woman said. "Eric's big sister."

"Hi," Alex said. She extended a hand, which was accepted.

"This is my husband, Carl," she said. A slightly balding but fit man offered his hand. Alex took it.

"Hello, Alex," he said. "Nice to meet you."

"Same."

"I've got the tickets here," Sarah said. "Let's go on in and find our seats."

"Sounds like a plan," Alex said.

They joined the line of ticket holders and proceeded into the theater. Sarah led the way. Alex engaged in small talk with Sarah's husband. Carl Myers, like his wife, was a pediatrician. They had met in medical school in Boston and remained together and were, conveniently enough, in the same practice along with four other doctors in a Boston suburb.

They walked down the right side aisle. Alex thought she would never stop walking. The house seats were in the fifth row in the center, among the best in the house, not surprisingly. Alex entered the row first and moved to the center. Sarah followed and sat next to her.

Sarah was a good conversationalist and easy to talk to. She and her husband were attending a convention of physicians at Columbia-Presbyterian Hospital, she said. The convention afforded them the occasion to visit her brother.

"Convenient," Alex said with a hint of irony.

"Very," Sarah answered.

"Not everyone has a brother who's a big star on Broadway."

Sarah shook her head and smiled. "He's still just a little kid to me," she said. "He's very special."

"I'm catching on," Alex said.

Then the lights went down. The orchestra played the overture and the show transported the audience seven decades into the past to a South Pacific island during the final days of World War II.

Eric Robertson made his entrance to great applause midway into Act One, playing US Marine Lt. Joseph Cable. He arrived on the island from Guadalcanal, having been assigned to take part in a dangerous spy mission against Imperial Japan.

Alex was transfixed. Here was her downstairs neighbor transformed into another person, another time. He was the tall good-looking guy from the hallways, the sidewalk, the grocery store, and the mail room, yet he was someone else. He seemed to take on an added stature and gravitas before an adoring live audience, even though he managed to slip the occasional surreptitious glance to his guests during the performance.

Thoroughly engrossed, Alex marveled at how smoothly Eric glided through his demanding role, spoken words and three musical numbers. Alex watched as Bloody Mary persuaded Lieutenant Cable to visit Bali Ha'i where he meets Bloody Mary's daughter, Liat, with whom he communicates in French.

Knowing that Liat's only chance at a better life is to marry an

American officer, Mary leaves Liat alone with Cable. The two are instantly attracted to each other. Alex watched him violate the racial taboos of the time by falling in love with a Tonkinese girl, and she almost felt jealous.

On stage, Bloody Mary encouraged them to continue their life on the island after the war and urged them to marry. Cable, in the second act, says he cannot marry a Tonkinese girl due to his prejudices. Cable, filled with self-loathing after losing a young girl he loved, realizes that his prejudice "is not something you're born with," yet it is an ingrained part of his upbringing.

He and the older Frenchman go off on their dangerous mission to a Japanese-held island. Eventually, Cable — Eric — is killed. And out of the blue, the tragedy in Kiev came back to Alex as she saw her new friend, Eric, "dead" on stage.

She found herself biting her lip and squeezing her own hands from the poignancy of it, something she understood too well but hadn't expected to be hit with so hard this evening. There were many eyes in the house that were not dry. Hers were among them. Eric's role that evening was finished, but he and the whole cast were rewarded with thunderous applause and five curtain calls, including one that Eric took individually and threw a mischievous wink to his guests as he did so.

After the show, a specially assigned usher came to the fifth row and guided Alex and Eric's family through a series of private corridors until they were backstage. The usher brought them to Eric's dressing-room suite. He greeted everyone with a hug. They waited as he quickly showered in a private area, then reemerged, having changed into jeans, a black T-shirt, and a jacket.

They made the rounds of the cast party, catered by Sardi's with champagne galore. Alex enjoyed the evening with a single glass of bubbly.

Then Eric took Alex and his sister by the hand and introduced them to the other stars. Alex felt herself drifting into the mode of a teenage girl again, stagestruck, and had the leads and supporting actors sign her *Playbill*, famous people whom she had seen in movies and on television for years. The evening dazzled. Alex could not remember a recent evening she had enjoyed more. It was a far, far universe away from snowy cemeteries in Switzerland, assassination squads in Venezuela, mortuaries in Egypt, and execution squads on Cuban beaches. She appreciated the change of venue.

They stayed at the backstage party for half an hour. Then Eric said to his sister, "Sarah, you know the drill getting out of here. Let's split."

"All too well, brother dear," she said with wry bemusement. Sarah turned to Alex and made a joke of it. "This is where dear little brother must be rescued from his adoring public. Either that or they will tear him apart, and we will never see him again in one piece."

"I get it," Alex said.

"In other words, we go on ahead, and his fans get to beat him up," Carl said. "Maurice gets to look after him."

"I'll follow you guys," Alex said.

Sarah motioned with a nod of the head. Then she led her husband and Alex out a stage door at the side of the theater which connected with Shubert Alley. The door opened onto New York's nightly posttheater chaos. A narrow pathway had been cleared for stars leaving, but behind wooden barricades hundreds of fans waited.

Some of the other actors from that evening's performance were making their way slowly out, signing *Playbills*. Sarah recognized the waiting limousine that picked up Eric every evening.

Maurice, the driver and bodyguard, stood sentry on the curbside, a powerful and authoritative figure. He smiled when he saw Eric's family and guest and guided them protectively to the vehicle. He greeted Alex by name, meaning Eric had been courteous enough to prep him. Alex was starting to like this.

They climbed into the back and waited.

Alex had a window seat. She turned and watched the stage door. There was no secret when Eric emerged. The air was filled with screams and shouts and applause from hundreds of his adoring fans. The older male lead was a huge star, a veteran of London and New York stages and many movies. But Eric was the young hunk, the person all the women were there to see, and some of the men as well.

Maurice, in his bodyguard mode, quickly joined Eric and loomed with him, a powerful bulky man of six four looking over a lanky athletic guy of six two. But Maurice didn't interfere. Maurice was a strong visual deterrent to anyone crossing a line, a silent but intimidating presence.

Eric smiled and moved patiently, signing as many *Playbills* as he could, moving slowly, taking time to lean into the crowd and allow some fans to have their picture taken with him. Clearly he enjoyed the adulation, much as his fans wanted to devour him.

Yet Alex was struck with how extraordinarily well Eric handled it, giving — it seemed — a little piece of himself to every admirer. She was also struck anew by how extraordinarily handsome he was. It took him fifteen minutes to navigate fifty feet to the car.

Finally he entered. "Is it like that every night?" Alex asked as he settled into a seat next to her.

He laughed. "Some nights it's worse," he said. "Or better, depending how you look at it." He shrugged. "Hey. These are the people who keep the show open," he said. "They pay good money. I don't get to do this if they don't buy tickets. They deserve a little extra. They deserve to go home happy."

Said by someone else, it might have sounded self-serving. The way Eric said it, it was self-deprecating.

Maurice opened the shotgun side door to the front and slid across into the driver's seat. "Where to, Mr. Robertson?" the driver asked.

"Let's go to Le Chien Blanc on East 67th Street," he said. "Everyone like French food?"

"I'm good," said Sarah. Her husband gave a thumbs up.

"Sounds great to me," Alex said.

"Then it's decided," Eric said. "Off to the infamous white dog."

Eric reached to her hand, squeezed it affectionately and released it, much like Robert used to. He called the address to his driver. "Thanks for waiting," he said to Alex. "Thanks for coming to the show. Did you enjoy it?"

"Are you kidding? What do you think?" she asked.

"Well," he concluded, "it is a pretty sound production. Anyway, I'm glad you enjoyed it."

The limo pulled away from Shubert Alley like a long gleaming panther. It traveled up Broadway several blocks, then continued up Sixth Avenue to Central Park, then to the east side of Manhattan where their restaurant reservations awaited them.

All the way, Maurice noticed, they were followed by a pale green Honda motorcycle. Maurice kept eyeing it in the rearview mirror but said nothing. He was used to paparazzi and other pests and always had his eye out.

Maurice wished people wouldn't do such dangerous things. Someday, he reckoned, someone was going to get killed.

FIFTY-NINE

Eric's been obsessed with *South Pacific* since he was sixteen," Sarah said over dessert and coffee two hours later. Eric rolled his eyes, suddenly in the goofy kid brother role. "I think he would have played Lt. Joe Cable for free if his brother hadn't intervened."

"My brother, Matthew, is my manager, Alex," Eric said.

"Well, you can trust your brother," Alex said. "I would hope."

"Completely," he said. He gave her a little pointing wag of the finger to indicate she was spot on. "Too many people in my profession get ripped off," he said.

"Back to *South Pacific*," Sarah said.

"Okay, okay," Eric said. "When I was a kid I loved to read. I read all of James Michener. Our family had a library of all those condensed books, you know, the ones Reader's Digest used to publish. I really liked Michener. He never published anything before he was forty years old, by the way. Did you know that? When I realized that *South Pacific* was based on a collection of short stories Michener had published in the late 1940s, I was blown away. I went to the library, got the short stories, read them, and was blown away again. Then this touring production came through Chicago in the early nineties. I went to see it. Everyone else was listening to Hootie and the Blowfish, and I'm listening to Rodgers and Hammerstein. But I was swept away! Tackling racial prejudice in the late 1940s ... can you imagine?"

"Eric's about to get on his soapbox," Sarah said. "He can't shut up about Michener and *South Pacific*. Not that he should. I'm just sayin'."

"Oh, Sis, you shut up for once," he said playfully. She stuck out her tongue at him and her husband, Carl, laughed.

"Hey, it's paying for this meal we're eating," Eric said with a wink.

Sarah laughed again. "I'm glad someone is," she said, "because I don't plan to."

"She's been a lovable mooch for thirty years," Eric said, grabbing Sarah and hugging her playfully. "I hope she never stops."

"How do you know so much about the past of the show, its history?" Alex asked Eric.

"You'll be sorry you asked," Sarah said good-naturedly.

"I'm sure I won't be," Alex said. "I want to hear it."

"Okay. When I was in drama school I did a thesis on Rodgers and Hammerstein. I was fascinated. Got to meet a lot of people who had worked with them or performed in their shows on stage. Hammerstein died fifty years ago but Rodgers was around until the late seventies."

"So it's a special subject of yours," Alex said. "Well, I can understand that."

"Hey, it's such a beautiful piece of work, *South Pacific*," Eric said. "That's why I'm so passionate about it. Fabulous music. 'South Terrific,' that's what one of the opening night critics called it in 1949. But look at the geometry of the story: Nellie fights to accept Emile's mixed-race children. In my role, as Lieutenant Cable, I have to battle the prejudice that I would face if I married an Asian woman and brought her home to the US. Michener had a Japanese wife, late in life, by the way. Here's a little Broadway history. You know that song I sang tonight, "You've Got to Be Carefully Taught?" Do you know that in 1949 and during the 1950s, that song was ripped as 'too controversial for the musical stage.' It was called procommunist, indecent, and — get this! — anti-American. What's wrong with people?"

"I warned you about the soapbox, right?" Sarah chimed in.

Carl laughed.

"When the show toured the South in the 1950s," Eric said, "the Georgia State assembly introduced a bill outlawing any entertainment containing 'an underlying philosophy inspired by

Moscow.' How do you like that? Moscow! One redneck legislator said that 'a song justifying interracial marriage was implicitly a threat to the American way of life.'"

Everyone at the table shook their head.

"It's easy to dismiss now," he continued, "but back then it was serious business. Can you imagine? Rodgers and Hammerstein defended their work. So did Michener, it goes without saying. Rodgers and Hammerstein said that this song represented why they had wanted to do this play, and the song was going to stay or there would be no production. God bless them all for that! That's why I've always admired them and this work; that's why I wanted to do it." Eric calmed slightly. "Needless to say, when I was an ugly zit-faced teenager in the Midwest in 1993, whom none of the girls would talk to, it never occurred to me that someday I'd be able to sing that same song on Broadway ..." He shook his head. "I'd never have believed it if you'd told me back then. I can barely believe it now."

"I doubt you were a homely teenager whom none of the girls would talk to," Alex said.

"Oh, I was, I was!" he insisted.

Sarah chipped in. "He was," she said. "Really. To me he still is."

"Thanks, Sarah," he said again. "Why did I invite you again?"

"Family ties," she said.

"Ah! That must be it," Eric said. He had a mock gesture of punching his sister on the arm. She made a mock gesture of being scared.

"What happened?" Alex asked.

"About what?"

"How did the pimply faced teen turn into the Broadway and movie star?"

He shrugged. "I grew up," he said, looking her in the eye. "I maintained some discipline and trained myself to work hard." He paused. He shook his head, highly animated. Alex was fascinated and started to feel herself falling completely under his spell. Eric added, "And I was blessed," Eric said. "That's how I prefer to look at it. To some degree, it's a mystery, but I prefer to let the mystery be. I tried to do the right things, follow my dreams, and thank God for the grace to allow me to live another day."

The waiter cleared the dessert plates.

"We were raised by the same parents," Sarah said, looking to Alex for sympathy. "There were three kids in the family. Eric was always the acolyte. I don't know what happened to him."

"You don't go anymore?" Alex asked Sarah.

"Go where?"

"Church."

"Christmas, Easter, weddings, and funerals," Sarah said. "So shoot me."

Carl chimed in. "Don't even ask me," he said with a grin. "I'm Jewish."

"So were Rodgers and Hammerstein," Sarah said.

"Actually, you're only partially correct," Eric said. "Richard Rodgers was Jewish. Hammerstein, the composer, was Oscar Hammerstein II. His father, the original Oscar was a theater impresario in the vaudeville days. He was a German Jew, well known and successful in his time. But he married a Protestant," he added.

"See? He knows everything," Sarah said.

"The composer, Oscar II, was raised as an Episcopalian," said Eric. "And we all know there's an Episcopalian cabal that controls the arts," he added with a wink.

"So, are you Episcopalian?" Alex asked.

"Yup. You okay with that?"

Before she knew it, a response was out of Alex's mouth. "That's what I am," Alex said. "An Episcopalian."

Eric turned on her fully and seemed startled. "Are you?" he asked. He laughed and touched her hand. "Were you raised Episcopalian?"

"I make an effort to keep up with it. I'm not perfect. But it keeps me focused. I was raised by a very religious mother," Alex said. "She was from Mexico. A Roman Catholic."

"Tell me about her," he said.

"Her faith was an important part of her life," Alex said. "She passed it on to me. I haven't been able to shake its influence on my life — not that I want to. And it was of tremendous value when I lost my fiancé." She spoke toward Sarah and Carl. "My fiancé was killed in an accident a year and a half ago," Alex said.

"I'm so sorry," Sarah said.

There was a ringing sound: Eric's cell phone. Eric reached into his inside jacket pocket. He glanced at the LED. "It's Maurice," he said, indicating his driver. Eric answered. His expression darkened. He listened. Then he clicked off and put the phone away. For a moment, he looked as if he didn't know what to do next, but was trying to make a decision.

"Problem?" Alex asked.

"A small one. Maurice is having a problem with some obnoxious fan on a motorbike. The guy is insisting on parking near us and won't go away."

"So what's happening out there?" Alex asked, her anxiety starting to build.

"Maurice called the police and the police haven't come. Nothing new about that," Eric said with annoyance. "The guy says he won't leave until I come out with the lady and let him take our pictures." He thought about it. "Fan or paparazzi, don't know which is worse. Let me go out there and help Maurice get rid of him. Sometimes you sign an autograph or let them take a picture, and they go on their way. It happens from time to time. Sorry. Excuse me."

"Motorbike?" Alex asked.

"Yes. Don't worry about it. I'll be right back."

Eric was on his feet in an instant. Then, in a second instant the whole scenario made sense to Alex. "Eric!" she called after him. "Wait!"

He gave her a smile and waved. He held up a finger indicating he would be back in one minute.

Alex called, rising quickly. "He's dangerous! He doesn't want you, he wants me!"

But the restaurant was noisy and Eric couldn't hear. Instead, he was politely working his way through the crowds to the front door.

To the shock of Eric's family, Alex bolted to her feet, reached under her blazer for her Glock. She kept a hand on it and gave chase. A crowd closed in behind Eric, however, and it slowed her progress to the door.

Eric emerged onto East 67th Street. It was shortly past 1:00 a.m. Maurice had the limousine parked down the block. Now he eased it forward into a more convenient spot in front of the awning of the restaurant. He jumped out and came around to open doors.

"No, no," Eric called. "We're not leaving yet. Where's the little pest?"

At that time, as Alex hit the street behind Eric, there was the buzz of a much smaller motor vehicle that kick-started from the corner at Madison Avenue. A rider in a helmet guided a green Honda motorcycle onto 67th and, as Eric watched quizzically, zipped toward the limousine.

Alex watched. Everything registered. Then Alex's instincts cranked in.

"Maurice! Look out!"

The man eased the Honda to a stop at a midpoint next to the limo on the street side. The Honda blocked the limo's easy exit and even bumped up against the limo with a loud clunk—metal hitting metal, the trunk of the motorcycle to the metal of the limousine—as the rider hurriedly jumped off.

The biker lifted his face mask and stared at Alex. Their eyes locked. That's when she knew. He reached into his pocket and drew a gun.

Alex moved hard to her left and raised her own weapon.

The man fired wild two shots that crashed into the restaurant window. The plate glass shattered and flew in all directions, one large slab crashing to the pavement and splintering. Eric ducked behind another car. Alex moved to the middle of the street in full sight of the bomber to pull his attention from other targets. Maurice stayed on the sidewalk but drew his own weapon. Alex fixed her Glock with both hands and began to fire at the same time as Maurice. The city street was suddenly a mini–war zone, alive with gunfire, screams, and the sounds of errant bullets battering buildings, cars, and windows.

Wildly, the assassin emptied his pistol at them but missed. He moved out to a position twenty feet from Alex and fired another erratic barrage of three bullets in her direction She kept moving away from his line of fire, though one bullet hit the ground so close to her that she could feel the particles of concrete kick up from the street.

Then Alex followed the potential killer with her own weapon and fired a shot meant to take him down. It found its target, hitting him in the upper chest and spinning him as he cursed wildly in Spanish. His pistol flew from his hand and clattered onto the asphalt. Then a barrage from Alex's weapon and an accompanying barrage from Maurice's threw him backward against the wall of a residential building. He spun into a low row of trash cans. His gun dropped and the echoes of bullets faded in the night. There he slumped to the pavement while blood poured from four massive wounds. The left side of his face was pulpy with blood: probably from Maurice's weapon, Alex reasoned, as she lowered her Glock. She had been aiming lower for the torso.

In the windows above 67th Street, lights began to go on. People came to windows and doorways. Eric emerged from behind a car, and when all was still he walked over to Alex.

"You all right?" he asked. He put an arm around her.

"I'm all right," she said.

Eric looked to Maurice, who gave him a nod. Maurice was unscathed also.

"And I thought *I* was in a tough business," Eric said.

Within another minute there were sirens, then an armada

of flashing lights, then, as accounts were given, the bomb squad appeared, and the block was evacuated.

Inevitable thereafter, there were reporters. Worlds again had collided.

Seven hours later in Queens, a final brief act played out when bomb maker Luis Rivera went to his pickup truck. He stepped in, turned on the ignition, and felt a momentary surge of panic when the vehicle gave an unusual shake.

Then a tremendous eruption roared upward from the underside of the chassis, blowing the truck and its occupant into more pieces than the police or ambulance crew could count.

Luis died instantly, some would say by his own hand, but surely by the bomb that he had put together himself.

SIXTY

In the weeks that followed, as the bizarre tale of the shooting on East 67th Street faded from the press, Alex returned to her office with a greater sense of vengeance than ever. The hurricane season ended in Florida and the warmth of a late autumn came to an end in New York. The Yankees concluded their latest championship quest during the back end of October, not unusual, and the Giants and Jets moved to the back page of the tabloids. Sometimes, due to the behavior of coaches and players, the football teams were on the front page. Such things would have only mattered tangentially to Alex, except that her relationship with Eric had moved forward as they discovered they had much in common. Eric also had friends in the world of sports and show business. So they frequently attended Giants home football games together in some of the better seats when there was no conflict with Broadway performances. Alex, with her new companionship, even developed a strange new affinity for football. Through Eric, and through his sports-and-show-business contacts, she got to meet Eli Manning, who graciously autographed a football for her.

Then on another weekend, on the spur of the moment, they took off on a Saturday to see Eric's old college team play at home in New Jersey against Dartmouth and spent a Saturday afternoon huddled together under orange and black blankets, caps, and scarves as a premature winter wind whipped Palmer Stadium. Eric's hand held hers. She loved being a world away from the world of crime and assassination, at least for a few hours.

South Pacific's initial limited run on Broadway came to an end. But then again, it didn't. The show continued to play near capacity, so — at the producer's request and to the delight of his ticket-buying public — Eric opted to stay in the show, passing on some film offers to do so. The movies would have taken him out of town for long stretches. He was finding contentment in the big city now.

Frequently, as was the case with friends and family of leading cast members, Alex came by after work to see the show again, or parts of it. She continued to enjoy it, though every night found it difficult or impossible to watch the scene in which young Lieutenant Cable, portrayed by Eric, is killed. It was too poignant and too personal, and the echo from Kiev was too loud.

Gian Antonio Rizzo and Mimi also passed through New York City in early November, returning from Brazil and Colombia where, against all odds, Mimi's project for cyberaccounting of livestock was off to an extraordinarily successful start. Who knew? "I did," Rizzo maintained. "The girl is a genius."

What Alex did not know, not yet anyway, was how the betrayal in Rome had come about and who had tipped off the Dosis and allowed them to escape. Figuring that out remained on her crowded agenda both in Rome and New York. If she could just find out that bit of information, it might also lift the curtain on much else.

Also, her suspicions about Lionel Dickey had not abated. Had Dosi influence touched him? Or was he just a CIA guy who had freelanced too much in South and Central America? She swore she would find that out too. And during Rizzo's two-day layover in New York, Alex assured him that she was not just safeguarding the silver fountain pen, she was putting it to good use.

Alex deputized three new assistants and farmed out all of her assignments to them except for one: the conclusion of Operation Párajo. The latter continued in not just the courtrooms of the world, but also in the streets and back alleys. The Justice Department allowed her to add some staff. Security was boosted at Fin Cen's headquarters and the war continued.

To Alex, and to all observers, it was clear that there could be only one ultimate resolution. When one side lost its queen, the match would end.

With time, however, a new factor had come into play in the endgame that would follow between Alex LaDuca and Yardena Dosi. The shadow of Robert's death in Kiev had finally lifted, making Alex's world brighter and more clear-eyed. She moved around the city with confidence, reckoning that it would take the Dosis at least a few weeks to launch a new attack against her. Now, quietly armed with seventeen new possibilities of indicting and extraditing them, she might be able to get them first.

So much for Alex's professional life.

On a personal level, she had found a loving relationship again, complete with enough room to allow it to progress, as Eric liked to put it, at its own pace and on its own terms. She began to believe again that God had a plan for her. Not that she had ever doubted it. But she knew she had questioned it.

She thought back. Sometimes she discussed these things with Eric. She felt open enough with him to do so, trusting enough.

Late one weekend night, they split a takeout pizza from Donatella's on Eighth Avenue. They brought it back to Eric's place and somehow waded into some theology and philosophy.

"My fiancé, Robert, and I used to go to church together when we lived in Washington," Alex said. "It was a special, peaceful time in the week for us. I liked it. I missed it after he was gone. I still do. I have to tell you, my faith is still very much shaken by what's happened. I try to believe, I want to believe, but it's not the easiest thing." She shrugged. "That's me. That's where I am these days."

"You want me to go with you sometime? Is that what you're asking?" he said.

"I guess I am," she said. "Sorry. I didn't mean to get going on that."

"Well, I'll tell you," Eric said, "not to get too ponderous late on a Saturday evening. But the spiritual questions, sometimes I have a lot of trouble with those. Whether I believe everything absolutely, I couldn't even begin to answer that question. But it keeps me focused on what's good and right. It keeps me humble.

I'm very humble you know, most actors are," he said with a wink. "But I also like the life that it brings me. The way I learn to appreciate the grace of God. I think it makes me a better person. Sometimes I go to a Sunday service and just sit there, listen, meditate, do the prayers, follow the service. It's not always a profound experience, but that's why it's called faith."

"I understand what you're saying," Alex said.

"Do you? I'm glad." He paused and his mood changed. "So then I throw a hundred bucks in the collection plate to cover myself and sneak out before people recognize me."

Alex was grateful again to be alive and to have found companionship again. Finding herself on the arm of an attractive man on weekends and some weeknights after a show as Broadway's marquees faded into night, was merely a bonus. She was enjoying not just one world now, but two, and was happy to go with God's plan, as she saw it, and see where it would lead her.

At work, she doubled down. Midway through November, Alex moved Párajo to a new phase, one that she hoped would be the final one. She summoned her entire staff into her office. As she waited, she sat with an open notebook and a blank page. At the top, she wrote: "Párajo Homicides, US Jurisdiction."

She began the list with Kevork, James; Vierra, Thomas; and Skypios, Nicholas. Then she added to the list every name that Juanita Mejías had given her. She added several more that her other sources had given her. There were twenty-nine in total.

When her staff was fully present she looked up. "Close the door," she said.

Someone did.

She looked back down on her list. She added Ivar Mejías' name, put a question mark after it, then circled the name with a silver fountain pen that she had reserved entirely for this case.

"Okay," she said, "listen up. The Dosis. Here's how we're going to get them."

The Cuban Trilogy

Hostage in Havana

Noel Hynd

From bestselling author Noel Hynd comes this new series, The Cuban Trilogy, bursting with intrigue and set against the backdrop of Havana, an explosive capital city of faded charm, locked in the past and torn by political intrigue.

U.S. Treasury Agent Alexandra LaDuca leaves her Manhattan home on an illegal mission to Cuba that could cost her everything. At stake? Her life ... and the solution to a decades-old mystery, the recovery of a large amount of cash, and the return of an expatriate American fugitive to the United States.

After slipping into the country on a small boat, Alex makes her way to Havana. Accompanying her is the attractive but dangerous Paul Guarneri, a Cuban-born exile who lives in the gray areas of the law. Together, they plunge into intrigue and danger in a climate of political repression and organized crime. Without the support of the United States, Alex must navigate Cuban police, saboteurs, pro-Castro security forces, and a formidable network of those loyal to the American underworld.

Bullets fly as allies become traitors and enemies become unexpected friends. Alex, recovering from the tragic loss of her fiancé a year before, reexamines faith and new love while taking readers on a fast-paced adventure. If you enjoy thrillers such as those by John le Carré, David Baldacci, and Joel Rosenberg, you'll love this series.

Available in stores and online!

Conspiracy in Kiev

Noel Hynd

A shrewd investigator and an expert marksman, Special Agent Alexandra LaDuca can handle any case the FBI gives her. Or can she?

While on loan from the Treasury Department, Alex is tapped to accompany a Secret Service team during a presidential visit to Ukraine. Her assignment: to keep personal watch over Yuri Federov, the most charming and most notorious gangster in the region.

But there are more parts to this dangerous mission than anyone suspects, and connecting the dots takes Alex across three continents and through some life-altering discoveries about herself, her work, her faith, and her future.

Conspiracy in Kiev — from the first double cross to the stunning final pages — is the kind of solid, fast-paced espionage thriller only Noel Hynd can write. For those who have never read Noel Hynd, this first book in The Russian Trilogy is the perfect place to start.

Available in stores and online!

The Russian Trilogy

Midnight in Madrid

Noel Hynd

When a mysterious relic is stolen from a Madrid museum, people are dying to discover its secrets. Literally.

U.S. Treasury agent Alexandra LaDuca returns from *Conspiracy in Kiev* to track down the stolen artwork, a small carving called *The Pietà of Malta*. It seems a simple assignment, but nothing about this job is simple, as the mysteries and legends surrounding the relic become increasingly complex with claims of supernatural power.

As aggressive, relentless, and stubborn as ever, Alex crisscrosses Europe through a web of intrigue, danger, and betrayal, joined by a polished, mysterious new partner. With echoes of classic detective and suspense fiction from *The Maltese Falcon* to *The Da Vinci Code*, *Midnight in Madrid* takes the reader on a nonstop spellbinding chase through a modern world of terrorists, art thieves, and cold-blooded killers.

Available in stores and online!

The Russian Trilogy

Countdown in Cairo

Noel Hynd

Why won't the dead stay dead?

Federal agent Alexandra LaDuca travels to Egypt to investigate the sighting of a former mentor, a CIA agent everyone thought was dead. She is thrown into the deadliest game of double cross of her career as the events that began in Kiev and continued in Madrid find their culmination in the volatile Middle East.

Her assignment is to locate a man she once knew. But to find the answers, Alex needs to move quickly into the underworld of the Egyptian capital, a nether society of crooks, killers, spies, and Islamic fundamentalists. And she must work alone, surviving by her wits, her training, and a compact new Beretta.

If you've been waiting for Alex LaDuca's next adventure, this fast-paced thriller is it. If you've never met Alex, *Countdown in Cairo* offers a first-rate introduction. You will be holding your breath from its explosive beginning to the very last twist.

Available in stores and online!

The Russian
Three Complete Novels

*Noel Hynd, Bestselling Author
of Cemetery of Angels*

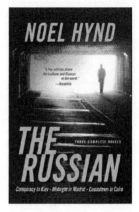

A thrilling compilation of three complete novels in bestselling author Noel Hynd's Russian Trilogy.

Conspiracy in Kiev

Working with the U.S. Treasury, federal agent Alexandra LaDuca travels to Ukraine to track a Russian-Ukrainian mobster named Yuri Fedrov during a visit by the American president. Personally and professionally, Alex's life will be changed forever by the explosive events that transpire in the Ukrainian capital.

Midnight in Marid

U.S. Treasury agent Alexandra LaDuca returns from *Conspiracy in Kiev* to track down stolen artwork, a small carving called The Pietà of Malta. It seems to be a simple assignment, but nothing about this job is simple, as the mysteries and legends surrounding the relic become increasingly complex with claims of supernatural power.

Countdown in Cairo

Alexandra LaDuca is smart, tough, and cool under fire. But when she travels to Cairo to investigate a former mentor who was believed to be dead, Alex is caught in a bizarre game of double cross, and her life is more perilously on the line than ever.

You'll be holding your breath from the explosive beginning to the very last twist!

Share Your Thoughts

With the Author: Your comments will be forwarded to the author when you send them to *zauthor@zondervan.com*.

With Zondervan: Submit your review of this book by writing to *zreview@zondervan.com*.

Free Online Resources at
www.zondervan.com

Zondervan AuthorTracker: Be notified whenever your favorite authors publish new books, go on tour, or post an update about what's happening in their lives at www.zondervan.com /authortracker.

Daily Bible Verses and Devotions: Enrich your life with daily Bible verses or devotions that help you start every morning focused on God. Visit www.zondervan.com/newsletters.

Free Email Publications: Sign up for newsletters on Christian living, academic resources, church ministry, fiction, children's resources, and more. Visit www.zondervan.com/newsletters.

Zondervan Bible Search: Find and compare Bible passages in a variety of translations at www.zondervanbiblesearch.com.

Other Benefits: Register to receive online benefits like coupons and special offers, or to participate in research.

ZONDERVAN®

ZONDERVAN.com/
AUTHORTRACKER
follow your favorite authors